Holger Michael Zellentin

The Qurʾān's Legal Culture

Holger Michael Zellentin

The Qurʾān's Legal Culture

The Didascalia Apostolorum as a Point of Departure

Mohr Siebeck

Holger Michael Zellentin: born 1976; 2007 PhD Princeton University; has taught at Rutgers University, the Graduate Theological Union, Berkeley, and at the University of California, Berkeley; teaches Jewish Studies at the University of Nottingham; 2012 Early Career Fellowship of the Arts and Humanities Research Council (UK).

ISBN 978-3-16-152720-3

Die Deutsche Bibliothek lists this publication in the Deutsche Nationalbibliographie; detailed bibliographic data is available on the Internet at *http://dnb.ddb.de*.

The book was typeset by Martin Fischer in Tübingen, printed on non-aging paper by Gulde-Druck in Tübingen and bound by Buchbinderei Nädele in Nehren.

Printed in Germany.

Table of Contents

Foreword

"For every constitution there is an epic,
for each decalogue a scripture."
– Robert Cover, *Nomos and Narrative*

"I [Jesus] am not come to abrogate the Law nor the prophets,
but to fulfill them. The Law therefore is not abrogated,
but the second legislation is temporary, and abrogated."
– *Didascalia* XXVI

"I [Jesus] confirm that which is before me of the Torah,
and to make lawful for you some of the things
that were forbidden to you."
– *Sūrat ʾĀl ʿImrān* 3:50

The following pages contextualize the Qurʾān's legal aspects within the religious culture of its time, the early seventh century of the Common Era. I hold that a majority of the laws promulgated in the Qurʾān, as well as its legal narratives about the Israelites and about Jesus, have close commonalities to the laws and narratives of the Didascalia Apostolorum. The legal and theological vocabulary of the Arabic Qurʾān likewise shows much affinity with that of the Syriac (Eastern Christian Aramaic) version of the Didascalia. This shared vocabulary corroborates the legal and narrative commonalities between the two texts. That said, the Qurʾān is not "based" on the Didascalia in any direct way. Detailed comparison of the two documents will illustrate the absence of textual influence in either direction. Both should rather be read against the background of the oral discourse shared by their audiences. I contend that, largely due to this shared oral tradition, the Qurʾān takes a stand on a significant part of the legal issues mentioned in the Didascalia, but without being constrained by the Didascalia's rulings.

The Didascalia Apostolorum, the "Teaching of the Apostles," is a Christian legal document (with affinities to Judaism) of which we have fragmentary Greek evidence from the third century, one complete Latin palimpsest from the fifth century, and an expanded Syriac version first recorded after 683 C.E. Additional evidence of the Didascalia's spread is offered by its rewritings (far less sympathetic to Judaism) from the fourth century C.E. onwards, the so-called Apostolic Constitutions tradition, which were circulating throughout the Near and Middle East. The Syriac Didascalia remained part of the Syriac legal tradition throughout the Middle Ages. Given its much earlier origins and ongoing later attestations, it is thus a document of plausible relevance for the Qurʾān's original audience.

The laws and narratives shared by the two documents allow us to illustrate the Qurʾān's continuity with contemporaneous forms of the Jesus movement, which in turn lets us integrate the Qurʾān's often neglected evidence more firmly into the study of Late Antique religions. At the same time, the proximity between the Qurʾān and the Didascalia highlights the remaining discrepancies between the two texts. These discrepancies afford an appreciation of the initial distinctness of the Arabic Qurʾān from the Syriac Didascalia, as well as an appreciation of the many ways in which the former not only accepts, but also develops and occasionally abrogates ritual laws imposed by the latter. The Didascalia as a text is therefore by no means the legal blueprint "behind" the Qurʾān; to reiterate, it is evidence merely of an oral discourse in which both texts participate.

The Didascalia encourages a legal approach to salvation in addition to a doctrinal one: practice and belief are inseparable. Vaguely comparable to the rabbinic literature of its time, the Didascalia is structured as a legal document that integrates its narratives within this legal framework; with some justification it has thus been called a "Christian Talmud." The Qurʾān similarly integrates law and narrative, albeit with more emphasis on the latter – a distribution more akin to the Hebrew Bible than to the Talmud. For the most part, a comparison between the laws and narratives of the Didascalia and the Qurʾān can be presented in a relatively straightforward manner. The presentation of my arguments, however, has to overcome two main challenges.

First, the evidence of the Didascalia's laws that are relevant for the Qurʾān is only mostly positive, i.e. constituted by legal agreement. The Didascalia also gives negative testimony through explicit legal disagreement, deploring that a small group of Jewish believers in Jesus within its own community endorses several laws of ritual purity additional to the ones its authorial voice endorses. The combination of the laws the Didascalia endorses with the ones it specifically rejects – the code, in other words, of its Jewish believers – overlaps even more with the legal corpus of the Qurʾān. When reading the Didascalia on its own, the historicity of this alleged group of Jewish believers in Jesus, and of their additional observances cannot be taken for granted. The Didascalia may simply be rehearsing traditional Christian discourse. The historicity of Judaeo-Christian groups past the fourth or fifth century is indeed more than uncertain. The historicity of

Judaeo-Christian *practice*, however, can also be supported by illustrating that most of the ritual observances rejected by the Didascalia are endorsed as requirements for *gentile* followers of Jesus not only by the Qurʾān, but also by the ("Pseudo"-)Clementine Homilies. This fourth-century Greek text of which we have later traces in Latin, Syriac, and Arabic is a text therefore of equally plausible direct or, more likely, indirect relevance to the Qurʾān's audience. Its insider discourse, endorsing ritual law in concrete terms and obliging its audience to follow it, cannot be assailed as stemming from mere heresiological tradition. I will use the triangular relationship between the three texts to trace the legal culture that the Qurʾān takes as its point of departure. I argue that Judaeo-Christian legal culture, as reconstructible with the help of the Didascalia, the Clementine Homilies, and the Qurʾān itself, holds a central place among the direct interlocutors especially of the longer surahs of the Qurʾān, which are often attributed to its "Medinan" period of composition. This study, then, combines two objectives. First, it outlines the Qurʾān's legal culture through its dialogue with a tradition embodied by the Didascalia's Christian community, broadened by comparison with the Christian and rabbinic traditions more broadly. Second, in doing so, this work assesses the persistence of Judaeo-Christian legal culture *within* establish Jewish and Christian communities.

A second factor that determined the shape of the present study is that, despite the proximity between the Qurʾān and the Didascalia, nearly all of the legal positions and narratives that are shared by these texts can also be traced to a plethora of other patristic and rabbinic sources, and often even to the Hebrew Bible or the New Testament (and their later Aramaic renderings). My claim does not exclude the relevance for the study of the Qur'ān of many other texts ranging from the Talmud to the sermons and narratives of many Syriac church fathers. Yet I seek to establish a hierarchy of relevance within the Late Antique context of the Qur'ān and maintain that, when it comes to legal material, the Didascalia occupies a position of special importance. While the legal practices and narratives in question and the lexemes used to describe them can be found throughout Late Antique Aramaic discourse, they are nowhere clustered, arranged, and inflected quite the way they are in the two central texts under consideration.

When writing this book, I faced not only the challenge of illustrating and assessing the similarity between the legal discourse of the Didascalia and the Qur'ān, but also of situating this specific similarity within and against the broader Biblical culture of Late Antiquity. Likewise, the pervasive lexical commonalities between the respective Arabic and Syriac terminology of the Qur'ān and of the Didascalia are meaningful only when viewed against the broader affinities among Semitic languages in general. It is against the background of this broad affinity that specific kinship must be assessed. Many of the legal and lexical similarities are simply the result of the fact that both texts were written within the same cultural milieu and in related Semitic languages. I took a middle path when trying to establish clarity within complexity. On the one hand, I have sought to contextualize both documents at least rudimentarily within the immense legal and narrative matrices of Jewish and Christian Late Antiquity. On the other hand, I drastically restricted any such comparative evidence and relegated much relevant information to the footnotes.

I am well aware that a full study may well be necessary for each of the comparison I suggest, and without doubt I have not always chosen the most pertinent illustration of the broader parallels. The necessary shortcoming of this initial study is not pointing in greater detail to the countless other parallels in Late Antique Jewish and Christian (not to mention early Muslim) culture in addition to the ones here offered. I hope that future studies will further contextualize how important a witness the text of the Didascalia is for reconstructing the Qur᾿ān's legal culture, and vice versa.

I have endeavored here to strike a balance between comprehensiveness and readability. Not every reader will appreciate the already dense amount of information offered in this book, nor will every reader agree with my selectiveness or with specific conclusions. Those who read to the end, however, will likely find it difficult not to acknowledge the extraordinary kinship between the legal cultures embodied in the Didascalia and the Qur᾿ān. If the current study would achieve nothing but inviting others to offer variant explanations for this kinship, I will consider it a success. A short summary of the following chapters will prove a useful reading guide.

Summary

The Introduction, entitled *Late Antique Legal Culture, Judaeo-Christianity, and the Qur᾿ān*, introduces the sources and the central methodological objective of this book: to read the Qur᾿ān historically within its legal focus and to understand law as a central aspect of its religious world view. For this purpose, I employ the well-established concept of "legal culture," constituted by actual law – *nomos* – as well as by the legal *narratives* justifying the law. The study of the Qurʾān's legal culture begins with short history of the "Decree of the Apostles" from the time of the Acts of the Apostles, where it is first attested, to the time of Athanasius of Bālād, writing in seventh-century Antioch. This short decree became the basis of a specific Judaeo-Christian ritual lawcode applied to gentiles in both the Didascalia and the Qurʾān. I define the concept of Judaeo-Christianity as the concomitant endorsement of Jesus and of a discrete set of observances of ritual purity *beyond* the requirements of the Decree of the Apostles. This religious tendency is traceable throughout Late Antiquity *within* established Jewish and Christian groups, yet not necessarily locatable as constitutive of social entities distinct from these groups. The Qurʾān stands in intimate dialogue with Judeo-Christianity as just defined, partially endorsing it, partially seeking to supersede it. Concluding this chapter, an illustrative example showing how the Qurʾān accepts and further develops a law preserved in the Didascalia – partially shared with other traditions, partially distinct – is taken from the two texts' jurisdiction on the wearing of the veil.

Chapter One, titled *The Didascalia's Laws and the Qurʾān's Abrogations*, considers the ways in which most of the Qurʾān's laws, as well as the legal narrative of the Ten Commandments, relate to their Biblical precedents. I claim that the Didascalia should be seen as a central source for any reconstruction of how Biblical law had been transformed from the times of the Israelites to that of the Qurʾān. Especially, I hold that the Qurʾān and the Didascalia conceive of the original revelation of law as consisting not only of the Ten Commandments, but also of a series of legal additions incumbent upon believers. Most of these additional laws are largely the same in both texts. The Qurʾān, at the same time as betraying a proximity to the ways in which Jews and Christians understand Biblical law in its time, can also be shown to develop extant laws, especially regarding central cultic practices, reflecting a break with established Jewish and Christian religious communities.

Chapter Two, titled *Ritual Law in the Didascalia, the Clementine Homilies, and the Qurʾān*, considers how the Didascalia's Judaeo-Christians and the Qurʾān's ritual law share a special continuity – a distinct set of purity laws – in addition to the general legal commonalities already established. This chapter illustrates in more detail the development of this set of ritual laws, whose core was originally formulated in the Decree of the Apostles (yet partially dismissed by most Christians). These laws fall far short of the entire biblical ritual code but go far beyond the Decree of the Apostles. They include washing after intercourse and before prayer, as well as the abstinence from intercourse during the menses, and from the consumption of pork. The Clementine Homilies provide an important intermediate step that allows us to conceive of a continuous development, further expansion and specification of Judaeo-Christian ritual laws imposed upon gentiles from the time of the Acts of the Apostles to the composition of the Qurʾān. Finally, this chapter discusses the heresiology of the Didascalia and the Qurʾān, arguing that both texts formulate similar anti-ascetic laws in response to shared depictions of antinomian ascetics.

Chapter Three, titled *Narratives of Law in the Didascalia and in the Qurʾān*, continues the comparative study of the Didascalia's and the Qur'ān's legal narratives in Chapter One, building on the basis of the two texts' presentation of the Ten Commandments and the original legal additions to them. I argue that both texts share an approach to the historical narrative of God-given law. This approach has an affinity with some early Greek and Latin patristic and with rabbinic sources, yet remains distinguishable from them. The Didascalia presents a clear-cut distinction between a primary, original divine law and a secondary law given to the Israelites as a punishment for sins such as the Golden Calf and other transgressions. Jesus is portrayed foremost in the role of a law-giver; he abrogates only *part* of the law, reinstating the original code. The Qur'ān's legal narratives repeatedly allude to such a distinction between original and secondary law and see Jesus similarly as abrogating only those laws given because of sins such as the Golden Calf.

Chapter Four, titled *Jesus, Muhammad, and Judaeo-Christian Food Laws*, shows how the legal history described in Chapter Three corresponds to the actual food laws of the Didascalia and the Qur'ān, both in the texts' past and present. For both the Qur'ān and the Didascalia, before the giving of the original law, no ritual law existed. Only a small number of purity laws were included in the original law, commensurate with a version of the Decree of the Apostles. The Israelites, however, sinned, and the secondary law was given to them as punishment, including additional dietary laws. Finally, Jesus abrogates these additional *food* laws for the Israelites, leading to a return to the stage of the original Torah, at least concerning food. In the Qur'ān, Muhammad mandates these food laws for Jews, Christians, and his own community.

The Conclusion, titled *The Didascalia's Judaeo-Christian Legal Culture as a Point of Departure for the Qurʾān*, summarizes the findings and seeks to assess the historical context of the legal culture shared by both texts. It problematizes the concept of and the historical evidence for Judaeo-Christianity, proposing a middle path between a minimalist and a maximalist position: either the complete disappearance of Judaeo-Christianity or the existence of hidden Judaeo-Christian communities in the sands of Arabia. In addition to the primary evidence of the Clementine Homilies and cognate texts, the Talmud, the Didascalia, and the Qurʾān itself, in my view, do not point to independent Judaeo-Christian groups, but testify to the survival of a Judaeo-Christian legal culture *within* the established Jewish and Christian communities. The Qurʾān takes this legal culture as one of its points of departure, constructing it as the original and true form of Christianity and Judaism alike. It thereby exhorts both rabbinic Jews and Christians to reform their ways by rectifying their respective positions on Jesus and on purity.

The Epilogue, entitled *The Qurʾān between Christianity and Rabbinic Judaism*, is set off from the rest of this study because it introduces the evidence of rabbinic Judaism into the interplay with that of the Didascalia. Its focus on philology is also more technical than the rest of this volume. I suggest a tentative reading of the Qurʾān's views on the Didascalia's religious officials in light of the present findings. I first consider the Qurʾān's sanctioning of the Jews' allegedly exaggerated veneration of rabbis and *ʾaḥbār* ("colleagues"), positing acute knowledge of pertinent rabbinic traditions among its audience. On the basis of this claim, I discuss the equally precise knowledge the Qurʾān presupposes of Christian elders (*qissīsīn*) and of the veneration of a class of church officials called *ruhbān*, which I argue to be "bishops" in Qurʾānic Arabic, corroborating the Qurʾān's knowledge of the ecclesiastical structure described in the Didascalia. The Qurʾān's simultaneous dialogue with several interlocutors, in addition to the Didascalia, is presented as a pathway for future studies, minimizing the danger of reductionism and enhancing the possibility of cross-fertilization between disciplines.

Methodology and Acknowledgments

The purpose of this study is to help explain the Qurʾān to the place in peoples' minds that is known as the "western" world. At the same time, however, a comparative study of the Qurʾān and a nominally "Christian" document such as the Didascalia Apostolorum requires the undoing of many conceptual distinctions at the very heart of western culture. Late Antiquity and the Middle Ages; Christianity and Judaism; the New Testament and the Talmud; the Qurʾān and the Bible; Jesus and Muhammad; and, more darkly, "us" and "them:" all of these are distinctions that define the identity of four billion people or more. Yet these distinctions, if constructed too neatly and too categorically, are as stereotypically false as any deictic dichotomy. This book situates the "origins" of Islamic legal culture within the Jewish and Christian debates that reach back to the first century C.E. It similarly prepares an argument for presenting the Qurʾān as critiquing the Christianity and the rabbinic Judaism of its time from within a Biblical tradition that sits squarely in between the Christian and the rabbinic orthodoxies of its time.

I do not discount the cultural continuity between the Qurʾān and its Muslim reception history, yet I emphasize the Qurʾān's intimacy with the Biblical culture of Late Antiquity more broadly – be it Christian, Jewish, or, especially, both. I reclaim the Qurʾān as a document at the apex of Biblical Antiquity since it integrates the rabbinic Jewish and the Christian traditions. It constitutes a bridge as much as a watershed between Late Antiquity and the Middle Ages. Hence, just as we have come to learn to read the Talmud without its medieval commentary (without ignoring the valuable insights given there), and just as we have learned to read the New Testament without its patristic reception history (as rich and valuable as it may be), so will I read the Qurʾān without relying on its later commentaries in the Tafsīr and the Sīra literature, the early commentaries on the Qurʾān and the biographies of the life of Muhammad (while still acknowledging that the Islamic tradition is largely responsible for accurately conveying the text of the Qurʾān and much of its meaning). While the answers I suggest here are, perhaps naïvely, beholden to historical objectivity, the questions I ask developed within my own personal and academic career. Summarizing the path to this book will give me a chance briefly to acknowledge some of the help and inspiration I received along the way.

I grew up in a liberal and largely secular Protestant German household. Through a grandmother active in improving German-Israeli relations, I was confronted early on with the complex realities of the state of Israel and the German atrocities that expedited its establishment. The first strong intellectual impulse of which I have memory, however, was to try to understand not so much the all but disappeared Jewish minority of the German past, but the living Muslim minority of the German present. As a teenager in 1989, I embarked on a comparative study of the stories of the patriarchs in the Hebrew Bible and in a German Qur'ān I had purchased. The project was ill-conceived and historically ignorant. I quickly abandoned it until I was introduced more properly to Islam while studying religion at the faculty of Protestant Theology in Strasbourg.

I was initially attracted to the breadth of humanistic education I hoped to receive in the study of Theology and Religious Studies and took a series of undergraduate and graduate degrees in this field, both in France and in the Netherlands. It was not until encountering rabbinic Judaism, however, that I felt any genuine academic fervor. I hence pursued a study of Judaism within the framework of a couple of degrees in Amsterdam, supplemented by literary and source-critical studies at the Departments of Hebrew Literature and Talmud in Jerusalem, and followed by a PhD at Princeton University under the tutelage of Peter Schäfer. Schäfer and his colleagues purged me of some of my all-too-intertextual impulses and allowed me to develop a historically contextualized understanding of Egyptian, Palestinian, and Mesopotamian Judaism in Late Antiquity.[1]

[1] Publications on Egyptian Judaism include Zellentin, "The End of Jewish Egypt: Artapanus's Second Exodus," in Gregg Gardner and Kevin Osterloh (eds.), *Antiquity in Antiquity, Jewish and Christian Pasts in the Greco-Roman World* (TSAJ 123; Tübingen: Mohr Siebeck, 2009), 27–73. On Mesopotamian and Palestinian Judaism see e.g. Zellentin, *Rabbinic Parodies of Jewish and Christian Literature* (Tübingen: Mohr Siebeck 2010); more recently see "Jerusalem Fell After Betar: The Christian Josephus and Rabbinic Memory," in

At Princeton, I also embarked upon my study of Arabic and of the Qurʾān and began a memorable reading of *Sūrat al-Baqarah* with two of my peers, Kevin Osterloh and Joshua Dubler. Once I was teaching as an Assistant Professor in Berkeley (at the Graduate Theological Union's Center for Jewish Studies and at the University of California), I again returned to the impulse of my teenage years. Inspired by a close collaboration with faculty in Islamic studies in Berkeley, and with helpful guidance of Michael Pregill, I dedicated myself to the study of the Qurʾān in its Late Antique context more fully, both in research and teaching. Initially, I sought to explore the ways in which the Qurʾān's statements on rabbis may enhance our understanding of the onset of the rabbinic tradition in Arabia. Yet very rapidly I realized that established categories of "Jewish," "Christian," and especially "Israelite" do not easily apply in the context of the Qurʾān. I therefore began with this preliminary study of the Qurʾān's legal culture, seeking to determine more precisely the role of Judaism, Judaeo-Christianity, and Christianity in a text that transforms the panoply of late antique discourse. I hope that my present study will prove better conceived and a little less historically ignorant than my first attempt.

My move to Nottingham in 2011 enabled me to dedicate myself more fully to the research for this book. The School of Humanities and the Department of Theology and Religious Studies at the University of Nottingham, as well as the British Arts and Humanities Research Council, which

---

Raʿanan Boustan et al. (eds.), *Envisioning Judaism: Studies in Honor of Peter Schäfer on the Occasion of his Seventieth Birthday* (Mohr Siebeck, Tübingen, 2013), volume 1, 319–67.

awarded me a generous fellowship in 2012–13, have made the completion of the present project possible.[2] In the process of research and writing, I have received invaluable feedback, constructive criticism, and encouragement from a larger number of friends and colleagues than can be acknowledged here; I beg for forgiveness for the inadvertent omissions of which I am surely guilty. Angelika Neuwirth has been a constant source of inspiration both in person and in writing. Jon Hoover has supported me as a scholar and as a colleague in Nottingham, as have Fred Astren, Erich Gruen, Ron Hendel and Lena Salaymeh in Berkeley. Many scholars have given me crucial feedback on many aspects of the project, not to mention their encouragement: Islam Dayeh, Nicolai Sinai, Sacha Stern, Guy Stroumsa and Daniel Weiss, as well as several others who have cho-

---

[2] I first presented the research here summarized at a conference I co-organized at the University of California, Berkeley, in October 2010, titled *Crosscurrents: Jewish and Islamic Cultural Exchange, 600–1250 C.E.*, followed by a presentation at the 2011 Annual Meeting of the Society of Biblical Literature in San Francisco, CA. Since then, I have repeatedly presented aspects of this study at a series of invited lectures and seminars: in 2012, at the Oxford Seminar *The Qur'an and Late Antiquity*, organized by Guy Stroumsa and Nicolai Sinai ("'Jewish Christianity' and the Qurʾān"); at the School of Philosophy, Theology and Religion at the University of Birmingham ("The Qurʾān on Rabbis and Judaism"); and in 2013 at Brown University at the Departments of Classics, History, and Religion ("Jesus and Ritual Purity in the Apostolic Literature and in the Qurʾān"). Most recently, with support from the University of Nottingham and from the British Arts and Humanities Research Council, I organized another conference dedicated to the subject matter, titled *Return to the Origins: The Qurʾān's Reformation of Judaism and Christianity*, held in Nottingham from 20–21 January 2013. A conference volume is in preparation, see <http://www.nottingham.ac.uk/theology/research/conferences/return-to-the-origins/return-to-the-origins.aspx>.

sen to remain anonymous. Jennifer Mann, Marton Ribary and Carol Rowe improved the text of this book by their careful copy-editing. Most importantly, the role of three of my colleagues in the formation of my scholarly approach, as it is reflected here, must be singled out (without seeking to blame them for remaining shortcomings).

First, I feel especially inspired by the work of Sidney Griffith on early Islam and Syriac Christianity, and especially by his respectful approach towards both, pointing to similarities without conflating the traditions. Over the past years, Father Griffith has offered me crucial support and criticism, especially on this study. Second, by organizing a series of conferences and publishing a seemingly endless stream of learned and insightful edited volumes, books and articles, Gabriel Said Reynolds may have done more than anybody else in the present century to advance the "Qurʾānist" approach to the text. Professor Reynolds, moreover, gave me the chance to participate in the Qurʾān Seminar he convened at the University of Notre Dame, a series of workshops held from 2012–13 that allowed for a rich scholarly exchange.[3] Joseph Witztum, last though certainly not least, has carefully read through two versions of this entire manuscript and has saved me from a number of embarrassing inaccuracies, both in form and in content. Dr. Witztum's stringent criticism and inspiring discussion has shaped the present form of this text in a broader manner than the acknowledgements of specific instances below will reflect.

---

[3] For the project see <https://quranseminar.nd.edu/> and Gabriel Said Reynolds and Mehdi Azaiez (eds.), *Collaborative Commentary on the Qurʾān* (2012–2013 Qurʾān Seminar at Notre Dame, IQSA Publishing, forthcoming).

A tragic post-script to this study has been constituted by my two brief encounters with Patricia Crone. I first met Professor Crone as a graduate student in Princeton, where she fervently encouraged me to pursue my studies of the Qurʾān. I reconnected with her this year after finishing the present manuscript, only to find out that she has in the meantime composed a study very much complementing the present one – a reading of Qurʾānic doctrine in the light of patristic evidence of "Jewish-Christianity" – and that her health is failing rapidly. Few agree with Professor Crone's early radical criticism of Muslim origins, yet none can deny that she has helped to move the field of Qurʾānic studies into the historical critical tradition. She constitutes one of her own most rigorous critics, in as far as she now fully embraces the historicity of Muhammad, reading the Qurʾān within a historical context not dissimilar to the one here proposed. While I could respond to some of her remarks on the present manuscript, her own study reached me too late to treat it in the present volume.

Editions and Transliteration

I transliterate Syriac as well as Jewish Aramaic and Hebrew in accordance with the early defective (i.e. non-vocalized) tradition, as follows: ʾ b g d h w z ḥ ṭ y k l m n s ʿ p ṣ q r š t; Arabic is transliterated according to DIN 31635 (1982). Text and translations of the Didascalia are based on the critical edition and translation of Arthur Vööbus, *The Didascalia Apostolorum in Syriac* I–IV, *Corpus Scriptorum Christianorum Orientalium* 401–2 and 407–8 (Louvain: Secrétariat du Corpus Scriptorum Christianorum Orientalium, 1979), occasionally emended to give a more literal sense; I have also consulted the fine new translation of Alistair Stewart-Sykes, *The Didascalia Apostolorum: an English Version with Introduction and Annotation* (Turnhout: Brepols, 2009). Citations from the Didascalia in the form of DA I, 1.1 denote chapter I, page 1, line 1 in Vööbus' Syriac. For previous editions of the Didascalia see Margaret Dunlop Gibson, *The Didascalia Apostolorum in Syriac, Edited from a Mesopotamian Manuscript with Various Readings and Collations of Other MSS* (Cambridge: Cambridge University Press, 2011 [1903]) and Paul de Lagarde, *Didascalia apostolorum syriace* (Leipzig: B.G. Teubner, 1854). The Latin text is that of R.H. Connolly, *Didascalia Apostolorum: The Syriac Version Translated and Accompanied by the Verona Latin Fragments* (Oxford: Clarendon Press, 1929). For a previous edition of the Latin text see E. Hauler, *Didascaliae Apostolorum fragmenta Veronensia latina* (Leipzig: Teubner, 1900). For the text of the Apostolic Constitutions see Franz Xaver von Funk, *Didascalia et Constitutiones Apostolorum* (Paderborn: Ferdinand Schoeningh, 1905), volume I. The text of the Clementine Homilies – falsely attributed to Pope Clement I in a later addition to the text, hence its usual epithet as "pseudo" – is that of Bernhard Rehm, *Die Pseudoklementinen I: Homilien* (Berlin: Akademie Verlag, 1969); the translation often follows, with many adaptations, Alexander Roberts and James Donaldson, *Ante-Nicene Christian Library, Volume XVII: The Clementine Homilies* (Edinburgh, T & T Clark, 1870). The vocalized text of the Qurʾān is that of ʿĀṣim (transmitted by Ḥafṣ), i.e. the Cairo text. Translations are largely based on the Sayyid 'Ali Quli Qara'i (ed. and trans.), *The Qur'an with an English Paraphrase* (Centre for Translation of the

Holy Qur'an: Qom, 2003), reprinted as *The Qur'an with a Phrase-by-Phrase English Translation* (Elmhurst, NY: Tahrike Tarsile Qur'an, 2006). Qara'i's translation seeks to preserve the original structure of much of the text and, more importantly, consistently translates Arabic words by using the same English word wherever possible. I regularly emend this translation in order to give an even more literal sense of the text. I have also consulted a number of standard English translations as well as the German of Rudi Paret, *Der Koran* (Stuttgart: Kohlhammer, 2004 [1966]). Most common names are rendered in their English equivalents. Biblical citations are based on the New Revised Standard Version. All other translations of ancient texts, unless otherwise noted, are my own.

Introduction

Late Antique Legal Culture, Judaeo-Christianity, and the Qurʾān

According to the most recent carbon dating of the parchment (not the ink) of the earliest evidence, a palimpsest, the Qurʾān may well have been largely redacted by the middle of the seventh century C.E., if not closer to the lifetime of Muhammad.[1] Its "implied author" is God, the same God who is called "the God of Abraham, the God of Isaac and the God of Jacob" in the Hebrew Bible (see Exodus 3:6) and in the New Testament (see Matthew 22:32). Muhammad is portrayed as a prophet in the mold of Abraham and

[1] See Behnam Sadeghi and Mohsen Goudarzi, "Ṣanʿāʾ 1 and the Origins of the Qurʾān," *Der Islam* 87 (2012): 1–129; cf. Elisabeth Puin, "Ein früher Koranpalimpsest aus Ṣanʿāʾ (DAM 01–27.1)," in Markus Groß and Karl-Heinz Ohlig (eds.) *Schlaglichter: Schriften zur frühen Islamgeschichte und zum Koran, Band 3: Die beiden ersten islamischen Jahrhunderte* (Berlin: Hans Schiler, 2008), 461–93; eadem, "Ein früher Koranpalimpsest aus Ṣanʿāʾ (DAM 01–27.1) – Teil II," in Markus Groß and Karl-Heinz Ohlig (eds.) *Vom Koran zum Islam: Schriften zur frühen Islamgeschichte und zum Koran, Band 4* (Berlin: Hans Schiler, 2009), 523–81; eadem, "Ein früher Koranpalimpsest aus Ṣanʿāʾ (DAM 01–27.1) – Teil III: Ein nicht-ʿuṯmānischer Koran," in Markus Groß and Karl-Heinz Ohlig (eds.) *Die Entstehung einer Weltreligion I: Schriften zur frühen Islamgeschichte und zum Koran, Band 5: Von der koranischen Bewegung zum Frühislam* (Berlin: Hans Schiler, 2010), 233–305. François Déroche has indicated to me in a personal communication that questions remain regarding the carbon dating as well as the palaeography of Ṣanʿāʾ 1, as he will detail in idem, *Qurʾans of the Umayyads: A Preliminary Overview* (*Leiden Studies in Islam and Society*; Leiden: Brill, 2014), forthcoming.

Jesus.[2] The Qurʾān's claim of divine authorship, however, is of limited relevance when seeking to understand it as a document of its time. Even God speaks the language of humans, as Rabbi Ishmael has taught us, implying that Scripture is meant to be understood – and for the historian, such understanding is locatable in history.[3] Conversely, positing Muhammad (or any other individual) as the Qurʾān's "historical author" is equally unsatisfying, for the Qurʾān, just like the Talmud, is not entirely a "written" text in the modern sense, as *Sūrat al-Furqān* illustrates:

The faithless say,
"Why has not the Qurʾān been sent down to him all at once?"
So it is, that We may strengthen your heart with it
And We have recited it (*wa-rattalnāhu*)
In a manner to be recited (*tartīlan*) (Q25:32)[4]

---

[2] The "prophetology" of the Qurʾān, as exemplified most clearly in *Sūrat ash-Shuʿarāʾ* (Q26), has recently been discussed by Sidney H. Griffith, *The Bible in Arabic: the Scriptures of the People of the Book* (Princeton: Princeton University Press, 2013), 54–96, see also page 95, note 26. The term "implied," or "abstract author" describes the sense of its author that a work as a whole conveys to its audience. It is distinct from the "historical," or "concrete author," who has actually written down the text. For a useful discussion of authorial terminology and associated problems, see Wolf Schmid, *Narratology: An Introduction* (Berlin: De Gruyter, 2010), esp. 36–50.

[3] The famous (minority) dictum of Rabbi Ishmael, insisting that Scripture can contain superfluous elements because it uses human speech, ("the Torah speaks in the language of humans," see e.g. Sifre *Bemidbar*, Shelach 6), does not inversely imply that humans would be able to attain the language of the transcendent God; see Azzan Yadin, *Scripture as Logos: Rabbi Ishmael and the Origins of Midrash* (Philadelphia: University of Pennsylvania Press, 2004), esp. 18–9 and 141.

[4] See also Q17:106 and Q73:4. Verses indicating a more constrained timeframe of revelation, such as Q2:185 (one month) and Q97:1 (one night) obviously designate specific portions of the text rather than the text as a whole. Much discussed in the exegetical tradition, the

The Qurʾān's own claim that it is given, perhaps most literally, in a "recitable manner" (*tartīlan*), as opposed to "all at once," implies a sequential composition. The veracity of this statement is amply illustrated by the Qurʾān's internal dynamic, lending credence to the traditional narrative that it was composed over decades – i.e. it should be read as the product of a long development and not as "published" all at once.[5] At the same time, the Qurʾān seems cohesive enough both from a literary and a legal point of view to

fact that such perceivably contradictory statements (and laws, see below) have been left in the Qurʾān side by side indicates minimal redactionist intervention during the collection of the text. As the cases of the Bible, the New Testament, and the Talmudic literature amply illustrate, editors almost always intervene in order to harmonize traditions; this is far less demonstrable in the Qurʾān than in other Scriptures.

[5] The question of the Qurʾān's inner development is obviously a difficult one. The core of traditional exegesis, as well as the German school of critical scholarship – from Nöldeke to Neuwirth – rests in one form or another on reading the Qurʾān along the prophet's career, an assumption neither easily proven nor entirely dismissed. The Qurʾān obviously has an internal history that is accessible with the proper historical and philological methods (its dialogue with outside sources being perhaps the most promising path). Yet the debate concerning the visibility of traces of the Qurʾān's redaction and over using legitimate historical and literary methods to discern its many layers continues to complicate the formation of a consensus. See Nicolai Sinai, "The Qurʾān as Process," in idem, Angelika Neuwirth, and Michael Marx (eds.), *The Qurʾān in Context: Historical and Literary Investigations into the Qurʾānic Milieu* (Brill: Leiden, 2010), 407–440. For a recent critique of the possibility of establishing an inner chronology, see Gabriel Said Reynolds, "Le problème de la chronologie du Coran," *Arabica* 58 (2011): 477–502. For an intriguing idiosyncratic stylometric reading influenced by the methods developed by Mahdī Bāzargān, see Behnam Sadeghi, "The Chronology of the Qurʾān: A Stylometric Research Program," *Arabica* 58 (2011): 210–99. For the importance of the Qurʾān's legal material for the

corroborate the traditional notion of its composition and redaction by a small group of people or by an individual. Any discussion of the Qurʾān's authorship, therefore, would have to take into account the effects of several volatile decades of a prophet's interaction with his community.

This longitudinal quality of the Qurʾān stands out in the cited passage for its rehearsal of the opinion of part of its audience, in this case "those who disbelieve" (*allaḏīna kafarū*). The Qurʾān gives clear evidence of the communal participation in its composition and should therefore be read as a text intended to be "heard" by a group rather than "read" by any individual. Angelika Neuwirth is correct in understanding the Qurʾān as the product of an intense dialogue of a prophet with his community.[6] This dialogue

dating of its layers and the present volume's likely contribution to the issue, see below, page 18, note 27.

[6] For a reading of the Qurʾān that pays close attention to the interaction between the prophet and his audience, and thereby to a "communal" composition, see Angelika Neuwirth, *Der Koran: Handkommentar mit Übersetzung. Band 1: Poetische Prophetie. Frühmekkanische Suren* (Berlin: Verlag der Weltreligionen, 2011); see also eadem, "Meccan Texts – Medinan Additions? Politics and the Re-Reading of Liturgical Communications," in Rüdiger Arnzen and Jörn Thielman, *Words, Texts, and Concepts Cruising the Mediterranean Sea: Studies on the Sources, Contents, and Influences of Islamic Civilization and Arabic Philosophy. Dedicated to Gerhard Endress on his Sixty-Fifth Birthday* (Leuven: Peeters, 2004), 71–93. For an argument of an even broader participation in the process see Claude Gilliot, "Reconsidering the Authorship of the Qurʾān: is the Qurʾān Partly the Fruit of a Progressive and Collective Work?" in Gabriel Said Reynolds (ed.), *The Qurʾān in its Historical Context* (London: Routledge, 2008), 88–108. I read the Qurʾān as *orally* composed and as composed *and* redacted in dialogue with its seventh-century emerging community, as suggested on page 33, note 42. This does not exclude the possibility that it contains elements of self-conscious, "secondary" orality as defined by Walter J. Ong, see idem, *Orality and Literacy:*

is the locus of authorial creativity. The dialogical nature of the Qurʾān allows us to use its testimony to address its historical audience more immediately than would be the case with an "authored" work such as, say, Augustine's *Confessions*. From the perspective of the historian, then, this communal involvement justifies attributing the text as we have it to "the Qurʾān" itself rather than to any specific person, as I will do in this book. (I likewise attribute Talmud's authorial voice to "the Talmud"). In reconstructing what the Qurʾān expects its audience to know, both on its discursive surface and in its cultural presuppositions, we can reclaim the Qurʾān as evidence of and for the culture of Arabia in the first half of the seventh century C.E.

Far too little is known about Arabia at this time. The way in which a slightly later outsider perceived the earliest Muslims in Antioch serves as a helpful – and contrasting – starting point to guide us towards appreciating the culture of the Qurʾān's original audience, particularly its attitude towards ritual purity. Such an outsider's perspective to which Robert Hoyland has drawn our attention is offered by the youngest of the many texts preserved in an important document in the Vatican library, Ms. Vatican Syr. 560 (on which more below). In the year 683/4 of the Common Era, merely two or three generations after the death of Muhammad, the Umayyad Caliphate had been established. Living under Muslim rule, Athanasius of Bālād, the Jacobite Patriarch of Antioch, writes an en-

---

The Technologizing the Word (New York: Methuen, 1982). A more nuanced discussion of the literary strategies the historian must employ to appreciate the Qurʾān would surpass the scope of the present work. The readings here suggested, however, may be a small contribution to this discussion, perhaps the most urgent one in the field.

cyclical letter condemning the intermarriage of Christian women with men he calls *ḥnp'*, a Syriac term denoting "pagans," or "gentiles."[7] Moreover, Athanasius lamented that Christians dine with these "pagans:"

"For a terrible report about dissipated Christians has come to the hearing of our humble self. Greedy men, who are slaves of the belly are heedlessly and senselessly taking part with the pagans in feasts together; wretched women have sexual intercourse (or: 'marry,' *mzdwgn*) anyhow with the pagans unlawfully (*l' nmws'yt*) and indecently, and all at times eat without distinction from their sacrifice (*dbḥ'*). They are going astray in their neglect of the commandments (*pwqdn'*) and rules (*wḥwqt'*) of the apostles who often would cry out about this to those who believe in Christ, that they should distance themselves from fornication (*znywt'*), from what is strangled (*ḥnyq'*) and from blood (*dm'*), and from the food of the pagan slaughter (*dbḥ' ḥnpy'*), lest they be by this associates of the demons and of their unclean table."[8]

Athanasius asks the rural bishops and inspectors to ensure that commensality cease and that the communities are reminded of the "canons of the church." Despite the alarming rhetoric, he exhorts them to exercise judgment and not to overreact: the women who have children from said relations should make sure these children are baptized; the

[7] On Athanasius' date see Omert J. Schrier, "Chronological problems concerning the Lives of Severus bar Mašqā, Athanasius of Balad, Julianus Romāyā, Yoḥannān Sābā, George of the Arabs and Jacob of Edessa," *Oriens Christianus* 75 (1991): esp. 78–80, see also Herman Teule, "Athanasius of Balad," in David Thomas and Barbara Roggema (eds.), *Christian-Muslim Relations: A Bibliographical History* (Leiden: Brill, 2009), volume 1, 157–9.

[8] Text cited according to François Nau, "Littérature canonique syriaque inédite," *Revue de l'Orient Chrétien* 14 (1909): 128–30, translation adapted from Robert G. Hoyland, *Seeing Islam as Others Saw It: A Survey and Evaluation of Christian, Jewish and Zoroastrian Writings on Early Islam* (Princeton: Darwin, 1997), 148.

women themselves, remarkably, are not, unlike Christian heretics, to be categorically barred from the Eucharist.[9] These women should simply "guard themselves from the meat of [the pagans'] sacrifice (*dbḥyhwn*) and from what is strangled (*wdḥnyq'*, i.e. meat) and from their illegal (*dl' nmwsyt'*) fellowship." Who, then, are the "pagans," or "gentiles" in Athanasius' community, who sacrifice and eat "strangled meat"? Are they other Christians, Muslims, "real" pagans, or a bit of each?

The Syriac term *ḥnp'* denoted "pagan" or "gentile" up to the seventh century; often, though not always, with a negative connotation. The persistence of paganism in some areas of the seventh-century Umayyad Caliphate, especially in formerly Byzantine territory, is highly marginal at best and would scarcely allow for such a reading of Athanasius' condemnation of Christian intercourse with actual pagans.[10] Athanasius' urgency and the public nature and pervasiveness of the perceived problem suggests that the term *ḥnp'* denotes not pagans, but a gentile group closer to Athanasius' Jacobite church itself.

In effect, Athanasius almost verbatim evokes the so-called *Decree of the Apostles*, as related in Acts 15. In the first Christian century, a compromise was allegedly struck between, on the one hand, those who demanded that the "gentiles" who believed in Jesus were to "keep the law of

---

[9] Athanasius emphasizes that "Nestorians, Julianists, any other heretic" are to be excluded from baptism and Eucharist, see Nau, "Littérature canonique syriaque inédite," 130.

[10] See the Hoyland, *Seeing Islam*, 149. On the persistence of paganism see Michael Morony, *Iraq after the Muslim Conquest* (Piscataway: Gorgias Press, 2005 [1983]), 280–430; John F. Haldon, *Byzantium in the Seventh Century: The Transformation of a Culture* (Cambridge: Cambridge University Press, 1990), 326–51; both cited by Hoyland.

Moses" (Acts 15:5) and, on the other hand, those like Peter and Paul, who insisted that one should not place "on the neck of the gentiles a yoke that neither our ancestors nor we have been able to bear" (Acts 15:10).[11] The compromise suggested in Acts is what Athanasius presupposes, here in the Peshitta's rendering:

For it seemed good to the Holy Spirit and to us
to impose on you [gentiles] no further burden than these essentials:
that you abstain from what has been slaughtered (*dbyḥ'*) to idols
and from blood (*dm'*)
and from what is strangled (*ḥnyq'*)
and from fornication (*znywt'*) (Acts 15:29)

By avoiding the impurity associated with idol worship, blood, strangled animals and improper sexual relations, the Decree of the Apostles maintains a minimum of ritual law as applicable to gentile believers in Jesus.

Why, then, when accusing his community of mingling and commensality with the "pagans" of his time, did Athanasius evoke the language of Acts? Is it simply that the list of prohibited foods and actions in the Decree of the Apostles had become the standard language regarding "whether one should eat meat that had been killed according to the procedure of another religious community," as Hoyland perceptively puts it?[12] In effect, Acts tries to integrate formerly pagan gentiles into its belief system, and thereby fur-

[11] The Peshitta of Acts 15:19 uses *'mm'* for gentiles, yet, as de Blois has noted, elsewhere (e.g. 18:4), Acts also uses *ḥnp* for gentiles, equally in a neutral way; see François de Blois "Naṣrānī (Ναζωραῖος) and ḥanīf (ἐθνικός): Studies on the Religious Vocabulary of Christianity and of Islam," *Bulletin of the School of Oriental and African Studies* 65 (2002): 21.

[12] Hoyland, *Seeing Islam*, 149.

nished Athanasius with powerful language for his attempt to exclude the gentile Muslims by portraying them *as* pagans. The early copyists of Athanasius' letter understood his coded language: in its two early manuscripts (as well as in most later ones), a later hand introduces Athanasius' letter as regarding a Christian's not eating "of the sacrifices of the Muslims (*mhgry'*) who now hold power."[13] For good reason, then, does Hoyland consider it "more likely that, though he may in general intend all non-Christians, Muslims were uppermost in Athanasius' mind."[14]

Using traditional language to describe new problems is a time-honored strategy to cope with radical change. By comparison, the rabbis equally avoided acknowledging the Christianization of the Roman Empire in the century after Constantine by refusing even to name Christians, instead portraying Christianity in terms of Roman paganism.[15] Likewise, Athanasius' association of Muslim sacrifices with demons reflects the standard attitude towards many a religious Other of his time. In the time of Acts, demons were associated with actual idol worship, yet demonological references had become commonplace in Christian polemics of the seventh century. While rabbis favored a technical and psychological approach to demons, Christians not only accused Muslims, but also Christians

---

[13] The Syriac term *mhgry'*, based on the Qur'ānic Arabic term *muhāǧirūn*, "emigrants," clearly denotes Muslim Arabs, see Sokoloff, *A Syriac Dictionary*, 719.

[14] Hoyland, *Seeing Islam* 149.

[15] See Zellentin, "Jerusalem Fell After Betar." Instead of naming it, the rabbis speak of Christianity in terms of Jewish heresy; the most likely rabbinic term exclusively used for gentile Christians is *nṣrym*, akin to the Qur'ānic *naṣārā*, and first attested (as a plural) in the Babylonian Talmud (see below, page 193, note 14).

of different denominations of being possessed by demons and showed their religious prowess by outdoing each other in exorcisms.[16]

At the same time as using standard accusations, Athanasius' language is subtle and precise in evoking Muslims. The "gentile" self-identity of the Qur'ān is actually reflected in its use of the Arabic term *ḥanīf* to depict the original gentile form of worship, going back to Abraham. Athanasius here employs the ambiguity of the cognate Syriac term *ḥnp'* in a polemical way by alluding to the Muslims' own language. He depicts the Muslims not as gentiles, but as pagans – a usage that became common only in the subsequent century.[17] The ambiguity of the term and the affinity

---

[16] See for example Gerrit J. Reinink, "Die Muslime in einer Sammlung von Dämonengeschichten des Klosters von Qennešrīn," in René Lavenant (ed.), *VI Symposium Syriacum 1992*, Orientalia Christiana analecta 247 (Rome: Pontificio Istituto Orientale, 1994), 335–46; Vincent van Vossel, "Le moine syriaque et son diable," in *Le monachisme syriaque aux premiers siècles de l'Eglise, IIe – debut VIIe siècle. I: Textes français*, Patrimoine Syriaque, Actes du Colloque V. Antélias, (Lebanon: Centre d'Études et de Recherches Orientales, 1998), 191–215; and Joseph Verheyden, "'The Demonization of the Opponent' in Early Christian Literature: The Case of the Pseudo-Clementines," in Theo L. Hettema and Arie van der Kooij, *Religious Polemics in Context: Papers Presented to the Second International Conference of the Leiden Institute for the Study of Religions (LISOR) held at Leiden, 27–28 April 2000,* Studies in Theology and Religion 11 (Assen: Van Gorcum, 2004), 330–359. For a recent discussion of the role of external and internal demons in rabbinic and patristic culture, see Ishay Rosen-Zvi, *Demonic Desires: "Yetzer Hara" and the Problem of Evil in Late Antiquity* (Philadelphia: University of Pennsylvania Press, 2011), esp. 36–43.

[17] See de Blois "Naṣrānī (Ναζωραῖος) and ḥanīf (ἐθνικός)," 16–27; Hoyland, *Seeing Islam*, 148; and Sidney Griffith, "The Prophet Muḥammad, his Scripture and his Message according to the Christian Apologies in Arabic and Syriac from the First Abbasid Century," in

between Syriac and Arabic gave Athanasius an easy way to associate Muslim-Christian commensality with idolatry.

In addition to commensality, the problem of intermarriage was equally acute for the patriarch. The Qurʾān explicitly allows intermarriage between the men of its community and Christian women (Q5:5); Athanasius' contemporaries discuss the topic as well.[18] By employing, once more, ambiguous terminology – the verbal (*etpaʿʿal*) form of the Syriac term *zwg* can denote both sexual intercourse in general and marriage in particular – the women's intermarriage can easily be portrayed as fornication (*znywt'*) and the terminology again evokes cognate Arabic terms.[19]

Athanasius' play with language goes further. As Hoyland noted, the term Athanasius uses to deplore the "sacrifice" to idols, *dbḥ'*, equally denotes simple "slaughter." Used in conjunction with the intimation of paganism, "sacrifice" naturally evokes idol worship through sheer guilt by association, even if the slaughter would originally fall well within ritual observance acceptable to Athanasius.[20] Again,

Toufic Fahd (ed.), *La Vie du prophète Mahomet. Colloque de Strasbourg (octobre 1980)* (Paris: Presses universitaires de France, 1983), 118–21.

[18] See Hoyland, *Seeing Islam*, 149.

[19] The Syriac term *mzdwg*, moreover, also evokes one of the Syriac terms for husband and wife, *zwwg'*, as well as the Arabic term for a spouse, *zawǧ*, possibly another way in which Athanasius alludes to his Muslim contemporaries. Hoyland translates "mingle," perhaps seeking to reflect both denotations of *zwg* – "to marry" and "to have sexual intercourse" – as well as the term's affinity to the verb *mzg*, "to mix," see Michael Sokoloff, *A Syriac Dictionary: A Translation from the Latin, Correction, Expansion, and Update of C. Brockelmann's* Lexicon Syriacum (Winona Lake, IN: Eisenbrauns, 2009), 369 and 732 and Hoyland, *Seeing Islam* 148.

[20] See Hoyland, *Seeing Islam*, 149.

ḏabḥ, the Arabic cognate of Syriac *dbḥ'*, is a homophonous cognate term for ritual slaughter (as well as for sacrifice). Athanasius' condemnation thereby likely evokes *Muslim* sacrifice or slaughter among his audience.

Why, then, did Athanasius use coded language, and why could he – why in other words, does the Arabic legal and ritual terminology correspond so closely to the Syriac? Self-censorship does not seem plausible. The allusions are too obvious, and the copyists of Athanasius' letter – still living under Muslim caliphs – did not see the need for such precautions. It may make more sense to understand Athanasius' references to paganism within the history of Christian heresiological discourse, and especially within the history of the Decree of the Apostles, showing that his accusations against commensality with Muslims may actually contain an aside against some Antiochian Christians. For the history of the Decree of the Apostles, in many ways, reflects the history of Byzantine and Syriac Christianity, as much as that of the Arabic Qurʾān.

The issue of ritual purity split Christianity before it was invented. The purported compromise in Acts, related in the late first or early second century C.E., stands in clear tension with the words of the historical Paul, who in the first half of the first century explicitly *permitted* the consumption of idol meat (1 *Corinthians* 8). Indeed, the Decree of the Apostles glosses over the bitter scars of a conflict that divided the early Jesus movement. John of Patmos, for example, writing in the second half of the first century, condemns the Jesus-believing congregations of Pergamum and of Thyatira because they eat "food sacrificed to idols" and "practice fornication" (*Revelation* 2:14 and 20). In other words, these congregations follow Pauline doctrine on the consumption of sacrificed meat and on marriage.[21] The charges Athanasius uses half a millennium later had already been stylized when first uttered.

The conflict between John of Patmos and a Pauline congregation was itself long forgotten in the time of Athanasius, yet attitudes towards ritual purity continued to define and divide Christians. While idol meat became a rarity within the Byzantine Empire, Paul's liberal approach had in the meantime been extended by some church fathers to apply to "blood" and "strangled meat" as well. The latter was deleted from the western manuscripts of Acts altogether, the former was contextualized to the point of abrogation.[22] For example, around 400 C.E., Augustine spoke out against any ritual meaning of the prohibition of blood and attributed a temporal and practical meaning to the decree.[23] More pertinent for the Eastern Church, and likewise writing at the turn of the fifth century in Constantinople, is John Chrysostom, who had spent most of his career in Antioch, the city over whose Jacobite community

---

[21] See esp. Martha Himmelfarb, *A Kingdom of Priests: Ancestry and Merit in Ancient Judaism* (Philadelphia: University of Pennsylvania Press, 2006), 115–86; and David Frankfurter, "Jews or Not? Reconstructing the 'Other' in Rev. 2:9 and 3:9," *Harvard Theological Review* 94 (2001), 403–27.

[22] For a history of the decree in its own time see Roland Deines, "Das Aposteldekret – Halacha für Heidenchristen oder Christliche Rücksichtnahme auf jüdische Tabus?," in Jörg Frey, et al. (eds.), *Jewish Identity in the Greco-Roman World* (Leiden: Brill, 2007), 323–95 and Markus Bockmuehl, "The Noachide Commandments and New Testament Ethics, with Special Reference to Acts 15 and Pauline Halakhah," *Revue Biblique* 102 (1995), 72–101.

[23] See *Contra Faustum* XXXII.13 (Roland Teske (trans.) and Boniface Ramsey (ed.), *The Works of St Augustine. Answer to Faustus, a Manichean* (Hyde Park, NY: New City Press, 2007), 415–6).

Athanasius would one day preside. Chrysostom comments on the Decree of the Apostles that the New Testament in effect did not "severely ordain" (διετάττετο) these prohibitions and that "Christ did not discourse on them."[24] The prohibitions in Acts, for Augustine and Chrysostom, were almost as obsolete as the rest of the Torah's ritual law.

In contrast to the Late Roman church fathers, the liberal opinion of Chrysostom regarding purity did not prevail in the Eastern Churches.[25] To the contrary, the Decree of the Apostles had become the ritual core of Athanasius' own tradition, as exemplified in the Didascalia Apostolorum. As I will discuss below, the Didascalia Apostolorum is a

---

[24] John Chrysostom *Homilia* XXXI, 32–33 (see J.-P. Migne (ed.), *Joannis Chrysostomi Opera Omnia. Patrologiae Graeca* 60 (Paris: Migne, 1860), 240.32–3).

[25] The prohibition of consuming blood was observed by some early church fathers; see Tertullian, *Apology* 9.13 (see T. R. Glover, *Tertullian: Apology; De spectaculis* (Loeb Classical Library 250; London: Heinemann, 1931), 50–3) taking the observance for granted, as, for example, do the following church fathers: Origen, *Contra Celsum* 8:30 (see Marcel Borret (ed. and trans.), *Origène. Contre Celse* (Sources chrétiennes 150) (Paris: Éditions du Cerf, 1969), ad loc, see also Henry Chadwick (ed.), *Origen's Contra Celsum* (Cambridge: Cambridge University Press, 1980), ad loc.); Cyril of Jerusalem, *Catechetical Lecture* 4:28 (see Wilhelm K. Reischl and Joseph Rupp, *S. Patris nostri Cyrilli, hierosolymorum archiepiscopi. Opera, quæ supersunt, omnia* (Hildesheim: Georg Olms, 1967 [1848], volume 1, ad loc., see also Leo P. McCauley and Anthony A. Stephenson (trans.), *The works of Saint Cyril of Jerusalem* (Washington, DC: Catholic University of America Press, 1969–1970), ad loc.); Socrates Scholasticus, *Church History* 5:22 (see Pierre Périchon et al. (eds.), *Socrate de Constantinople, Histoire ecclésiastique (Livres IV–VI)* (Paris: Éditions du Cerf, 2006), ad loc); the observance is also endorsed by the *Synod of Gangra*, Canon II (JJ-P. Migne (ed.), *Dionysii Exigui justi, facundi opera omnia. Patrologia Latina* 67 (Paris: Migne, 1848), 55–6); the observance is reaffirmed in the epitome, ad loc.

church order whose origins may well go back to the third century C.E., yet nothing certain can be said about its content or form before the fifth century, from which we have a Latin text – as in the case of the Qurʾān, a palimpsest. The oldest manuscript of the Syriac version of the Didascalia, more likely translated from a lost Greek text than from the preserved Latin one, is Ms. Vatican Syr. 560, the same manuscript that also contains the oldest copy of Athanasius' letter. Indeed, the Syriac Didascalia is placed at the very beginning, the place of honor in this remarkable manuscript, a large collection of legal documents.[26] In turn, the youngest document in this collection is Athanasius' letter, whose earliest copy thereby constitutes the Syriac Didascalia's *terminus ad quem*.

The present text of the Syriac Didascalia, hence, likely developed between Latin and the Syriac version, between the fifth and the seventh century C.E., and the Didascalia, just like Athanasius, fully endorses the Decree of the Apostles. Its twenty-fourth chapter includes a paraphrase, prohibiting "that which is sacrificed" (*dbyḥ'*), "blood" (*dm'*), "that which is strangled" (*ḥnyqa'*), and "fornication" (*znywt'*). (DA XXIV, 236.9–10, 237.3–4). The Qurʾān does of course prohibit fornication (*zinā*, e.g. Q17:32) as well. Its own catalogue of prohibited meat likewise endorses the Decree of the Apostles, including the following central verse:

---

[26] The manuscript is a parchment codex, which "contains the corpus of legislative sources incorporating acts of ecumenical councils, canons of Greek and indigenous origin, monastic canons and civil legislation, laws as well as related materials" (Vööbus, *The Didascalia Apostolorum in Syriac*, volume 1, *11, see also Vööbus, *Syrische Kanonessammlungen. Ein Beitrag zur Quellenkunde*, *Corpus Scriptorum Christianorum Orientalium* 307 (Louvain: Secrétariat du Corpus Scriptorum Christianorum Orientalium, 1970), 200–2.

You are prohibited carrion,
Blood (*ad-dam*), the flesh of swine,
And what has been offered to other than God.
And the animal strangled (*al-munḫaniqatun*) or beaten to death,
And that which dies by falling or is gored to death,
And that which is mangled by a beast of prey
– barring that which you may purify –
And what is sacrificed (*mā ḏubiḥa*) on stone altars,
And that you should divide (*tastaqsimū*) with arrows.
All that is transgression. (Q5:3)

The similarity of this verse to the Decree of the Apostles will receive due attention below. Here already, we can state that Athanasius' evocation of the consumption of "blood" and "strangled" meat especially would fit many Christians who followed Augustine and Chrysostom quite well – certainly better than the patriarch's complaint would apply to observant Muslims, who share with Athanasius precisely the observances of which he accuses the *ḥnp'*. This ritual sameness, the large overlap between Muslim and Jacobite ritual law, may be the ultimate reason why Athanasius evoked, against likely law-abiding gentile Muslims, the standard charges of eating demon meat and fornication we already saw John of Patmos hurl at the Pauline congregations. From Athanasius' point of view, too little divided his community from that of the Muslims. Hence, accusing them of standard charges of eating strangled meat, he could reaffirm his own commitment to ritual purity – not least against the Byzantine Christians just across the border of the Caliphate, or against their Melkite (i.e. Roman) associates within it.

The Qur'ān, in the meantime, requires purity observances above and beyond those endorsed by Athanasius and the Didascalia. For among the Qur'ān's catalogue of ritual observances, the prohibition of pork (*ḫinzīr*, Q5:3) and of sexual intercourse during the menses feature centrally, as do the requirement to wash before prayer and after intercourse. The Didascalia, in turn, specifically rejects those who singularly add pork (*dḥzyr' blḥwd*, DA XXIII, 230.19) to the list of prohibited meats, together with those who wash before assembling for prayer and after intercourse, and even those who abstain from intercourse during the menses, denouncing such observances as obsolete.

The Didascalia, hence, gained acute relevance after the Muslim conquest: its rejection of Judaeo-Christian additions to the Syriac catalogue of ritual observance such as ritual washing and abstinence from pork, would mark Christian difference from the ruling Muslims. It is quite possible that the Didascalia was given its prominent place in Ms. Syr. Vatican 560 for precisely this reason. Some of the Syriac Didascalia's details may even have been changed in response to the Muslim conquest. Yet as a text and as a discourse, the Didascalia predates the Qurʾān by far, and it is this original context of the Didascalia that I see as reflecting a shared legal culture with the Qurʾān. The present volume will investigate the history of law that gave rise to the complaints of Athanasius and will seek to reconstruct the legal culture of the early seventh century C.E. that stood behind the two central documents of his time: the Qurʾān and the Didascalia.

Legal Culture

In this volume, I will claim that both the majority of the Qurʾān's laws as well as its internal legal dynamics and developments – including its partial self-abrogation known as *naskh* – can be related more precisely to the *nomos* and the *narrative* of Late Antiquity than hitherto established.[27] *Nomos* is constituted by the continuum of criminal, civil, social and ritual laws, *narrative* by the continuum of legal, theological, political and ethical narratives justifying these laws.[28] Based on a momentous trend in recent legal theory,

---

[27] It has long been noted that most of the Qur᾽ān's legal material is to be found in the longer surahs that appear at the beginning of the Qur᾽ān. This fact may make the present study especially pertinent to those students of the Qur᾽ān who argue that a precise inner chronology of the text can be established, and who generally see many of these surahs as part of the later, "Medinan" period of revelation; see above, page 3, note 5. Mehdi Azaiez has recently submitted a conference paper titled "Eschatological Counter-Discourse: Intratextual and Intertextual Approaches" (at the occasion of the conference *Return to the Origins: The Qur᾽ān's Reformation of Judaism and Christianity*, Nottingham, 20–21 January, 2013. A conference volume is in preparation; see page XXI, note 2). Azaiez argues that the increased intertextuality in the "Medinan" surahs opens a more objective approach to the Qur᾽ān's chronology. Accordingly, it is the "Meccan" period, or more precisely the fifth year of the Hijrah, which Shlomo Dov Goitein identified as "the Birth-Hour of Muslim Law," stipulating that increased contact with rabbis led Muhammad to formulate an independent lawcode; see idem, "The Birth-Hour of Muslim Law," *The Muslim World* 50 (1960): 27 and below, page 21, note 30. Such contact between the emerging Muslim community and the rabbis is likely, and should be expanded to include Christian legal traditions as well.

[28] Based on the work of Peter Berger, Robert Cover may be the most important legal theorist insisting that the entirety of the "normative universe" must be taken into account when studying any aspect of law. The *nomos*, any given "set of legal institutions," Cover writes, does not exist "apart from the narratives that locate it and give it meaning. For every constitution there is an epic, for each decalogue a scripture. Once understood in the context of the narratives that give it meaning, law becomes not merely a system of rules to be observed, but a world in which we live. In this normative world, law and narrative are inseparably related. Every prescription is insistent in its demand to be located in discourse – to be supplied with history and destiny, beginning and end, explanation and purpose," (idem, "The Supreme

I consider nomos and narrative as mutually constitutive, jointly establishing what I will call *legal culture*.[29] The thesis I put forward is that, on the one hand, the Qurʾān's

---

Court, 1982 Term – Foreword: Nomos and Narrative," *Harvard Law Review* 97 (1983), 4–5). See also Peter L. Berger, *The Sacred Canopy: Elements of a Sociology of Religion* (New York: Doubleday, 1967).

[29] The term "legal culture" has been used to describe the continuum of culture and law, see for example the volume edited by Csaba Varga, *Comparative Legal Cultures* (New York: NYU Press, 1992). Austin Sarat has already advocated that law shapes "society from the inside out by providing the principal categories in terms of which social life is made to seem largely natural, normal, cohesive and coherent" (idem, "Redirecting Legal Scholarship in Law Schools: Review of Paul W. Kahn, *The Cultural Study of Law* (Chicago: Chicago University Press, 1999)," *The Yale Journal of Law & the Humanities* 12 (2000): 134). Yet, the mutually constitutive relationship of law and culture has especially been emphasized by Naomi Mezey, who states that "law is both a producer of culture and an object of culture" and advocates the crucial insight that we must see "law *as* culture" (eadem, "Law as Culture," *The Yale Journal of Law & the Humanities* 13 (2001): 46). For the present considerations, we should remember that law is never stable; it is shaped in a constant state of internal or external conflict. It has been argued by Robert C. Post that even today, it is at times "better legally to impose fundamental cultural values than to face the unacceptable consequences of costly and destructive cultural conflict" (idem, "Law and Cultural Conflict," *Chicago-Kent Law Review* 78 (2003): 508); see also idem, *Law and the Order of Culture* (Berkeley: University of California Press, 1991). One needs not endorse Post's views to see how they allow us to appreciate the pressures on any given legal culture already in antiquity. The continuity of ancient Jewish law and culture has been elegantly demonstrated by Barry Wimpfheimer, *Narrating the Law: A Poetics of Legal Stories* (Philadelphia: University of Pennsylvania Press, 2011); see my review in *The Journal of Religion* 93 (2013): 117–9. An attempt to establish a specifically Muslim legal culture in contemporary Morocco has been undertaken by Lawrence Rosen, *The Anthropology of Justice: Law as Culture in Islamic Society* (Cambridge: Cambridge University Press, 1989), cf. the critical review by Ann Elizabeth Mayer, "Islam Inside and Out," *The Journal of Interdisciplinary History* 22 (1991): 89–100.

legal culture largely remains within the matrix established by Jewish and Christian tradition broadly defined. On the other hand, in all aspects of its legal culture – its laws and its legal narratives, including specific formulations, concepts, and terminology – the Qurʾān engages a specific tradition that can be tentatively reconstructed based on its comparison with the Syriac Didascalia, whose *nomos* and narrative it takes as one of its points of departure. The Qurʾān, in my view, assumes its audience to be familiar with a legal culture comparable to the one reflected and constituted by the Didascalia. This legal culture reaches ultimately back to the Acts of the Apostles and the Revelation of John of Patmos, yet a search for "origins" would not do justice to its dynamic development. Rather, the Qurʾān as a whole testifies to the persistence of this legal culture up to its own time; the Qurʾān largely affirms this legal culture and partially, but decidedly, alters it in dialogue with the *oral* culture of a *living community*.

How the Didascalia relates to other forms of Judaism and Christianity of its time is a question for which I can only sketch an answer in the following pages. As is the case with the Qurʾān, there is little in the Didascalia for which one would not be able to cull comparable examples from a variety of rabbinic and patristic sources – yet never from *one* single text. The argument for the affinity and distinctness of the Qurʾān and the Didascalia, hence, is necessarily cumulative at best, and may appear tendentious at worst. Yet reading the Didascalia as a pertinent source allows us partially to reconstruct the Qurʾān's distinct legal culture, even if this culture must be understood within the exegetical and legal grammar shared with the broader Biblical culture of Late Antiquity.

In short, the Didascalia and the Qur'ān share a large part of their actual lawcode and both present Jesus as abrogating parts of the law that were given to the Israelites as a punishment for the many sins of which both texts accuse them, as epitomized by the Golden Calf.[30] Moreover, the Didascalia attributes an expansion of its own legal code, encompassing additional observances of ritual purity, to

[30] The affinity of the legal code of the Didascalia and the Qur'ān extends to many fields of law, ranging from what we would classify as criminal and civil to ritual law, and includes the prominence of law in and of itself. Shlomo Goitein concluded that "proportionally the Qur'ān does not contain less legal material than the Pentateuch, the Torah, which is known in world literature as 'The Law'" (idem, "The Birth-Hour of Muslim Law," 24). As exaggerated as the claim may be, it still rectifies a prevailing scholarly lack of emphasis on Qur'ānic law. More importantly yet, the modern distinction between different aspects of law, just as between law, culture, and religion mentioned in the previous note, becomes less prominent the more law is presented as part of religion. We can easily see how Goitein's depiction of the Shari'a is rooted in the Qur'ān itself: it "does not differentiate between purely legal matters, such as contracts or the law of inheritance, and religious duties, such as prayers and fasting; all alike are part of the Holy Law" (see ibid., 23). The discussion about the admissible extent of human participation in the process of formulating and implementing divine law, as advocated by the rabbis, has been the subject of Jewish-Christian polemics since the first century, with an early culmination in the fifth through seventh centuries, see e.g. Shaye Cohen, "Antipodal Texts: B. Eruvin 21b–22a and Mark 7:1–23 on the Tradition of the Elders and the Commandment of God," in Ra'anan Boustan et al. (eds.), *Envisioning Judaism: Studies in Honor of Peter Schäfer on the Occasion of his Seventieth Birthday* (Mohr Siebeck, Tübingen, 2013), volume 1, 965–83; Zellentin, *Rabbinic Parodies of Jewish and Christian Literature* (Tübingen: Mohr Siebeck 2010), 213–27 and idem, "Jesus and the Tradition of the Elders: Originalism and Traditionalism in Early Judean Legal Theory," in L. Jenott, P. Townsend et al. (eds.), *Beyond the Gnostic Gospels: Studies Building on the Work of Elaine H. Pagels* (*Studies and Texts in Antiquity and Christianity* (Tübingen: Mohr Siebeck, 2013), 379–403.

a group in its midst of formerly Jewish believers in Jesus. Their observances are distinct from those of rabbinic Jews, instead constituting a distinct set of practices based on a partial selection of biblical observances above and beyond the requirements in Acts, such as ritual washing after intercourse and before prayer, the avoidance of pork, and the prohibition of intercourse during the menses.[31]

I will adduce comparative rabbinic and patristic evidence in order to try to situate the legal culture shared by the Qurʾān and the Didascalia within Late Antiquity more broadly. Yet I will veer from my focus on the Didascalia only in one case, namely by turning to the evidence of the "Clementine" homilies in order to confirm the historicity of the practice of the Jewish believers in the midst of the

[31] We do not know, of course, what the practices of non-rabbinic Jews would have been in the early seventh century, and it is not impossible that the practices here designated as Judaeo-Christian would constitute a selection of biblical observances similar to that of other non-rabbinic Jewish groups. This fact, however, would not make the religious identity any less distinct from those who combined these observances with a belief in Jesus' status as central to salvation history. On (non-rabbinic) Common Judaism, see E.P. Sanders, *Judaism: Practice and Belief 63 BCE–66 CE* (London: SCM Press, 1992). For further readings see also Seth Schwartz, "Was there a 'Common Judaism' after the Destruction?" In Raʿanan Boustan et al. (eds.), *Envisioning Judaism*, Volume 1, 3–22; Seth Schwartz, *Were the Jews a Mediterranean Society? Reciprocity and Solidarity in Ancient Judaism* (Princeton: Princeton University Press, 2010); Shaye J.D. Cohen, *From the Maccabees to the Mishnah* (Louisville: Westminster John Knox Press, 2006 [1987]); Martin Goodman, "Jews and Judaism in the Second Temple Period," in ibid. (ed.), *The Oxford Handbook of Jewish Studies*, (Oxford: Oxford University Press 2002), 53–78; cf. Martin Hengel and Roland Deines, "E P Sanders' 'Common Judaism', Jesus, and the Pharisees," (Trans. D.P. Bailey), *Journal of Theological Studies* 46 (1995): 1–70.

Didascalia. Crucially, the Clementine Homilies not only record the observances they impose upon Jews, who simply have to follow the Torah, but they also specify ritual observances for Gentiles, whose belief entails "doing the things spoken by God:"

> For even the Hebrews who believe Moses, and do not observe (φυλάσσοντες) the things spoken by him, are not saved, unless they observe (φυλάξωσιν) the things that were spoken to them ..... Neither is there salvation in believing in teachers and calling them lords (καὶ κυρίους αὐτοὺς λέγειν)... For on this account Jesus is concealed from the Jews, who have taken Moses as their teacher, and Moses is hidden from those who have believed Jesus. For, there being one teaching by both, God accepts him who has believed either of these. But believing a teacher is for the sake of doing (ποιεῖν) the things spoken by God.[32]

The Clementine Homilies operate with a clearly defined pattern of two alternate paths to salvation: either through Moses, by observing the Torah, or by believing in Jesus and observing the practices imposed on gentiles. No patristic heresiologist notes this crucial difference and its absence mars many an academic study of Judaeo-Christianity to this day. Yet focusing on these gentile practices will allow us to establish a clearly defined *Judaeo-Christian ritual lawcode*. In addition to the Decree of the Apostles, gentiles in this tradition should observe:

- ritual washing after intercourse and before prayer
- the prohibition of intercourse during the menses
- the strict and expanded prohibition of carrion
- and the avoidance of pork.

[32] Clementine Homilies 8:5–6.

This expanded ritual lawcode is not all of Moses' law, yet it is presented and rejected as "too Jewish" in great detail by the Didascalia. Corroborating the historicity of this outsider's perspective from the inside, the Clementine Homilies and the Qurʾān largely endorse this code and impose it explicitly on gentiles. The additional ritual affinities between the Didascalia's Judaeo-Christians, the Clementine Homilies, and the Qurʾān allow us to see how exactly the Qurʾān brings about a parting of the ways not only with Judaism and Christianity, but more pointedly and decisively with the Judaeo-Christian legal culture described in the Didascalia. Its parting of the ways presupposes prior proximity.

My definition of the Judaeo-Christian ritual lawcode raises a few broader issues I cannot address here. For example, we saw the sketched continuity of the Pauline rejection of any ritual purity requirements for gentiles with church fathers such as Augustine and Chrysostom, as opposed to their continued embrace from Acts to Athanasius of Bālād. When taking the Decree of the Apostles as a benchmark, we should differentiate not only between Christian and Judaeo-Christian law, which adds to the Decree, but also between Christians and Pauline Christians, who subtract from it. My definition of Judaeo-Christianity leads to a disproportionate emphasis on the differences between the position of the Didascalia and Athanasius, on the one hand – based on the Acts of the Apostles – and, on the other, the Clementine Homilies and the Qurʾān, who take the law further. "Judaeo-Christianity" as a category, in my view, was created by Christian heresiologists and perpetuated by scholars who sought to deflect attention from the simple fact that their Christian tradition, in leaving behind ritual purity entirely, rejected a fundamental trait of the first two Christian centuries, as embodied for example in John of Patmos and the Acts of the Apostles.

Redefining all of Christianity based on its legal requirements, however, while attractive in principle, would surpass the scope of this volume by far. Hence, I will henceforth employ the term "Christian" to denote gentile groups following the ritual requirements of the Decree of the Apostles or less. Despite my reservations concerning the scholarly construct of "Judaeo-Christianity," I will use the term for lack of a better one as designating the combined endorsement of ritual purity beyond the Decree of the Apostles – by endorsing the Judaeo-Christian lawcode – and of Jesus' elevated status. I will advocate a critical reconsideration of the theses of Shlomo Pines and others who present the Qurʾān as familiar, but not commensurate with "Judaeo-Christianity."[33]

[33] See Shlomo Pines, "Notes on Islam and on Arabic Christianity and Judaeo-Christianity," *Jerusalem Studies in Arabic and Islam* 4 (1984): 135–52, notes 75 and 112. Most scholarly approaches to "Judaeo-Christianity" rely on the biased evidence of the heresiological tractates of Epiphanius and other church fathers, which, on the one hand, cannot be dismissed entirely, but, on the other, do not serve as a stable point of departure. (Patricia Crone is currently composing a study titled "Jewish Christianity and the Qurʾān," which surveys much of the pertinent patristic literature. Professor Crone was kind enough to share a draft of her study with me, yet it reached me too late to respond to its many worthwhile observations.) The combined evidence of the Didascalia, the Clementine Homilies, and the Qurʾān, however, provides us with three partially overlapping views of "Judaeo-Christian" legal culture, as I will discuss in more detail below. What I am not claiming here is that Judaeo-Christianity, however defined, was a movement that was socially independent from Judaism and Christianity at any point in history. Such a scenario, in which a Judaeo-Christian Church would have separated from other groups before or during the height of the anti-Jewish polemics in the fourth

It is well-established that the Qur'ān seeks to supersede rabbinic Judaism and Christianity, certainly in its Syriac and likely in its Jacobite forms, as becomes increasingly clear.[34] The argument here is that, from a legal point

century and carried on an undocumented existence in remote locations, is of course not impossible, and not even implausible. However, we do not have any evidence for it either. Rather, it seems to me that Judaeo-Christianity constituted an integral part of various forms of Judaism and Christianity throughout Late Antiquity, as evidenced by the explicit statements of the Didascalia and by the preservation of its heritage in the Qur'ān. The following pages will attempt to integrate these two main witnesses for the phenomenon into the broader religious history; I will return to the topic of Judaeo-Christianity in my Conclusion.

[34] On the alleged importance of "monophysite" Christianity for the Qur'ān, cf. John Bowman, "The Debt of Islam to monophysite Syrian Christianity," *Nederlands Theologisch Tijdschrift* 19 (1964/5): 177–201 and already Henri Grégoire, "Mahomet et le monophysitisme," in *Mélanges Charles Diehl: Études sur l'histoire et sur l'art de Byzance* (Paris: Ernest Leroux, 1930), 107–19. For the alternative view, emphasizing Nestorian Christianity, see Tor Andrae, *Der Ursprung des Islams und das Christentum* (Uppsala: Almqvist & Wiksells, 1926), e.g. 158, 188, and 195, but cf. 3 for Andrae's insistence on a variety of Christian interlocutors of the Qur'ān. For recent trends on the question, see below, page 34, note 43, see especially Joseph Witztum's criticism of Bowman and Andrae in Witztum, *The Syriac Milieu of the Quran: The Recasting of Biblical Narratives* (PhD Dissertation, Princeton, NJ, 2011), 36–49. For a recent study emphasizing the diversity of Christian groups before and after the coming of Islam see Jack Tannous, *Syria between Byzantium and Islam: Making Incommensurables Speak* (Ph.D. dissertation, Princeton University, 2010). While a new approach to the Jewish presence in Arabia that would integrate the Qur'ānic evidence remains a desideratum, Gordon Newby's broad overview remains helpful, even if often overstated, see idem, *A History of the Jews of Arabia: From Ancient Times to Their Eclipse Under Islam* (Columbia, SC: University of South Carolina Press, 2009 [1988]). A more careful approach is offered by Robert Hoyland, "The Jews of the Hijaz in the Qur'ān

of view, the Qur'ān's engagement with the broader legal culture of Late Antiquity is secondary to its much more focused affirmation and alteration of a particular form of Judaeo-Christian observance that can be reconstructed with the help of the overlap between the Qur'ān, the Syriac Didascalia and the Clementine Homilies. While I argue that the legal culture based on these observances can be traced backwards to the time of the Didascalia, and possibly to an even earlier tradition, I reserve judgment on the existence of Judaeo-Christianity as a social entity distinct from other Jewish and Christian groups. Without negating this possibility, I rather imagine adherents of Judaeo-Christian practice and belief to be part of other Jewish and Christian social structures, known to us or not.

Throughout this study, I seek to strike a balance between two strongly formulated positions regarding the existence of Judaeo-Christianity throughout Late Antiquity and especially past the fourth century. On the one side, some scholars have long suspected a Judaeo-Christian "heresy" at the origins of Islam, presupposing or actually claiming that a distinct community must have been responsible for the transmission of Judeo-Christian thought into the Qur'ān's milieu, most recently so de Blois.[35] The

---

and in their Inscriptions," in Gabriel Said Reynolds, *New Perspectives on the Qur'ān: The Qur'ān in Its Historical Context 2* (Abingdon: Routledge, 2011), 91–116.

[35] De Blois suggests that "the 'Jewish Christians' in the environment of primitive Islam were ... those that it calls *naṣārā*, the Nazoraeans. ... The realization that the *naṣārā* of the Quran are not simply Christians, but 'Jewish Christians', who maintained, against Paul, the continued validity of the law of Moses, explains why the quranic notion of Abraham the *ḥanīf*, gentile, stands in polemical juxtaposition not only to the Jews, but also to the Nazoraeans. This suggests

Qur'ān's Judaeo-Christian tendencies, for them, are proof enough of the actual presence of Judaeo-Christians. On the other side, scholars have denied any historical affinity between Judaeo-Christianity and the Qur'ān, most recently Sidney Griffith. The absence of clear evidence for the survival of Judaeo-Christian groups for these scholars is proof enough for their nonexistence. As Griffith puts it,

> "it is important to recognize the probability that themes and turns of phrase that can also be found in earlier Jewish Christian sources had long since entered the stream of mainline Christian discourse, especially in the Aramaic/Syriac-speaking communities of the early seventh century. The Qur'ān's seeming espousal of positions earlier owned by some Jewish Christians hardly constitutes evidence for the actual presence of one or another of these long-gone communities in its seventh century Arabian milieu."[36]

---

that the primitive Muslim community had contact with Nazoraeans. But the author of the Quran must have had some knowledge also of the teachings of Pauline (or rather pseudo-Pauline, presumably catholic) Christianity. One does not, however, gain the impression that catholic Christians were perceived as a serious rival to nascent Islam." De Blois, "Naṣrānī (Ναζωραῖος) and ḥanīf (ἐθνικός)," 26. De Blois does not differentiate between the Judaeo-Christian requirements for Jews and for gentiles (Clementine Homilies 8:5–7, see pages 22–5 above) and erroneously understands the entirety of the Mosaic law, rather than the Judaeo-Christian ritual lawcode alone, to apply to the latter. Blois also constructs the Judaeo-Christians as a discrete "Nazorean" group distinct from the established Christian and Jewish community, for which there is no evidence. In my Conclusion, I will develop Griffith's argument against de Blois that the Qur'ān's view of the *naṣārā* is pre- rather than descriptive, suggesting that the *naṣārā* are indeed "Pauline," and that these are indeed among its main "rivals" – all the while being seen as part of ("true") Israel. In my view, the Qur'ān enjoins these "Pauline" Christians to become more Judaeo-Christian.

[36] Griffith, *The Bible in Arabic*, 37.

De Blois obviously cannot dismiss Griffith's charge that no outside evidence corroborates the existence of independent Judaeo-Christian groups; yet Griffith never explains which Judaeo-Christian "themes and turns of phrase," or as he puts it earlier, "texts and turns of phrases," actually can be found in Syriac Christianity in the seventh century, or where exactly to find them.[37] More importantly, he does not consider the fact that the continuity of actual Judaeo-Christian practice in the Qur'ān goes far beyond doctrine, themes, texts, and turns of phrase.

It is easy to see how a long-ranging debate in the study of Late Antiquity is spilling over into the study of the Qur'ān. It had long been held that Judaeo-Christianity basically ceased to exist in the second century, and Judaeo-Christian texts edited in the fourth century and later – especially the Clementine Homilies – were long read with a focus on their much earlier "Grundschrift." Scholars such as Annette Yoshiko Reed (on whom more below) have challenged such a "historicization" of Judaeo-Christianity, pointing to the fact that Judaeo-Christian authorial creativity in the fourth and fifth centuries and beyond presupposes that someone must have leaned towards ritual purity.

Yet we need not equate tendencies or observances of people with independent groups. Observing the Judaeo-Christian ritual lawcode, marked by abstinence from certain foods and by activities as mundane as washing at appropriate times, can be done very discretely. Griffith's argument from silence – the church fathers ceased complaining about Jewish observances and Judaeo-Christians groups – may or may not attest to the end of Judaeo-Chris-

---

[37] See Griffith, *The Bible in Arabic*, 28.

tian groups. Yet the intense focus on the Christological debates that swept through all Syriac churches in the fifth and sixth centuries would have allowed for a broad spectrum of attitudes towards ritual purity to flourish unnoticed or even be endorsed by the authorities.

A careful reading of all sources leads to a position in between Griffith and de Blois. On the one hand, Griffith's argument from silence that few Greek or Syriac church fathers past the fourth century mention independent Judaeo-Christian groups by no means proves that they ceased to be, yet the possibility seems likely. In my view, then, the perspectives on Judaeo-Christians that we find in the Didascalia, the Qurʾān, and, as we will see below, in the rabbinic tradition, corroborate Griffith in as far as these texts portray Judaeo-Christians to be located *within* the established Jewish and Christian communities. On the other hand, the commonalities of the legal culture of the Qurʾān, the Clementine Homilies and the Didascalia corroborate de Blois in that they strongly suggest the persistence of Judaeo-Christianity in some way – and practice can be much more stable than mere doctrine.[38]

It seems to me most likely, then, that we should posit the Didascalia's Jewish believers, as well as the gentiles who follow the purity laws imposed on them in the Clem-

---

[38] Pierre Bourdieu's notion of "doxa" proves helpful here; see idem, *Outline of a Theory of Practice* (Cambridge: Cambridge University Press, 1979 [1972]), esp. 167–9. Judaeo-Christian observances, in other words, may have been more widespread within Syriac Christianity than hitherto appreciated. In an intellectual environment that focused on Trinitarian debates, especially from the fifth century onwards, such observances could have been part of the *doxa* of individuals or communities without necessarily inciting official reprimands, as I will argue in Chapter Two.

entine Homilies, precisely where these two texts posit them: within established Christian and Jewish community respectively, and among the people of the book, as the Qurʾān puts it (see my Conclusion).

Reading the Qurʾān in light of its affinities with Judaeo-Christian legal culture will corroborate this suggestion. Likewise, Griffith's claim that many Judaeo-Christian "texts," "themes," and "turns of phrase" were actively circulating in the Syriac milieu of seventh-century Arabia is indeed supported by the Didascalia itself, adding "laws" more broadly. While the Didascalia's origins can be traced centuries before the Qurʾān, we should in turn understand it as continuously in circulation, informing oral discourse and being informed by it. Both documents are reflective of part of the oral legal discourse prevalent throughout Arabia and its environs in the early seventh century C.E.[39] A closer look at the historical evidence for the circulation of the Didascalia will suggest that it played a continuous,

[39] As Wael B. Hallaq puts it, when "Muhammad embarked on his mission of establishing a new religion and building a state, he and his collaborators were well acquainted not only with the political and military problems of the Fertile Crescent, but also with its cultures and much of its law. While law as a doctrine and legal system does not appear to have been on the Prophet's mind during most of his career, the elaboration of a particularly Islamic conception of law did begin to emerge a few years before his death. The legal contents of the Quran, viewed in the larger context of already established Jewish law and the ancient Semitic-Mesopotamian legal traditions, provide plentiful evidence of this rising conception" (idem, *The Origins and Evolution of Islamic Law* (Cambridge: Cambridge University Press, 2005), 4). I agree with Hallaq, though I would add the Didascalia as an important part of the evidence for "Jewish" and "Semitic-Mesopotamian" legal traditions. On the putative timing of the Qurʾān's legal material see also above, page 18, note 27, and page 21, note 30.

albeit marginal, role in shaping the legal culture in the Near and Middle East and in Northeast Africa from the third through the seventh centuries C.E. and beyond, and thereby influenced the legal culture which the Qurʾān assumes as established among part of its audience.[40]

The Veil in the Didascalia and in the Qurʾān

As the example of the veil will illustrate, the Qurʾān's specific affinity with the Didascalia points less to any direct *literary* relationship between the two texts, and more towards the Qurʾān's familiarity with the *oral* legal discourse of which the Didascalia gives evidence.[41] While the

[40] The Qurʾān, without being reducible to its legal predecessors, participates in and departs from a legal culture that can best be appreciated in its comparison with the Didascalia – analyzing cultural similarity is meaningful only if the purpose is to evaluate cultural difference. As Joseph Witztum puts it, we should try to understand "how the Quran appropriated, revised and adapted its building blocks in order to convey its own message. ... [It] is more productive to ask in what ways the Quran reflects earlier trends and in what ways it develops its received traditions in new directions," in idem, *The Syriac Milieu of the Quran*, 4; see also the following note.

[41] For a summary of the recent critical discussions of the concepts of "dependence" and "influence" in cross-cultural intertextuality in rabbinics, see Holger Zellentin, *Rabbinic Parodies*, 21–2; for a discussion in Qurʾānic studies, see Michael Pregill, *The Living Calf of Sinai: Polemic, Exegesis, and "Influence" from Late Antiquity to the Islamic Middle Ages,* a study in preparation building on *The Living Calf of Sinai: Orientalism, "Influence," and the Foundation of the Islamic Exegetical Tradition* (PhD Dissertation, New York, NY, 2007), which Professor Pregill kindly shared with me. For the Qurʾān's own cognate view of the history of subsequent revelations, see Angelika Neuwirth, *Der Koran als Text der Spätantike. Ein europäischer Zugang* (Berlin: Insel Verlag, 2010), 128–34.

establishment of such an oral discourse is by definition elusive, the Qurʾān's endorsement and development of the legal culture constituted by the Syriac version of the Didascalia follows an established pattern. Recent scholarship emphasizes the Qurʾān's familiarity with Syriac Christian and, to a lesser degree, also with rabbinic, narrative Scriptural traditions, equally in the framework of orality.[42] The Qurʾān uses these Syriac and Aramaic narrative traditions in order to criticize the perceived "excesses" of rabbinic Judaism and Christianity (see e.g. Q2:111, Q4:171, Q5:77, Q9:30–1). Likewise, the Qurʾān's recasting of the Judaeo-Christian legal culture, which can be reconstructed with the help of the Didascalia, shows evidence of its intimate dialogue with, as well as its clear emancipation from, distinctive aspects of the Judaism and Christianity

[42] For the orality of scriptural traditions in Arabia, see Griffith, *The Bible in Arabic*, esp. xii–iii, 43–6, and 90–1. Using orality as a central aspect of ancient Jewish or Christian culture has been long established, but has yet to be fully integrated in Qurʾānic studies. For the importance of orality in the formation of the Qurʾān, see Angelika Neuwirth, "Two Faces of the Qurʾān: Qurʾān and Muṣḥaf," *Oral Tradition* 25 (2010): 141–56; and Daniel A. Madigan, *The Qurʾān's Self-image. Writing and Authority in Islam's Scripture* (Princeton: Princeton University Press, 2001). The methodologies developed in Late Antique studies may be helpful when seeking further to enhance our understanding of the Qurʾān's orality. "The oralist approach to the rabbinic text," Martin Jaffee writes, "is a variant of the intertextualist approach to literary interpretation combined as well with a kind of 'audience-response' sensibility" (idem, "What Difference Does the 'Orality' of Rabbinic Writing Make for the Interpretation of Rabbinic Writings?" in Matthew Kraus (ed.), *How Should Rabbinic Literature Be Read in the Modern World?* (Piscataway, NJ: Gorgias Press, 2006), 20). For Christian orality see e.g. Samuel Byrskog, *Story as History – History as Story: The Gospel Tradition in the Context of Ancient Oral History* (WUNT 123; Tübingen: Mohr Siebeck, 2000).

of its time – such as the pervasive religious dominance of the Aramaic language.[43]

[43] The Qurʾān sees itself as an "Arabic" confirmation of Scripture (see Q46:12) and thereby shows acute awareness of the linguistic difference between itself and what it considers previous revelation. The Qurʾānic emphasis on Arabic only makes sense if its audience was also exposed to other languages; among those, Jewish and Christian forms of Aramaic, i.e. Jewish Aramaic and Syriac, were likely the most prominent. The growing importance of the Jewish and Christian Aramaic languages and literatures (and especially of the *memre* of Jacob of Serugh and the Syriac Gospel of Matthew) for the study of the Qurʾān is well exemplified in two recent dissertations: Joseph Witztum, *The Syriac Milieu of the Quran* (see also idem, "The Foundations of the House (Q2: 127)," *Bulletin of the SOAS* (2009): 25–40); and Emran al-Badawi, *Sectarian Scripture: The Qur'an's Dogmatic Re-Articulation of the Aramaic Gospel Traditions in the Late Antique Near East* (PhD Dissertation, University of Chicago, 2011); while al-Badawi may occasionally overstate his case, the main thrust of his argument seems valid. See also the weighty contributions by the two volumes edited by Gabriel Said Reynolds, *New Perspectives on the Qurʾān* and *The Qurʾān in its Historical Context*; especially Sidney H. Griffith, "Christian Lore and the Arabic Qurʾān: The 'Companions of the Cave' in Surat al-Kahf and in Syriac Christian Tradition," in ibid., 109–37; Kevin van Bladel, "The Legend of Alexander the Great in the Qurʾān 18:83–102," in ibid., 175–203; and Joseph Witztum, "Joseph Among the Ishmaelites: Q12 in Light of Syriac Sources," in Reynolds (ed.), *New Perspectives on the Qurʾān* , 425–448. On Jacob of Serugh see also below, page 45, note 55. For a bibliography of the classical works on the question of the relationship of the Qurʾān with Aramaic and esp. Syriac literature see Witztum, *The Syriac Milieu of the Quran*, 10–65 and Claude Gilliot, "Language and Style of the Qurʾān," in Jane Dammen McAuliffe (ed.) *Encyclopaedia of the Qurʾān* (Brill: Online, 2013, <http://referenceworks.brillonline.com/browse/encyclopaedia-of-the-quran>), ad loc.; a missing reference in Gilliot is Karl Ahrens, "Christliches im Qoran: Eine Nachlese," *Zeitschrift der Deutschen Morgenländischen Gesellschaft* 84 (1930): 15–68 and 148–90.

After the opening example of the veil, this introduction will proceed by summarizing the nature and the dynamic development of the Didascalia throughout Late Antiquity, focusing on its Syriac iteration. I then present the Didascalia's laws and its (mutually constitutive) legal narratives in conceptual comparison and contrast with those of the Qur'ān. I will make reference throughout to the broader legal culture and lexicon of Late Antique Judaism and Christianity to which both the Qur'ān and the Didascalia belong, in order to show how both texts share a distinct subset of laws and legal narratives. Likewise, I will note the stylistic and lexical commonality between the respective presentation of legal and ritual concepts in the Syriac of the Didascalia and in the Arabic of the Qur'ān. Given the contentiousness of the recent "Syriac turn" in Qur'ānic studies, it may be apposite to illustrate what the lexical commonality proves, and what it does not.[44] Namely, the

---

[44] In light of the recent advances – and derailments – of the use of Syriac materials for the reading of the Qur'ān, it must be emphasized that lexical affinity between two literary corpora has limited significance in and of itself. The Didascalia and the Qur'ān are both simply written in Semitic languages and will naturally share many lexemes. More concretely, both of the Semitic texts from Late Antiquity are reflective of a similar tradition of preserving and interpreting Scripture in and around Arabia and will naturally share stylistic elements. The lexical affinity between the Didascalia and the Qur'ān, however, remains a doubly potent device of inquiry, first by guiding us towards the especially close lexical affinity in matters of law and ritual, and second by corroborating the adjacent conceptual affinities. For a clear warning against the excesses of the "Syriac turn" see, e.g., Walid Saleh, "The Etymological Fallacy and Qur'anic Studies: Muhammad, Paradise, and Late Antiquity," in Neuwirth et al. (eds.), *The Qur'ān in Context*, 649–698; Sidney H. Griffith, "Syriacisms in the 'Arabic Qur'ān': Who were those who said 'Allāh is third of three' according

Didascalia endorses the veiling of women in a way that may have been endorsed and altered by the Qur᾿ān:

If you want to become a believing woman (*mhymnt'*),
Be beautiful (*špr'*) for your husband (*lb'lky*) only.
And when you walk in the street,
Cover your head with your garment (*blbwšky*),
That because of your veil (*tḥpytky*) your great beauty (*dšwprky*) may be covered.
And paint not the countenance of your eyes,
But have downcast looks
And walk being veiled (*mḥpy'*). (DA III, 26, 5–11)[45]

The Didascalia's admonition is hardly surprising in the light of centuries of Jewish and Christian discourse on female modesty and veiling.[46] The Qur᾿ān also shares this

to al-Mā'ida 73?" in Meir M. Bar-Asher et al. (eds.) *A Word Fitly Spoken: Studies in Mediaeval Exegesis of the Hebrew Bible and the Qur᾿ān, Presented to Haggai Ben-Shammai* (Jerusalem: The Ben Zvi Institute, 2007), 83*–110*; and Angelika Neuwirth, "Qur'an and History – A Disputed Relationship. Some Reflections on Qur'anic History and History in the Qur'an," *Journal of Qur'anic Studies* 5 (2003): 1–18.

[45] See also Apostolic Constitutions I.8 (ibid., 27) for the current passage, see also page 41, note 48, and pages 46–7, note 57 below.

[46] Veiling of women is attested since ancient times, see Karel van der Toorn, "The Significance of the Veil in the Ancient Near East," in David P. Wright et al. (eds.), *Pomegranates and Golden Bells: Studies in Biblical, Jewish, and Near Eastern Ritual, Law, and Literature in Honor of Jacob Milgrom* (Winona Lake, IN: Eisenbrauns, 1995), 329–30; for references to the veil in Islamic tradition see Mona Siddiqui, "Veil," McAuliffe (ed.), *Encyclopaedia of the Qur᾿ān*, ad loc. Some trends in rabbinic law require married women to cover their hair. See esp. Mishna *Ketuboth* 7.7, which lists as one of the transgressions against Jewish law to go out with "a wild head" (*wr'šh prw'*). See also Mishna *Ketubot* 2.1, Sifre *Bemidbar* 11, Yerushalmi *Ketubot* 2.1 (26a, 75–26b, 5), Bavli *Ketubot* 72a–73a, Bavli *Gittin* 90a, Bavli *Yoma* 47a; as well as Arthur Marmorstein, "Judaism and

aspect of the broad heritage of Scriptural culture, instructing the veiling of women. Yet within the broader legal cultural framework, we should also consider the more precise conceptual, stylistic and lexical affinities between the ways in which the Didascalia presents its teaching and the Qur'ān's respective rendering:

Christianity in the Middle of the Third Century," *Hebrew Union College Annual* 10 (1935): 233; and "Veil," in Michael Berenbaum and Fred Skolnik (eds.), *Encyclopaedia Judaica* (Detroit: Macmillan Reference, 2007), 20, 489. In the Christian tradition, the veil seems to have been introduced as a requirement for worshipping women early on (see 1Cor. 11:3–15); the practice was later extended as a permanent garment to consecrated virgins and widows, see for example Tertullian, *On the Veiling of Virgins* (see Tertullien, *Le Voile des vierges (De uirginibus uelandis)*, *Sources Chrétiennes* 424 (Intr. by Eva Schulz-Flügel, trans. by Paul Mattei) (Paris: Éditions du Cerf, 1997); *Acts of Thomas* 13–14 (see Paul-Hubert Poirier and Yves Tissot (eds.), *Écrits apocryphes chrétiens* I, *Bibliothèque de la Pléiade* (Paris: Gallimard, 1997), 1341–2); and Ephrem, *On Virginity* 17 (see Edmund Beck (ed.), *Des heiligen Ephraem des Syrers: Hymnen de Virginitate*, *Corpus Scriptorum Christianorum Orientalium* 224 (Louvain: Secrétariat du Corpus Scriptorum Christianorum Orientalium, 1962), 11). For the veiling of women in Najran see Eleanor A. Doumato, "Hearing Other Voices: Christian Women and the Coming of Islam," *International Journal of Middle East Studies* 23 (1991): 177–99. For veiling of nuns see Jeffrey F. Hamburger and Susan Marti, *Crown and Veil: Female Monasticism from the Fifth to the Fifteenth Centuries* (New York: Columbia University Press, 2008). For a general overview see Roland de Vaux, "Sur le voile des femmes dans l'orient ancien," *Revue Biblique* 44 (1935): 397–412. The extent to which women in Byzantium, as well as in Arabia and Persia, were veiled in general remains disputed; see the lucid summary by Timothy Dawson, "Propriety, Practicality, and Pleasure: the Parameters of Women's Dress in Byzantium, A.D. 1000–1200," in Lynda Garland, (ed.), *Byzantine Women: Varieties of Experience 800–1200* (Aldershot: Ashgate, 2006), 41–75.

Tell the believing men (*mu'minīna*) to cast down their looks,
And to guard their private parts
And tell the believing women (*mu'mināti*)
To cast down their looks
And to guard their private parts,
And not to display their beauty (*zīnatahunna*)
Except for what is outward
And let them draw their veils (*ḫumurihinna*) over their bosoms
And not display their beauty (*zīnatahunna*),
Except to their husbands (*buʿūlatihinna*)
Or their fathers,
Or their husband's fathers …
Or children uninitiated
To women's parts (*ʿalā ʿaurāti'n-nisā'i*) (Q24:31)

The similarity between both texts, to begin with, goes far beyond the broadly shared tradition of the veil. Both texts here agree on the veiling of married women, and both construct a narrative of sexual modesty around it. Rather than condemning sexual attraction, as is common in the ascetic strands of the Christian tradition, both texts channel it into the approved sphere of matrimony. Most importantly, both the Didascalia and the Qur'ān formulate their instructions in very similar ways, indicated in italics, using partially overlapping lexemes:

- Both texts are addressed to the *believing* women (*mhymnt'*, *mu'mināti*).
- Both indicate that these women should *cast down* their *looks*, likely in order to avoid unwanted attention, as the Qur'ān spells out in the parallel passage Q33:59.
- According to both texts, such attention should also be avoided by *covering/not displaying* the women's *beauty* from the general public, and reserve it for the *husbands* (*lbʿlky*, *buʿūlatihinna*).

– And of course, both exhort married women to wear a *veil* over part of their bodies in order to achieve this end.

Hence, the manifold conceptual overlaps in the presentation allow us to speak of a shared aspect of the legal culture between the Qurʾān and the Didascalia insofar as both texts endorse the same law and justify it with the same minimal, yet recognizable narrative about modesty, female beauty, and matrimony. This commonality extends to part of the lexicon common to both Syriac and Arabic when describing central concepts: "faith" and "husband," based on the shared Semitic roots *'mn* and *bʿl*, are identical in both languages.

Because of the lexical affinities, the texts' differences are all the more noteworthy: the Qurʾān's choice to use the vernacular Arabic stands out as starkly against the Didascalia's Syriac as Luther's German did against the Vulgate's Latin. The Syriac *šwpr'* denotes "beauty" first of all and "adornment" only secondarily, while the Arabic term employed for the women's *zīna* more often denotes "adornments" than "natural beauty" – even if the context of the Qurʾānic passage here suggests reading these "adornments" as being mostly natural, as explicated with the reference to "women's parts."[47] Further, the terms here employed in both texts for "veil," "casting down" and even "looks," share no kinship whatsoever. While this

[47] Note that the respective distinct lexemes for "*beauty*," *šwpr'* and *zīna*, both occur *twice* in each text. For the Syriac term *šwpr'* denoting "beauty" and "adornment" see Sokoloff, *A Syriac Dictionary*, 1533–4. In the Qurʾān, esp. in Q24:60, *zīna* seems to imply a similarly "natural" adornment of older unmarried women that is to be covered; however, in Q7:26, 31 and 32 for example, the "adornment" is clearly external to the body.

fact could be explained with the distinct lexicon of both languages, we should consider also the structural dissimilarities between the two passages, which far outweigh the parallels.

Distinctness is apparent on the conceptual level, perceived with particular clarity against the background of shared aspects. While the Didascalia emphasizes the veiling of the head, the Qurʾān emphasizes that of the bosom (even if later Muslim tradition understood it in line with the Didascalia). The Qurʾān moreover demonstrates a stricter stance toward veiling, *expanding* the shared injunction for married women to veil in some way to include apparently unmarried "daughters" (Q33:59), and likely all "women of the believers," unless they be of advanced age and without intent to marry (Q24:60). Along the same lines, the Qurʾān extends the instruction to females to "cast down their looks" to include believing men as well. Finally, the Qurʾān *exempts* other close male family members, in addition to the Didascalia's "husbands," from the prohibition to see the women unveiled.

Hence, as striking as the conceptual, stylistic, and, to a lesser degree, lexical commonalities may be, they are at the same time very limited and do not point to the Qurʾān's rephrasing of a written text. Rather, the combination of partial sameness and broad difference between the Qurʾān and the Didascalia testifies to the Quran's participation in an oral tradition at least partially approachable through the Didascalia, as well as to its development of an independent legal stance.

The laws of behavior regarding the veil were likely iterated and more importantly applied countless times between the time of the Didascalia's composition and that of the Qurʾān, making a direct textual line between the two texts seem unlikely.[48] To summarize, the example of the veil affords us a glimpse of the Qurʾān's participation in and development of an established legal culture for which the Didascalia, in my view, is our best witness. This becomes apparent in the Qurʾān's doubly broadened application of both the established law (to include unmarried women) and its exemptions regarding the veil (to include male relatives); similarly, the Qurʾān presents all of its shared laws with greater specificity than the Didascalia and tends to make allowance for reasonable exemptions (on which more below).

The Didascalia Apostolorum from the Third to the Seventh Century C.E.

Before turning to the further legal and narrative comparison, a few words on the nature of the Didascalia are necessary. The Didascalia Apostolorum is a church order that circulated in a number of languages throughout Late Antiquity and early Islamic times. It is presented as writ-

[48] A comparison of the Qurʾān with the adaptation of the Didascalia's instruction for veiling in the Apostolic Constitutions I.8 (Funk, *Didascalia et Constitutiones Apostolorum,* volume I, 27), to be found in note 57 on page 46–7 below, shows that the Qurʾān's affinity with the Didascalia is closer than with the Didascalia's retelling in the Apostolic Constitutions. While the Apostolic Constitutions continue to share a few of the similarities we saw between the Didascalia and the Qurʾān – the casting down of eyes appears here, as do the instructions to focus on husbands, and the covering of the women – other significant aspects do not appear, such as the veil itself, and the repeated focus on "beauty." At the same time, the Apostolic Constitutions introduce additional stylistic elements not shared with the Qurʾān, such as the exhortation to "pay attention."

ten by Jesus' disciples who then became the apostles.[49] Its affirmative attitude towards divine law as essential for salvation, as well as its legal hermeneutics more broadly, can be understood within, or at least in dialogue with the intellectual framework of "Judaeo-Christianity," as Charlotte Fonrobert and more recently Joel Marcus note.[50] In my view, however, the Didascalia's rejection of many aspects of ritual purity and its self-designation as *krysṭyn'* (DA I, 13.6), "Christian," merely incorporates momentous rabbinic and Judaeo-Christian elements while remaining Christian. Hence, the voice of its implied authors – the

[49] On the identity of the apostles behind the Didascalia, including Jesus' original disciples, Peter (DA XXIII, 229.17) and Matthew (DA X, 118.17), as well as later Clement (DA Proem, 10.15.), see Stewart-Sykes, *The Didascalia Apostolorum*, 22–5; see also Georg Schöllgen, "Pseudapostolizität und Schriftgebrauch in den ersten Kirchenordnungen. Anmerkungen zur Begründung des frühen Kirchenrechts," in: idem and Clemens Scholten (eds.), *Stimuli: Exegese und ihre Hermeneutik in Antike und Christentum. Festschrift für Ernst Dassmann* (Münster: Aschendorff, 1996), 96–121.

[50] Charlotte Elisheva Fonrobert, "The Didascalia Apostolorum: A Mishnah for the Disciples of Jesus," *Journal of Early Christian Studies* 9 (2001), 483–509 and Joel Marcus, "The *Testaments of the Twelve Patriarchs* and the *Didascalia Apostolorum*: A Common Jewish Christian Milieu?," *Journal of Theological Studies* 61 (2010), 596–626. In many of the Didascalia's later manuscripts, we find an additional proem in which the Didascalia's self-designation indeed has shifted from *krysṭyn'* (DA I, 13.6), "Christians," to *nṣry' mšyḥy'*, "Messianic Christian," (DA *Proem*, 10.16); here we also find the attribution to Clement (see the previous note). The proem, however, is extant only in manuscripts E F G H I J K N (see Vööbus, I, 36*–37*). The evidence from these manuscripts should best be bracketed; it may equally be the result of post-Qurʾānic developments or a reflection of the Arabic environment of later scribes, as François de Blois aptly notes, see idem, "Naṣrānī (Ναζωραῖος) and ḥanīf (ἐθνικός)," 8 note 41. On the identity of the Qurʾān's Christians see also my Conclusion.

apostles – represents what I will call a "Christian group," as opposed to a heteropractical "Judaeo-Christian group," within its congregation that I will discuss at length. In the case of the Didascalia, it seems more efficient to speak of communal "authors" than in the case of the Qurʾān. In contrast to the role that orality played in the composition of the Qurʾān, the Didascalia is a text that claims apostolic authorship in the first place and whose text was revised over centuries; it is simply much more a "written" text than the Qurʾān.

The Didascalia's "origins" can be traced to a Greek composition of the third century C.E. of which only fragments remain. The Didascalia is in turn partially modeled on earlier texts, such as the *Didache*; the Syriac version also incorporated the *Teaching of the Apostles* and other materials in its third chapter.[51] Epiphanius attests that the Didascalia circulated in Syria in the fourth century C.E. and we possess one complete Latin translation whose survival in the fifth century *Verona Palimpsest* is nothing short of a literary miracle.[52] The earliest manuscript that

[51] On the textual history of the added materials in Chapter Three of the Didascalia, among them the "Teaching of the Apostles," see Vööbus, *The Didascalia Apostolorum in Syriac*, volume II, *39–*43. On the Didascalia's relationship to the *Didache*, see esp. R.H. Connolly, "The Use of the *Didache* in the *Didascalia*," *Journal of Theological Studies* OS 24 (1923): 147–157 and Steward-Sykes, *The Didascalia Apostolorum*, 4.

[52] On the origins of the Didascalia and a possible redaction history, see esp. Stewart-Sykes, *The Didascalia Apostolorum*, 22–44; W. Witakowski, "The Origin of the 'Teaching of the Apostles,'" in: Han J.W. Drijvers et al. (eds.), *IV Symposium Syriacum, 1984: Literary Genres in Syriac Literature (Groningen – Oosterhesselen 10–12 September)* (Rome: Pontificium Institutum Studiorum Orientalium,

contains the Syriac version is the long collection of legal text, Ms. Vatican Syr. 560, which also contains the letter of Athanasius of Bālād, written in 683. To reiterate, the Didascalia is given the place of highest prominence in the copyist's legal canon.[53]

The fact that pre-Islamic manuscripts have survived only for the materials contained in the Syriac Didascalia's third chapter does not affect the cumulative secondary evidence for the pre-Qurʾānic date of the translation as a whole.[54] The respective scholarly consensus is based on its use of archaic Syriac, its affinity with Christian practice in Syria and Mesopotamia, and its likely spread among Syriac-speaking communities indicated by its echoes among

---

1987), 161–171; Arthur Vööbus, *The Didascalia Apostolorum in Syriac*, volume I, 11*–69*; and Paul Galtier, "La date de la Didascalie des Apôtres," *Revue d'histoire ecclésiastique* 42 (1947): 315–351. For Epiphanius' evidence on the Didascalia see Frank Williams, *The Panarion of Epiphanius of Salamis* (Leiden: Brill 1994), volume II, 412–3. Epiphanius' *heresiological* attribution to a quartodeciman group is of secondary interest for the present inquiry, but happens to correspond to the Didascalia's calendar according to Chapter XXI; see Sacha Stern, *Calendars in Antiquity: Empires, States and Societies* (Cambridge: Cambridge University Press, 2013), 415–22. For an argument that the Didascalia circulated in yet another recension, see James John Charles Cox, "Prolegomena to a Study of the Dominical Logoi as Cited in the Didascalia Apostolorum. II: Methodological Questions," *Andrews University Seminary Studies* 15 (1977): 1–15 and 17 (1979): 137–167.

[53] See page 15, note 26.

[54] Ms. London Br. Mus. Add. 14, 644, dated to the fifth or sixth century C.E., and Ms. London Br. Mus. Add. 14, 531, dated to the seventh or eighth century, both contain the Teaching of the Apostles which the Didascalia incorporates in Chapter Three, see above, page 43, note 51 and Vööbus, *The Didascalia Apostolorum in Syriac* I, 50–1*.

some Syriac church fathers.[55] Hubert Kaufhold correctly emphasizes that there is no clear proof that the translation of the Syriac Didascalia dates before Athanasius. Hence, if future research were to date all of the extant Syriac translations of the Didascalia closer to the time of the Qur'ān, it would further strengthen the ongoing relevance of this text for later religious culture. Inversely, while the extant Syriac translations of the Didascalia may well incorporate

[55] Vööbus has drawn attention to the Didascalia's use of archaic terms such as *tlyty'* (for "mediator") and *dyr'* (for "fold") which would allow us a dating to the time of Aphrahat in the fourth century C.E. – these terms are even translated into later Syriac ones in the marginal notes of some manuscripts; see idem, *The Didascalia Apostolorum in Syriac* I, 26–7, based on Connolly, *Didascalia Apostolorum*, xvii; see also Stewart-Sykes, *The Didascalia Apostolorum*, 90. For the relationship to patristic literature, esp. Aphrahat, see also Michael Pregill, *The Living Calf of Sinai*, Chapter Three. Vööbus has also recognized several affinities between the gospel quotations of the Didascalia and those of the fourth-century Syriac writer Evagrius Ponticus, as well as those of the sixth-century writings of Philoxenus of Mabbug and, intriguingly, of Jacob of Serugh; see Vööbus, *Studies in the History of the Gospel Text in Syriac, Corpus Scriptorum Christianorum Orientalium* 128, Subsidia, 3 (Louvain: Secrétariat du Corpus Scriptorum Christianorum Orientalium, 1951), 112 and idem, *Studies in the History of the Gospel Text in Syriac*, volume II, *Corpus Scriptorum Christianorum Orientalium* 496, Subsidia, 79 (Louvain: Secrétariat du Corpus Scriptorum Christianorum Orientalium, 1987), 148. My gratitude to Steven Ring for bringing these works to my attention. Temporal proximity to writers such as Jacob of Serugh would in turn reinforce the recent scholarship highlighting the importance of this church father for the study of the Qur'ān mentioned above on page 34 in note 43. See also Maria Doerfler, "Didascalia," in Sebastian Brock et al. (eds.), *Gorgias Encyclopedic Dictionary of the Syriac Heritage* (Piscataway: Gorgias Press, 2011), 124–5; Reinhold Meßner, "Die 'Lehre der Apostel' – eine syrische Kirchenordnung," in: Konrad Breitsching and Wilhelm Rees (eds.), *Recht – Bürge der Freiheit. Festschrift für Johannes Mühlsteiger SJ zum 80. Geburtstag* (Berlin: Duncker & Humblot, 2006), 305–335.

minor changes reflective of the Muslim conquest, the text as a whole clearly predates the Qurʾān.[56]

There is no consensus regarding the Coptic translation of the Didascalia, of which only one alleged fragment exists, yet this fragment allows us to appreciate how fluid the Didascalia tradition really was – and how much closer the Qurʾān's affinity is with the Syriac Didascalia than with either this Coptic fragment or the Didascalia's later iterations.[57] In the late fourth century, the Didascalia

[56] The consensus of an "early" Syriac Didascalia has been challenged by Hubert Kaufhold, who cautions that the evidence for the Syriac Didascalia even in the seventh century is insufficient; see "La littérature pseudo-canonique syriaque," in: M. Debié et al. (eds.), *Les apocryphes syriaques* (Paris: Geuthner 2005), 157. Kaufhold's views would place the Syriac Didascalia in even closer temporal proximity to the Qurʾān – in his view even perhaps *later*. Still, if one were to judge solely on manuscript evidence, as Kaufhold here suggests, other literary artifacts, for example the *entirety* of the rabbinic corpus (whose earliest manuscripts are early medieval) would have to be re-dated by as much as half a millennium; cf. the debate inspired by Peter Schäfer (see idem, "Research into Rabbinic Literature: An Attempt to Define the Status Quaestionis," *Journal of Jewish Studies* 37 (1986): 139–152). How the Didascalia was understood by Syriac Christians after the establishment of the Caliphates is an intriguing question that deserves further study. There are, however, no clear traces of any response to Islam in the earliest extant Syriac versions, with two possible exceptions. First, for the self-designation as *nṣryʾ mšyḥyʾ*, "Messianic Christian," in the later manuscripts (DA *Proem*, 10.16), which may reflect the Arabic term *naṣārā*, see above page 42, note 50; and second, for the Syriac Didascalia's explicit permission for intercourse during the menses in contrast to the prohibition preserved both in an earlier passage in the Syriac Didascalia and in the Latin, see below page 91, note 21. Neither case would fundamentally alter the conclusion of this study should they be proven to be post-Islamic.

[57] For the alleged Coptic version of the Didascalia see Alberto Camplani, "A Coptic Fragment from the Didascalia Apostolorum (M579 F.1)," *Augustinianum* 36 (1996): 47–51. Camplani concludes

was thoroughly revised and incorporated, as chapters one through six, into the Greek *Apostolic Constitutions*, further attesting to the Didascalia's pre-Qurʾānic use and circulation, likely including North Africa from the on-

---

correctly that he is dealing with "different stages of a very fluid canonical writing," (ibid., 50), but then he insists that the fragment he examines represents the Didascalia rather than the Apostolic Constitutions, simply because it includes a quotation of Proverbs that is attested in the former but missing in the latter. One may ask what such an omission can prove, especially since Camplani correctly states that "the omission and the addition of biblical quotations is one of the features of the compiler of the [Apostolic Constitution]" (ibid., 51). Moreover, when discussing the preserved Coptic passage about the veiling of women "[if you] want to become believing, take care especially to please your husband only and cover your head in the streets so that your beauty remains hidden" (Camplani's translation, ibid., 48), Camplani correctly states that only the Syriac and the Latin Didascala, but not the Coptic fragment under discussion, mention a garment (*lbwš/ueste*) or veiling (*tḥpyt/uel[atio]*, DA III, 26, 5–11, Connolly, *Didascalia Apostolorum*, 27) with which to cover the head. Likewise, the women's *walking* in the streets is found in the Latin and Syriac only, but not found in the Greek Apostolic Constitutions – or in the Coptic fragment under discussion. Camplani simply dismisses as "not meaningful" the strong argument according to which the Coptic fragment is a translation of the Apostolic Constitutions rather than of the Didascalia (ibid. 49). Most egregiously, Camplani does not note that the Greek Apostolic Constitutions and the Coptic fragment not only share the cognate Greek and Coptic lexeme for faith, *pistis* (as may be expected), but also the introductory instruction of "paying attention," equally using the cognate Greek and Coptic lexeme *proseḳe*; this specification again is *not* part of the Latin and Syriac Didascalia. While the fragment may require further study, in my view, the extant evidence strongly suggests that no Coptic fragment of the Didascalia has been transmitted and that the extant version is part of the "Apostolic Constitutions" tradition. The comparison here also reconfirms that the text of the Apostolic Constitutions in any language does not share the Syriac Didascalia's close affinity with the Qurʾānic passage discussed above.

set. The Apostolic Constitutions increase the anti-Jewish polemic and lack the residual openness towards Jews and Judaism found in the Didascalia.[58] The repeated bans of the

[58] Anton Baumstark argues that part of the Apostolic Constitutions is actually of Egyptian origin; see idem, "Aegyptischer oder antiochenischer Liturgietypus in AK I–VII?" *Oriens Christianus* 7 (1907): 388–407; Baumstark's arguments for an Egyptian setting are accepted by Stephen Gero, "The So-Called Ointment Prayer in the Coptic Version of the Didache: A Re-Evaluation," *The Harvard Theological Review* 70 (1977): esp. 73 and 81. On the Christian Identity of the Apostolic Constitutions, see F. Jacob Eliza Boddens Hosang, *Establishing Boundaries: Christian-Jewish Relations in Early Council Texts and the Writings of Church Fathers* (Leiden: Brill, 2010), 118–22, and Michele Murray, "Christian Identity in the Apostolic Constitutions: Some Observations," in Zeba A. Crook and Philip A. Harland (eds.), *Identity and Interaction in the Ancient Mediterranean: Jews, Christians and Others: Essays in Honour of Stephen G. Wilson* (Sheffield: Sheffield Phoenix Press, 2007), 179–194. On the Apostolic Constitutions and their fate in Eastern and Western churches more broadly, see Kaufhold, "Sources of Canon Law in the Eastern Churches," in Wilfried Hartmann and Kenneth Pennington (eds.), *The History of Byzantine and Eastern Canon Law to 1500* (Washington: The Catholic University of America Press, 2012), 266–70; and Heinz Ohme, "Sources of the Greek Canon Law to the Quinisext Council (691/2)," in ibid., 28–33; Frances Margaret Young, "The Apostolic Constitutions: a Methodological Case-Study," in Maurice F. Wiles et al. (eds.) *Studia Patristica, Volume XXXVI: Papers Presented at the Thirteenth International Conference on Patristic Studies Held in Oxford 1999. Critica et Philologica, Nachleben, First Two Centuries, Tertullian to Arnobius, Egypt before Nicaea, Athanasius and His Opponents* (Leuven: Peeters, 2001), 105–115; Eva Maria Synak, "Die Apostolischen Konstitutionen – ein 'christlicher Talmud' aus dem 4. Jh," *Biblica* 79 (1998): 27–56; David A. Fiensy, "Redaction History and the Apostolic Constitutions," *Jewish Quarterly Review* 72 (1982): 293–302; Georg Wagner, "Zur Herkunft der Apostolischen Konstitutionen," in: Bernard Botte (ed.), *Mélanges liturgiques offerts au R.P. dom Bernard Botte, O.S.B., de l'Abbaye du Mont César, a l'occasion du cinquantieme anniversaire de son ordination sacerdotale (4 juin 1972)* (Louvain: Abbaye du Mont César, 1972), 525–537.

Apostolic Constitutions in Roman Christianity attest to their continuing circulation there as much as their endorsement by John of Damascus in the Eastern Churches. The Apostolic Constitutions were in turn rewritten in Syriac and likely translated into Coptic, as well as into Arabic and Ethiopic, leading to substantial revisions. These documents hence evolved continuously in the context of their own ecclesiastical settings. Especially in the case of the (very likely post-Qurʾānic) Ethiopic and Arabic Apostolic Constitutions, it may be preferable to speak of independent works rather than seeking to press the later works into the conceptual mold of the former ones.[59]

[59] Note that the Apostolic Constitutions are sometimes, confusingly, referred to as Didascalia Apostolorum. For a synoptic edition of the Latin Didascalia and the Greek Apostolic Constitutions, see Funk, *Didascalia et Constitutiones Apostolorum*, volume I; for part of the cognate Arabic and Ethiopic literature, see ibid., volume II, 98–136; see also Marcel Metzger (ed.), *Les constitutions apostoliques, Sources Chrétiennes* 320, 329, and 336 (Paris: Le Cerf, 1985–7). For the Syriac of the Apostolic Constitutions, see Arthur Vööbus, "Die Entdeckung der ältesten Urkunde für die syrische Übersetzung der apostolischen Kirchenordnung. Neue Quellen für die syrische Version," *Oriens Christianus* 63 (1979): 37–40; the oldest Syriac manuscript dates from the eighth century. The first Arabic version of the Apostolic Constitutions seems to have been translated before the eleventh century from a Coptic Bohairic text and the second Arabic version in the thirteenth century from a Coptic Sahidic text. (Note that Camplani misrepresents this thirteenth-century Arabic translation of the Apostolic Constitutions by Abu Isḥāq ibn Faḍlallāh as being a translation of the Didascalia; see idem, "A Coptic Fragment from the Didascalia Apostolorum," 51.) The so-called Ethiopic "Didascalia," in effect much closer to the Apostolic Constitutions than to the Didascalia, seems to have greatest affinity with this second Arabic version; see the excellent overviews by Kaufhold, "Sources of Canon Law in the Eastern Churches," 266; and Alessandro Bausi, "Didəsqəlya," in Siegbert Uhlig (ed.) *Encyclopaedia Aethiopica*:

For the present purposes, hence, we can state that the evidence for a pre-Qurʾānic circulation of the Didascalia around Arabia is beyond doubt and that its impact on the oral discourse within seventh-century Arabia was likely greatest in the context of Syriac Christianity and rabbinic Judaism. The rabbinic inroads into Arabia in the sixth and seventh centuries are well-known; Christians had formed a presence there for centuries, as Sidney Griffith has recently summarized:

> "[B]y the dawn of the seventh century Christians had long been pressing into the Arabian heartland from all sides. Arabia was literally surrounded by Christian enclaves, in the towns and villages of South Arabia, in Ethiopia and Egypt, in Sinai, Palestine, Syria, Mesopotamia, and Iran."[60]

D-Ha (Wiesbaden: Harassovitz, 2005), 154–55; see also Georg Graf, *Geschichte der christlichen arabischen Literature* (Rome: Biblioteca Apostolica Vaticana, 1944), I, 564–9; J. M. Harden, *The Ethiopic Didascalia* (London: Society for Promoting Christian Knowledge, 1920) and C. H. Turner, "Notes on the Apostolic Constitutions," *Journal of Theological Studies* OS 16 (1915): 523–538 (all pace François Nau, "'Note sur le prologue de la Didascalie arabe et sur quelques apocryphes arabes pseudo-clémentins," *Journal asiatique* X, 17 (1911): 319–323, who argued for a Syriac original of the Ethiopian). For modern translations of other parts of the Ethiopic Didascalia, in addition to Harden, see Thomas Pell Platt (ed. and trans.), *The Ethiopic Didascalia: or, the Ethiopic Version of the Apostolical Constitutions, Received in the Church of Abyssinia* (London: Richard Bentley, 1834) and J. Françon, "The Didascalie éthiopienne traduit en français," *Revue de l'Orient Chrétien* 16 (1911): 161–166 and 266–70; 17 (1912): 199–203 and 286–293; and 19 (1914): 183–87.

[60] Griffith, *The Bible in Arabic*, 8; see also above, page 26, note 34 and page 35, note 44; on the Didascalia's respective affinity with rabbinic Judaism, see pages 88–89, note 14 below. The burden of explaining the numerous affinities between the Didascalia and the Qurʾān in a geographic or cultural context different from that of the Hijaz in the early seventh century should be put on those who

Would the teachings of the Didascalia have been among those literary materials circulating in Arabia in the early seventh century C.E.? Griffith concludes that

"by the time of the Qur'ān, knowledge of the Christian Bible, the Christian creed and liturgy had already spread orally among the Arabs, presumably transmitted originally from those Arabs living on the Arabian periphery, who were in more immediate contact with the Syriac and Ge'ez-speaking Christians whose

---

argue for relocating Muhammad's life altogether. Stephen Shoemaker has recently argued that Muhammad went to Palestine towards the end of his life (idem, *The Death of a Prophet: The End of Muhammad's Life and the Beginnings of Islam* (Philadelphia: University of Pennsylvania Press, 2012)). Likewise, Patricia Crone writes that the "suspicion that the location [of Muhammad's career in the Hijaz] is doctrinally inspired is reinforced by the fact that the Qur'an describes the polytheist opponents as agriculturalists who cultivated wheat, grapes, olives, and date palms. Wheat, grapes and olives are the three staples of the Mediterranean; date palms take us southwards, but Mecca was not suitable for any kind of agriculture, and one could not possibly have produced olives there." Crone suggests to locate Muhammad "somewhere in the Dead Sea region," (see eadem, "What do we actually know about Mohammed?" http://www.opendemocracy.net/faith-europe_islam/mohammed_3866.jsp, accessed October 30, 2012). Crone's suggestion is intriguing and will hopefully be spelled out in more detail. However, if the choice of Mecca in Islamic tradition is "doctrinally inspired," the same should be said about the *depictions* of the environs of the prophet in the Qur'ān, as Simeon Chavel has pointed out to me in private communication. One need not go further than the Garden of Eden to realize that ancient ideology often portrayed any blessed region as especially fertile. Large swaths of the Dead Sea region, moreover, are not exactly ideal for the type of agriculture described in the Qur'ān either, see M. Broshi, "Was There Agriculture at Qumran?," in Katharina Galor et al. (eds), *The Site of the Dead Sea Scrolls: Archaeological Interpretations and Debates, Proceedings of the Conference Held at Brown University, November 17–19, 2002* (Leiden: Brill, 2006), 249–81. Finally, as far as I know, there are no specific references in the Qur'ān to the geographic or political details of Cis- or Transjordanian Palestine.

faith and practice the Qur'ān echoes. For [...] very few traces of Christian texts in Arabic prior to the rise of Islam have so far come to light."[61]

The Didascalia, as written or as oral document, certainly circulated among the Syriac-speaking Christian communities, and possibly also among Arabic and Ge'ez-speaking Christians. Given the attestation of the Didascalia in various languages and renderings, we should construe the legal culture which has grown up around this text very broadly and understand the Didascalia itself as a living tradition, a multi-screen movie of which nothing but a few still frames have survived.[62]

I hold that the broader Didascalia tradition in whichever language had a possibly peripheral, though continuous, impact on the legal culture of the Sasanian and Byzantine Empires from the third century onwards, and early on also reached Arabia and its environs. While future studies may clarify the Qur'ān's interaction with the legal cultures of Ethiopia and Egypt, I still see myself coerced here to disregard the Coptic, Ethiopic, and even the Arabic

[61] Griffith, *The Bible in Arabic*, 15.

[62] For an approach to the Didascalia as a fluid tradition see Joseph G. Mueller, "The Ancient Church Order Literature: Genre or Tradition?," *Journal of Early Christian Studies* 15 (2007): 337–380; for discussions of genre of the text as preserved, see also Karl Olav Sandnes, "The Teaching of the Apostles (Didaskalia apostolorum) and the Syriac Tradition: 'Avoid All the Books of the Gentiles'," in idem (ed.), *The Challenge of Homer: School, Pagan Poets and Early Christianity* (London/New York: T&T Clark, 2009), 102–110; and Georg Schöllgen, "Die literarische Gattung der syrischen Didaskalie," in Han J. W. Drijvers et al. (eds.) *IV Symposium Syriacum, 1984: Literary Genres in Syriac Literature* (*Groningen – Oosterhesselen 10–12 September*) (Rome: Pontificium Institutum Studiorum Orientalium, 1987), 149–59.

witnesses of the Didascalia, whose extant versions were written after the Qur'ān, and also those of the Apostolic Constitution, which stand farther apart from it. I focus instead on the Latin Didascalia as a proof of the tradition's antiquity and especially on what is most likely the *closest* written echo of the fluid and oral legal culture in which the Qur'ān participated: the Syriac Didascalia (henceforth simply Didascalia).

Chapter One

The Didascalia's Laws and the Qur'ān's Abrogations

When it comes to obliging non-Jews to observe certain biblical commandments, we will see that the Didascalia and the Qur'ān both stand in the line of the "Christian" legal tradition which is based on the Decalogue, on the seven commandments in *Ezekiel* (18:1–32), and on the four commandments found in the Decree of the Apostles (in *Acts of the Apostles* 15:29). Part of the difficulty we face when seeking to realize the specificity of the legal culture shared by the Qur'ān and the Didascalia is geometrical. We must compare specific conceptual overlaps that are contained within their immense shared framework of the common Late Antique Jewish and Christian legal culture. In order to remain within the scope of this study, and at the risk of appearing naïve, I will largely focus on specific affinities between the Didascalia and the Qur'ān. At the same time, I will sketch the broader legal overlaps only through exemplary, though necessarily incomplete and idiosyncratic, references to cognate aspects of legal culture in the Syriac and Greek patristic and the Palestinian and Babylonian rabbinic traditions. There is hardly any legal aspect exclusively shared between the Qur'ān and the Didascalia; yet other than the Didascalia, there may be no other *single* post-biblical document with which the Qur'ān shares so much of its legal culture.

The Qur'ān itself emphasizes the fact that it shares and develops the fundamental Jewish and Christian legal narrative. To begin with the obvious, the Qur'ān has long been shown to endorse the *nomos* as well as the *narrative* of a "Decalogue," the original law given to Moses, as well as the individual commandments we find in the Jewish and Christian versions thereof – with important additions, omissions, and differences of emphasis, as Sebastian Günther persuasively argues.[1] Indeed, Günther emphasizes that "unlike their Biblical counterparts, the Qur'anic lists of the Commandments specifically emphasize human values such as giving one's kinsman his due, not slaying one's children because of poverty, trading correctly and fairly;" according to him, these discrepancies "make it impossible to speak of *one code* common to and equally binding on all three monotheistic religions."[2]

What, however, if there were another list of the Commandments that specifically emphasized human values such as giving one's kinsman his due, not slaying one's children because of poverty, and trading correctly and fairly? Considering the legal and narrative framework in which the Qur'ān presents the Decalogue in comparison with the cognate framework of the Didascalia will demonstrate, in response to Günther's keen observation, that the Qur'ān stands in a legal tradition with the broader Jewish

[1] See Sebastian Günther, "O People of the Scripture! Come to a Word Common to You and Us (Q. 3:64): The Ten Commandments and the Qur'an," *Journal of Qur'anic Studies* 9 (2007): 28–58. On the Decalogue and the Qur'ān as such see also W. M. Brinner, "An Islamic Decalogue," in idem and S. D. Ricks (eds.), *Studies in Islamic and Judaic Traditions* (Atlanta: Scholars Press, 1986), volume 1, 67–84.

[2] Günther, "O People of the Scripture," 45.

and Christian additions to the Decalogue. Further, a comparative consideration will point to the Didascalia as an ideal witness for the Qurʾān's general continuity with the Biblical legal culture of Late Antiquity, hence preparing my broader claim of a privileged relationship between this text and the Qurʾān (in an oral setting).

Accordingly, like many other Late Antique traditions, the Qurʾān depicts the tablets given to Moses as follows:

And We wrote for [Moses] in the tablets
Advice concerning all things
And an elaboration of all things (*tafṣīlan li-kulli šayʾin*)
(Q7:145)

The Qurʾān clearly handles a broad concept of what was written on these tablets (as do some rabbis as well), as is implied by the fact that the tablets concern "an elaboration of all things." Crucially, the Qurʾān also references itself as an "elaboration of all things" (*tafṣīla kulli šayʾin*, Q12:111); this "elaboration" hence points to a broad concept of core commandments that remain in force in the time of the Qurʾān itself.[3]

What the Qurʾān states, it also implements, as becomes clear when considering its cognate presentation of legal material. For example, the Qurʾān explicitly presents prayer and charity as part of a broadly conceived "Deca-

[3] The term "elaboration of all things" is also applied to the Bible in Q6:154; the Qurʾān is called an "elaboration" in Q10:37 (see also Q17:12). See also Angelika Neuwirth's lucid discussion of the relationship of the heavenly book to Moses' tablets in the Qurʾān (eadem, *Der Koran als Text der Spätantike*, 133–9), and below, page 138–9, note 13 on the Qurʾān's confirmation of the heavenly book. The rabbinical teaching that the entirety of the written and the oral Torah were already given at Sinai goes back to the Palestinian Amoraic tradition; see below, page 143, note 19.

logue," the cornerstones not only of its own community, but also of the "Israelite" tradition more broadly:

And we took a pledge (*mīṯāqa*)
From the Children of Israel
Worship no one but God,
Do good to parents, relatives, orphans (*al-yatāmā*),
And the poor (*al-masākīn*),
And speak kindly to people,
And maintain the prayer (*aṣ-ṣalāta*),
And give charity (*az-zakāta*) (Q2:83, see also Q4:162)

This text has been understood as the Qur'ān's presentation of the Scriptural "Decalogue," or, in the view of Neuwirth and others, as the "Medinan" revision of an earlier "Meccan" version thereof. Neuwirth rightly interprets the passage at hand as constructing core legal observances as part of the *mīṯāq*, the "covenant" given to the Israelites, and as defining the Qur'ān's own code as well.[4] We should note that the Qur'ān has a very clear sense of God's "universal law:" namely, the text understands care for orphans (*yatāmā*), prayer (*ṣalāh*), care for the poor (*masākīn*), charity (*zakāh* and *ṣadaqa*), ideally given discretely (see Q2:264 and 271), and, mentioned in the same context, fasting (*ṣawm*, see e.g. Q2:183–85), as incumbent on its own

[4] Angelika Neuwirth, "The Discovery of Evil in the Qur'an: Contemplating Qur'anic Versions of the Decalogue in the context of Pagan-Arab Late Antiquity," (forthcoming), and eadem, "Meccan Texts-Medinan Additions?" 71–93. Neuwirth regards Q17:22–39 to be the first ("middle Meccan"), Q6:151–53 the second ("late Meccan"), and Q2:83–85 to be the last ("Medinan") Qur'ānic iteration of its "Decalogue;" she plausibly sees the entire sequence as reflective of intellectual developments in the prophet's community. The passage on the tablets of Moses (Q7:145) is also usually read as belonging to the late Meccan period; see e.g. Günther, "O People of the Scripture!" 30.

audience precisely because it presents these observances as "given" to Jews and Christians.

Such a *narrative* of a broad canon of divinely ordained positive law is shared by the Didascalia, as will be discussed in Chapter Three: the Didascalia also handles a broadened concept of the Decalogue which consists of both the "Ten Words and the judgments" (DA XXVI, 243.2). These additional "judgments," akin to the Qur'ān's "elaborations," go far beyond the Bible's Ten Words, but are equally understood as part of the same covenant: indeed, the Didascalia also shares the specific *nomos*, the laws which the Qur'ān sees as valid for its own community. Using similar lexemes, the Didascalia likewise emphasizes care for orphans as central (*ytm'*, esp. chapters DA VIII, DA XVII, DA XVIII) and contains elaborate discourses on prayer (*ṣly*, *b'y*, DA passim) and fasting (*ṣwm*, DA XV, DA XIX, DA XXI). Just like the Qur'ān, the Didascalia exhibits a preoccupation with the care of the poor (*mskn'*, esp. DA XIV) and the giving of alms (*zdqt'*, esp. DA XV).

One might well wonder: are such laws not far too widespread to adduce them as evidence for specific legal affinities? Indeed, the general importance of practices such as fasting and praying in Christian and Jewish culture, and including possible pre-Islamic Arabian practices, hardly needs to be established.[5] In order to assess more precisely

[5] Commonly shared observances are furthermore depicted by shared roots in all Aramaic cultures. The affinities between Syriac and Arabic terms for ritual observances are especially strong, though neither complete nor exclusive to the Didascalia. As has long been recognized, the same lexical affinities could be established in rabbinic Aramaic. The Arabic term *ṣadaqa*, for example, is related to the Syriac term *zdqt'* as well as to Jewish Aramaic *ṣdqh* and *ṣdqt'* without being entirely cognate with either; see Sokoloff, *A Syriac Dictionary*, 365–6,

the posited relationship between the legal cultures preserved in the Qurʾān and in the Didascalia, we would have to locate it within a much broader web of general Late Antique observances than can be done in the scope of this volume. Even then, we should not only consider the shared legal concepts, style, and lexicon, but also the ways in which the Qurʾān explicitly presents its own laws as both *in continuity with* and *as a departure from* certain established observances. The Didascalia, in other words, contains not only many laws that the Qurʾān endorses, but it also contains many laws that the Qurʾān modifies, adapts, or tells its audience to leave behind, even though they were valid up to its own time, as the examples of alms, prayer, and fasting illustrate.

Alms

Concluding a longer passage that instructs widows never to disclose from whom they received alms, the Didascalia quotes the Matthean exhortation: "When you do alms (*zdqtʾ*), sound not the trumpet before men to be seen of them, as the hypocrites do; verily I say unto you, they have received their reward" (DA XV, 169.24–170.3, see Matthew 4:2).[6] At the same time, the Didascalia gives hope

---

idem, *A Dictionary of Jewish Palestinian Aramaic of the Byzantine Period* (Baltimore: Johns Hopkins University Press, 1992), 458, and idem, *A Dictionary of Jewish Babylonian Aramaic of the Talmudic and Geonic periods* (Baltimore: Johns Hopkins University Press, 2002), 952. For a comprehensive overview of classical and current studies of Qurʾānic and later Muslim ritual observances, with a focus on prayer, fasting, alms, and the pilgrimage, see the volume edited by Gerald Hawting, *The Development of Islamic Ritual* (Aldershot: Ashgate, 2006).

[6] The prominence of Matthean material in the Qurʾān has most re-

that God will remember the one who gave alms *anonymously* on "the day of your judgment" (*bywm' dpwr'nk*, DA XV, 168.2). The Qur'ān endorses the exhortation preserved in the Didascalia, stating that "if you hide [alms] and give them to the needy ones (*al-fuqarā'*), that is better for you" (Q2:271). The Qur'ān warns that it may "render your charity (*ṣadaqātikum*) void" if one behaves "like those who spend their wealth to be seen by people and have no faith in God and the Last Day" (*al-yawm l-'āḫir*, Q2:264). In this example, the Qur'ān fully endorses previous legal culture by effectively repeating the combined injunction to give alms discretely and by expounding it in the context of a narrative that emphasizes the relationship between alms and the judgment day, just as we saw in the Didascalia. Indeed, the audience's assumed knowledge of a promise of reward for anonymous alms-giving on judgment day, as recorded in the Didascalia, would make the cognate Qur'ānic association of anonymity in alms-giving and the last day much more precise. At the same time, the Qur'ān adapts the narrative to its Arabian context. Following Neuwirth, I suggest that the Qur'ān's specific reference to "spending one's wealth" attests to the way in which it hears the Matthean exhortation in the light of an echo of the traditional Arabic poetic trope of reproaching the flamboyant squanderer.[7]

---

cently been demonstrated by Emram al-Badawi, *Sectarian Scripture*. His findings hold true especially when considering the Gospel of Matthew less in the first century context of its composition and more so in the (Syriac) Late Antique context of its reception, for which the Didascalia and the Clementine Homilies are of special significance. See also above, page 34, note 43.

[7] Neuwirth sees special affinity with the figure of the *'ādhila*, "the female reproacher," "a fictitious counter-figure of the poet hero

Prayer

The Didascalia insists on prayer directed towards the East (*lwqbl mdnḥ'*, DA XII, 144.8); it elsewhere specifies: "pray (*mṣlyn*) towards the East, because 'as the lightning which lightens from the East, and is seen even to the West (*lm'rb'*), so shall the coming of the Son of Man be,' that by this shall we know and understand that he appears from the East suddenly" (DA III, 41.3–7). Conversely, regarding the direction of prayer (*ṣalāh*), the Qur'ān explicates that it departs from a specific previous practice. It notes that its community appears to have "turned away from the direction [of prayer, *qiblatihim*] they were following," (Q2:142), indicating "direction" with the lexeme *qbl* that we also saw in the Didascalia. The Qur'ān then instructs its audience from now on to turn towards "the esteemed place of worship" (Q2:144), most likely Mecca. There has been much discussion whether, before this change, the Qur'ān's Qiblah was Jerusalem or the East; the conceptuality and language the Qur'ān shares with the Didascalia could indicate that the practice presupposed in the Qur'ān is the same as in the Didascalia.[8] For the Qur'ān then justifies the new direction by insisting that "to God belong the East and the West" (*maġrib*, Q2:142), repeating the language of East and West we saw in the Didascalia with another

whose function it is to reprimand the flamboyant and boastful hero with pragmatic arguments," see eadem, "The Discovery of Evil in the Qur'an," (forthcoming).

[8] The abrogated Qiblah in the Qur'ān, a prominent topic in the discussion about "Islamic Origins" has been argued to be either towards Jerusalem or towards the East. No final judgment can be made, yet the present evidence for the East may bear on the debate. Cf. Richard Kimber, "Qibla," McAuliffe (ed.), *Encyclopaedia of the Qur'ān*, ad loc.

shared lexeme (*'rb / ġrb*).[9] Most importantly, against the background of the Didascalia's Christological argument for its Qiblah, the Qur'ān's change of *nomos* – of the direction of prayer – allows us to appreciate its cognate change of *narrative*. Not only that the East and the West belong to God, as it spells out, but they also belong to God *alone*, and are certainly not shared with His Christ, as we now see it implies – if it presupposes knowledge of a dictum as the one recorded in the Didascalia.

Fasting

The Didascalia calls its audience "Christian" and exhorts it to fast (*ṣymyn*) "not according to the custom (*'yd'*) of the former people (*d'm' qdmy'*), but according to the new covenant (*dytyq' ḥdt'*) which I have set up for you" (DA XXI, 208.14–5), a pattern of weekly and paschal fasts that sets apart the new Christian from the previous Jewish fasts. As Pines notes, the Qur'ān uses a lexeme cognate to the Didascalia's *dytyq'* in order to distinguish between the covenant (*mīṯāq*) made with the Israelites and the one made later with "those who say we are Christians," (Q5:14), i.e. *naṣārā* (understood by some as "Nazarenes" or "Judaeo-Christians," on which more in the Conclusion).[10]

---

[9] Shlomo Dov Goitein remarks that "it is interesting to note that the Talmudic passage dealing with the direction of prayer [i.e. *Bava Batra* 25a] also utters the opinion that God's presence is everywhere;" see idem, "Prayer in Islam," in idem, *Studies in Islamic History and Institutions* (Leiden: Brill, 1966), 86. Again, much that is shared between the Qur'ān and the Didascalia is equally shared by other texts – though not as closely.

[10] See Shlomo Pines, "Notes on Islam and on Arabic Christianity and Judaeo-Christianity," 140; Pines only discusses the Syriac term *dytyq'*, not its occurrence in the Didascalia.

The Qurʾān then modifies what it presents as an established fasting calendar by introducing Ramadan, and, like the Didascalia, also does so with reference to established legal culture. Yet in this case it emphasizes continuity rather than change: "prescribed for you is fasting (*aṣ-ṣiyāmu*), as it was prescribed for those who were before you (*ʿalā'l-laḏīna min qablikum*), so that you may be Godwary" (Q2:183). While fasting is clearly a widespread practice throughout the Near and Middle East and beyond, the Didascalia again allows us to construct a specific shared *nomos* and *narrative*. In both texts, fasting is obligatory and justified with reference to previous law, and both texts evoke a *second* covenant with Jesus-believers, in addition to the one on Mount Sinai (on which more in Chapters Three and Four) – which allows us to perceive the Qurʾān's continuity with foregoing legal culture as well as its innovation. In effect, the Qurʾān's return to tradition, in light of the Didascalia's departure therefrom, in this case may constitute a full turn of the hermeneutical screw.

In the three cases of prayer, alms, and fasting, the establishment of the Qurʾān's "pre-Islamic Arabian" context should hence include the "Jewish" and the "Christian" contexts. While the affinities between the legal culture of the Qurʾān and the Didascalia here and elsewhere is extensive, it is not difficult to find differences between the two legal corpora under consideration, and my argument for continuity should not be misunderstood as implying complete legal/narrative consonance.[11] Instead, I argue that

[11] As Joseph Witztum reminds me, an obvious counterexample to full legal overlap would be the missing discussion of the spoils of war or the land tax in the Didascalia, legislated by the Qurʾān in

within the broader Late Antique legal culture of pre-Islamic Arabia and especially within its Syriac and rabbinic iterations, the Qur'ān and the Didascalia share a legal culture that can best be illustrated by assessing the Qur'ān's similarities and continuities vis-à-vis the Didascalia. The similarities highlight the Qur'ān's divergences and alterations of the laws recorded in the Didascalia.[12] The evidence here presented will have to be validated against a study more inclusive of the Aramaic tradition as a whole, yet it suffices in my mind to point to the existence of one text that allows us to begin reconstructing the Qur'ān's legal culture – should another *single* text rival the proximity of

---

e.g. in Q8:41 and Q23:72. In addition, the Didascalia's instructions regarding bishops, elders, and widows may be the most obvious examples of difference – widows occupy no official functions in the communal space of the Qur'ān, which consists of imam and believers only, whereas "bishops" and "elders" may be depicted as governing the *naṣārā* (see my epilogue). On the independence of the Qur'ān's legal injunctions called "God's boundaries," as well as their possible affinity with aspects of the Didascalia, see below, page 116, note 51. On contract law in the Qur'ān and the *Syro-Roman Law Book*, see the following note.

[12] The Qur'ānic requirement for a written contract, signed in the presence of witnesses (Q2:282) is another good example of the limits of its affinity with the Didascalia. Legal witnesses and contracts are not discussed in the Didascalia. The Qur'ān's law instead has specific affinity with the *Syro-Roman Law Book*, as well as with aspects of rabbinic law; see Reimund Leicht, "The Qur'anic Commandment of Writing Down Loan Agreements (Q2:282) – Perspectives of a Comparison with Rabbinical Law," in Neuwirth et al. (eds.), *The Qur'ān in Context*, 593–614 (published in German as "Das Schriftlichkeitsgebot bei Darlehensverträgen im Koran," in Dirk Hartwig et al. (eds.), *"Im vollen Licht der Geschichte": Die Wissenschaft des Judentums und die Anfänge der kritischen Koranforschung* (Würzburg: Ergon, 2008), 203–222).

the legal aspects of the Didascalia to those of the Qurʾān, then the following inquiry will have to be amended. With this in mind, we can now turn to the broader legal culture of the two texts, first to their codes (in the remainder of this Chapter, and in Chapters Two and Four), and then to their legal narratives (in Chapter Three).

The Shared Legal and Ethical Code of the Didascalia and the Qurʾān

Establishing a full taxonomy of positive and negative Qurʾānic precepts, perhaps along the lines of Islamic legal theory, would not only surpass the scope of this work, but it would also miss the point of the present focus on fundamental legal and ritual observances. For the present discussion, it suffices to summarize the Qurʾān's precepts without distinction between minor and major commandments, or between exhortations and law. The following summary of precepts covers the basic catalogue of core observances presented as God-given positive law in both the Qurʾān and the Didascalia, yet it is necessarily simplistic and subjective. Taking the example of the veil, for a woman to veil her *zīna*, "adornment," for example, may or may not in itself be considered as one of these core observances, yet the veil is presented as part of the core principle of avoiding *zinā*, "fornication" (as the affinity of the terms evokes), and can therefore be included.

I touched on the affinity of the Qurʾān's and the Didascalia's narratives of a Decalogue above; the texts' *nomos* shares as much. The Late Antique attitude towards the Decalogue and its laws is of course generally positive, and one may take their observance as self-evident not only in

Jewish, but also in Christian cultures.[13] Still, a comparison between the Qurʾān and the Didascalia's respective attitudes towards these laws proves a useful starting point that will lead us to appreciate the further specific laws both texts *add* in the context of presenting the Decalogue. As is well-known, the Bible (Exodus 20:1–17 and Deuteronomy 5:4–21) commands its audience to

- Have no other gods besides God
- Not to make an image of any form of life, or to bow to such an image
- Not to misuse God's name
- To observe Shabbat
- To honor one's parents
- Not to murder
- Not to commit adultery
- Not to steal
- Not to bear false witness
- Not to covet one's neighbor's property or wife.

The Didascalia, to begin with, never enumerates the Decalogue, yet the repeated discussion of its importance (on which more below) and the Didascalia's precision in dealing with scriptural citations allows us to take the validity

[13] For an explicit endorsement of the Decalogue, see for example Wayiqra Rabbah, 2:10; Augustine of Hippo, *Qvaest. Exodi LXXI* (see J. Fraipont and D. De Bruyne (eds.), *Quaestionum in Heptateuchum libri VII. Locutionum in Heptateuchum libri VII. De octo quaestionibus ex veteri testamento* (Leuven: Brepols, 1958), 102–6); Aphrahat, *Demonstration I (On Faith)*, 11 (see Kuriakose Valavanolickal (trans. and ed.), *Aphrahat Demonstrations I* (Changanassery : HIRS Publications, 1999, 27–8). For the Didascalia, see Marcus, "The *Testaments of the Twelve Patriarchs* and the *Didascalia Apostolorum*: A Common Jewish Christian Milieu?," 616.

of these commandments for granted, as is common in the Christian tradition – with the exception of observing Shabbat rather than Sunday, to which we shall return.[14] The Didascalia also preserves a list of prohibitions taken from the biblical tradition that overlaps more specifically with some of the Qur'ān's requirements, i.e. the catalogue of capital sins in Ezekiel 18:1–32. In the Didascalia's extensive paraphrase, this list includes:

- Again, idol worship
- Again, intercourse with a woman married to another man
- To approach (*ntqrb*) one's wife during menses (to be discussed in Chapter Two)
- Robbery
- Oppression of the poor (*mskn'*)
- Usury (*rbyt'*) (DA VI, 66.18–70.4).

Finally, the Didascalia contains a long list of transgressors it perceives as so despicable that their charity cannot be accepted (DA XVIII, 180.18–181.13). Among them, we find:

- Again, those who oppress the poor (*lmskn'*)
- Painters of pictures
- Makers of idols
- Those who alter weights (*mšḥlpy mtql'*)
- Those who measure deceitfully (*dmkylyn bnkl'*)
- Murderers

[14] In addition, the Didascalia repeatedly draws conclusions which assume the prohibition of transgressions that figure among the Decalogue such as theft and murder (DA XIX), idolatry (passim), and bearing false witness (DA V).

- Perverters of judgment who, for (reasons of) theft deal in wickedness and in deceit (*bnkl'*) with the peasants and with all the poor (*mskn'*)
- Idolaters
- Those who take usury (*rbyt'*).

The Didascalia's list is of course entirely biblical and any Christian or Jew of Antiquity would have largely endorsed it. Still, the selection of commandments is remarkable in its conceptual and lexical affinity with that of the Qur'ān. For just as the Bible is at the same time "everywhere and nowhere" in the Qur'ān, to use Sidney Griffith's fortuitous phrase, so the Qur'ān's Decalogue is everywhere in its legal code, yet nowhere fully cited. As we saw in the case of the Didascalia, familiarity with the concept and content of the Decalogue is presupposed, yet its details are never fully elaborated.

We do find commandments assumed by the Qur'ān that are closely related to the Biblical Decalogue, such as pertaining to coveting, theft, the creation of images and the use of God's name.[15] Yet more typically, these laws are presented along with others, such as prayer and charity described above. The following excerpt contains additions to the original biblical Decalogue; namely, the "servants of the All-beneficent" are described as follows:

---

[15] Coveting property or children is addressed in Q4:32 (see also Q57:20 and Q102:1); theft is addressed e.g. in Q5:38 (see below pages 74–76); the prohibition of misusing God's name can easily be inferred from the Qur'ān's insistence on the importance of God's names throughout the Qur'ān; and the prohibition of creating and bowing to images is amply illustrated in the discussion about the Golden Calf (on which more in Chapter Three).

Those who do not invoke another god besides God,
And do not kill a soul
[whose life] God has made inviolable,
Except with due cause,
And do not commit fornication …
Those who do not give false testimony (*lā yašhadūna'l-z-zūr*)
And when they come upon vain talk,
Pass by nobly. (Q25:68–72)

The Qurʾān, on the one hand, shares the giving of the "Decalogue" as well as its content – both as *narrative* and as *nomos* – with the broad Jewish and Christian tradition. The detail that concerns us in the present inquiry, on the other hand, is the Didascalia's and the Qurʾān's specific *additions* to broadly shared observances. In the present passage, the Qurʾān, going straight back to the biblical *leges talionis* (and their Matthean updating), excludes the killing of a murderer from the prohibition on taking a life.[16] More importantly, it also here adds the exhortation

[16] The Biblical *leges talionis*, the laws of retribution (as formulated esp. in Exodus 21:18–35, Leviticus 24:17–21 and Deuteronomy 19:21) oscillate between mandating a *quid pro quo* exchange either physically (life for life, i.e. substitution of people) or through monetary compensation. Christian tradition, based e.g. on Matthew 5:38–42 ("You have heard that it was said, 'An eye for an eye and a tooth for a tooth,' but I say to you, do not resist an evildoer …") has generally understood the Biblical laws as demanding retributive killings or other types of physical punishment and has in turn discarded the laws of retribution altogether. The rabbinic tradition reflects both views, but clearly decides in favor of the latter option (see e.g. Mishna *Bava Qamma* 8.1), perhaps in reaction to Matthew's distortions, as Sandra Jacobs suggested to me in conversation. The Qurʾān goes back to the Biblical law, combining aspects of the rabbinic and the Christian attitude along the way, reflecting its notion of the continuity of the Torah and the Gospel (see e.g. Q2:136). In Q25:68–72 and elsewhere (Q2:178; Q4:92–93; Q5:45; Q17:33–35, and Q25:63–72), the Qurʾān holds fast to the Biblical mandate – as understood especially in the

against "vain talk" to the prohibition of acting as a false witness. Even though this added observance also has a basis in the Bible, we should note that a cognate *combined* exhortation to keep oneself from false witness (*mshd*) and from "slander" and "disparagement" can also be found in the Didascalia (DA IV, 56.20–25).[17] Both texts enlarge the biblical concept in cognate ways that are important for

Christian tradition – that the heirs of a killed person can decide to kill the perpetrator. In line with the rabbinic view, it then emphasizes the option of the heir of the slain person to accept monetary retribution instead. Unlike the rabbis, however, and more akin to the Matthean exhortation, the Qur'ān portrays the option to accept the compensation *as* a divine *raḥmah*, "mercy." Its legal hermeneutics may be most closely related to, but not commensurate with, a passage of Ptolemy's "Letter to Flora" (quoted by Epiphanius in his *Panarion* 33.5.3), who comments on the *leges talionis* that "in any case this commandment was and is just, though owing to the frailty of its recipients it was given in violation of the pure law. But it does not fit with the nature and goodness of the Father at all." The Qur'ān, like Ptolemy, combines the Torah and the Gospel, but unlike Ptolemy it allows the heirs of the slain person to avenge the death (without excess!) or to forgive it – it is in this sense that the Qur'ān states that there is "life in retribution" (Q2:179). I am inspired here by Genevieve Gobillot, "Der Begriff Buch im Koran im Licht der pseudoklementinischen Schriften," in M. Gross and K.-H. Ohlig, *Vom Koran zum Islam* (Hans Schiler, 2009), 339–445; Gobillot's references to anti-Manichean debates about the laws of retribution in the Hebrew Bible and in the Gospel, such as *Acta Archelai* 31 and 40, also seem worth exploring in more depth.

[17] See also the exhortation to keep oneself "from empty speech and from words of levity and impurity" (DA XXI, 203.4–5); similar language is very common in rabbinic (e.g. Bavli *Shabbat* 30a) and patristic discourse, e.g. Chrysostom, *Homilies On Ephesians*, Homily 17 (see J.-P. Migne (ed.), *Patrologiae cursus completus (series Graeca)* 62 (Paris: Migne, 1862), 119.37–122.59); and Ephrem, *Homily on Admonition and Repentance,* esp. 6 and 13 (see John Gwynn, *Selections Translated into English from the Hymns and Homilies of Ephraim the Syrian, and from the Demonstrations of Aphrahat the Persian*

the shared approach to biblical law. Likewise, a cognate Qurʾānic list of observances (in what Neuwirth considers the first, "middle Meccan," version of the Qurʾān's Decalogue) adds a few other observances that are also cognate to the aforementioned additions of the Didascalia:

Do not set up another god besides God,
Or you will sit blameworthy, forsaken.
Your Lord has decreed
That you shall not worship anyone except Him
And [He has enjoyed] kindness to parents.
…
Give the relatives their right,
and to the poor (*al-miskīna*) and the traveler
…
Do not kill (*lā taqtulū*) your children for the fear of penury,
we will provide for them and for you.
Killing them (*qatlahum*) is a great iniquity.
Do not approach fornication (*az-zinā*),
It is indeed an indecency and an evil way
Do not kill a soul
[Whose life] God has made inviolable
Except with due course.
Do not approach the orphan's (*al-yatīmi*) property
Except in the best of manner
Until he comes of age
And fulfill the covenants;
Indeed all covenants are accountable
Observe fully the measure (*al-kayla*) when you measure (*kiltum*),
And weigh with an even balance
That is better and fairer in outcome
…
Do not walk exultantly on the earth. (Q17:22–37)

Sage (*Nicene and post-Nicene Fathers of the Christian Church*, Series 2, XIII), 334.

The Qurʾān's list of core observances shares much with the Didascalia, which likewise includes measuring honestly (using *kyl*, e.g., in Didascalia DA XVIII, 181.4–5) and the use of an "even balance"/"unaltered weights" (DA XVIII, 181.3–4), the just stewardship for orphans (using *ytm* throughout the Didascalia), and charity for the needy (using *mskn* e.g. in DA XVIII, 180.18). Likewise, the Qurʾān prohibits usury (*ribā*, Q2:275–80, Q3:130, Q4:161, Q30:39), as we saw in the Didascalia as well (*rbyt'*, e.g. DA XVIII, 181.13), equally using cognate lexemes. In addition to prohibiting murder, the Qurʾān emphasizes the prohibition of the slaying of children, just as we read in the Didascalia: "you shall not kill (*tqṭwl*) a child through destruction, nor after he is born shall you kill him (*tqṭlywhy*)" (DA III, 33.15–16; fear of penury is not mentioned here).

The Qurʾān's prohibition "do not walk exultantly on the earth" (*lā tamši fī'l-ʾarḍi maraḥan*) in turn recalls the Didascalia's exhortation not to be a boaster (*šbhrn'*, DA III, 34.6) or vainglorious (*sryq šwbḥ'*, DA III, 36.7). The Qurʾān uses lexemes different from those of the Didascalia precisely in the context of the Qurʾān's rejection of traditional Arabic poetical topoi, as highlighted by Neuwirth, yet its laws still dovetail with those of Judaeo-Christian ethics.[18]

Hence, in response to Günther's statement that it is "impossible to speak of *one code* common to and equally binding on all three monotheistic religions" (see above), the concept of "three monotheistic religions" may need to

[18] See Angelika Neuwirth, "The Discovery of Evil in the Qur'an," (forthcoming), note 39. In the Didascalia, see also the cognate exclusion from the ministry of "those who are high-minded and lifted up in arrogance or pride" (DA III, 48.3–4).

be modified to accommodate at least the legal culture we find in the Didascalia – which of course shares much with other church canons, and with the rabbis. In other words, the Didascalia complicates any rigid differentiation between Christian, Jewish, and Muslim law. If one compares not only the Hebrew Bible and the Qur'ān, but also the reception history of the former in the Didascalia, a legal code emerges that is much closer to the Qur'ān than Günther realized. This code's underlying legal culture constitutes a fundamental element of legal continuity throughout Late Antiquity, in addition to other Christian and Jewish traditions, that has hitherto been overlooked.

The Didascalia speaks from a position that assumes ecclesiastical, but not executive power. When considering theft, for example, its main concern is that a Christian is not mistakenly apprehended as a thief by non-Christian authorities (DA XIX, 187.16–188.8). The Qur'ān, like the Didascalia, usually discusses justice in general terms and speaks of punishment in the hereafter. Yet in contrast to the Didascalia, the Qur'ān occasionally moves to apply criminal law. The best example may be the famous verse on cutting off a thief's hand in Q5:38, offering a drastic (possibly rabbinically or Persian inspired) punishment when applying criminal law – a scenario which the Didascalia never faced.[19] In such cases, one could conceive of (espe-

[19] Cutting off a hand is a punishment mentioned in Deuteronomy 25:12. The punishment of Deuteronomy, a woman that touches a man's genitals during a fight, is commuted to monetary compensation in Bavli *Bava Qamma* 28a, yet in rabbinic law, different other instances of cutting off a hand are – at least metaphorically – upheld for cases of indecency or violence; see Mishna *Nidah* 2:1, Tosefta *Nidah* 2:6, Bavli *Nidah* 13b, Bavli *Shabbat* 108b and Bavli *Sanhedrin* 58b. Bavli *Keritot* 28b presents severing of the hand as a random punishment

cially the "Medinan" parts of) the Qur'ān as representing an initial stage of the process to turn into applied law a concept of justice that is quite close to the one embodied in the Didcascalia. In any case, it is the list of commandments found within the two documents, not the punishments for their transgression, that are the most closely related and on which both texts focus.

In effect, the Didascalia's list of legal and ethical commandments overlaps with the Qur'ān's expansion of core commandments specifically, and with its sense of justice more generally. This list emphasizes similar commandments – such as the prohibition of vain talk, the care for

---

applied by a Judean king (see also Bavli *Pesachim* 57a–b), and as an arbitrary punishment, it was common – none less than Maximus Confessor suffered it at the hands of the Byzantine authorities. I am not aware, however, of any pre-Qur'ānic attestation of cutting off hands for theft as a generally prescribed punishment and disagree with Andrew Marsham on his readings of an ancient Anatolian and Late Antique Sasanian case. The Anatolian Alalakh treaty discusses a case in which a town harbours a runaway slave; the mayor and five elders are therefore considered thieves and their hands are indeed cut off (in addition to a hefty fine). However, as Ignacio Márqez Rowe states, "we do not know whether that was the general treatment of thieves; the fact that it is expressly described only for this provision might actually suggest the contrary" (idem, "Alalakh," in Raymond Westbrook (ed.), *A History of Ancient Near Eastern Law* (Leiden: Brill, 2003), volume I, 715). Likewise, the *Letter of Tansar*, likely a sixth-century text written under the Sasanian king Khosrau I, depicts cutting off a thief's hand as an obsolete punishment meted out in the past. The punishment is commuted to a monetary fine by the Sasanian king; see Mary Boyce (ed. and transl.), *The Letter of Tansar* (Rome: Istituto Italiano per il Medio ed Estremo Oriente, 1968), 42–3. The letter can hardly be taken as proof of Persian practice, cf. Marsham, "Public Execution in the Umayyad Period: Early Islamic Punitive Practice and its Late Antique Context," *Journal of Arabic and Islamic Studies* 11 (2011): 117 note 48 and 119.

orphans, and the prohibition of false measures, the additions highlighted by Günther, as well as many others – in addition to the Biblical Decalogue. I would therefore propose the following preliminary conclusions: first, the Qurʾān's legal code stands in far-reaching continuity with Late Antique Near Eastern Law, which in turn emerges from the Ten Commandments. Second, the Didascalia, as a legally oriented document, seems to be an ideal source for demonstrating this continuity since it explicates many of the Qurʾān's additions to the Decalogue. Third, the legal affinity between the two texts also points to a lexical continuity between them and invites a comparative consideration, first, of their ritual law and, then, of their legal narratives. Should the ritual law and legal narratives of the Qurʾān and the Didascalia display the same conceptual and lexical affinity, while simultaneously lacking evidence for direct literary influence, we might confidently consider both texts as sharing a distinct legal culture within the broader legal discursive space inhabited by other Late Antique forms of Judaism and Christianity.

Chapter Two

Ritual Law in the Didascalia, the Clementine Homilies, and the Qurʾān

In addition to the continuity of many of their legal and ethical commandments as illustrated in Chapter One, both the Didascalia and the Qurʾān stand in a demonstrably shared tradition that requires gentiles to observe certain biblical purity laws regarding food and sex: the gentile commandments first formulated in *Acts* 15:29. While these "gentile" commandments found wide circulation in the Christian tradition (as shown in the Introduction), they also became a key element of the Didascalia, which endorses and quotes the list in these terms:[1]

- Stay far from that which is sacrificed (*dbyḥ'*)
- And from blood (*dm'*)
- And from that which is strangled (*ḥnyqa'*)
- And from fornication (*znywt'*)

(DA XXIV, 236.9–10, 237.3–4).

The Qurʾān's own catalogue, including abstinence from meat sacrificed (*mā ḏubiḥa*) on stone altars (*ʿala n-nuṣubi*) or offered to another entity than God, blood (*ad-dam*) and strangled (*al-munḫaniqatu*) meat (Q5:3), and fornication (*az-zinā*, e.g. Q17:32), thus far overlaps conceptually with that of the Christian tradition in general and, given the lexical commonalities, with the Syriac iteration thereof – as illustrated by the Peshitta, the Didascalia, and by Athana-

[1] See above, pages 7–16.

sius of Bālād – in particular.[2] At the same time, the Qur'ān expands on the list of "strangled" animals by adding pork (*al-ḫinzīr*) and other forms of an animal's accidental death that preclude consumption. Apparently all "dead" meat that is not properly slaughtered is prohibited (Q2:173; Q5:3, Q16:115), yet this general prohibition is juxtaposed to a specific list. In addition to strangled animals, one must not eat animals beaten to death, animals killed by falling or being gored (Q5:3), and animals mangled by a beast of prey (Q5:3), and meat "that you should divide with arrows" (Q5:3, see below on arrows).

The Qur'ān's additions, including animals that have died a natural death or were torn by wild animals, can again be found in the Hebrew Bible – yet neither the rabbis nor Christian tradition, (including the Didascalia) applies this expansion to gentiles.[3] The Qur'ān's acceptance and

---

[2] It is not clear whether the Qur'ān's prohibition of animals sacrificed on stone altars depicts idol sacrifices in general, or the use of stone altars in particular. Should the latter option be the case, we should note that the use of hewn stones to build altars is prohibited in the Hebrew Bible in Exodus 20:24–25 and Deuteronomy 27:5–6; the Didascalia in turn cites these verses in its polemic against sacrifice in general (in association with circumcision); see DA XXVI 243.18–244.8.

[3] See e.g. Exodus 22:31 and Leviticus 17 and 18, which are the basis of the rabbinic notion of impure food as well (see e.g. the tractates *Hullin* in the Mishna, the Tosefta, and the Talmudim). It will become clear that the Qur'ān has a closer affinity to the legal tradition of the Didascalia than to the tradition of the rabbis' own formulation of seven commandments for the gentiles, the so-called "Noahide Laws" (sometimes spelled "Noachide"), which only partially overlap with the Qur'ān; see Tosefta *Avodah Zarah* 9.4, Yerushalmi *Avodah Zarah* 2.1 (40c, 14–25; here, thirty laws are mentioned, but not spelled out), Bavli *Sanhedrin* 56a–60b; see also Bockmuehl, "The Noachide Commandments and New Testament Ethics," 72–101, cf. Deines, "Das Aposteldekret," 323–95.

further development of the *ritual* aspects of an established legal culture, however, can still be illustrated, if we read it in conjunction with the Didascalia and a third Late Antique text with close proximity to both the Didascalia and, as Pines notes, with the Qur'an, the Clementine Homilies.[4] These Homilies allow us to grasp the link between the ritual laws of the Didascalia and that of the Qurʾān in terms of developing practice.

The Clementine Homilies, like the Qurʾān, expand the list we find in Acts and in the Didascalia of "animals which have been suffocated," prohibited not only to Jews but also explicitly to Gentiles. The Homilies include "dead

[4] On the affinities between the Qurʾān and Clementine Literature, see esp. Pines, "Notes on Islam and on Arabic Christianity and Judaeo-Christianity," esp. 140–41, and below, page 137, note 12; see also Joachim Gnilka, *Die Nazarener und der Koran: Eine Spurensuche* (Freiburg: Herder, 2007) 109–10; François de Blois, "Elchasai – Manes – Muḥammad: Manichäismus und Islam in religionshistorischem Vergleich," *Der Islam* 81 (2004), 44–6; Andrae, *Der Ursprung des Islams und das Christentum*, 167, and Ignaz Goldziher, *Vorlesungen über den Islam* (Heidelberg: Carl Winter's Universitätsbuchandlung, 1925 [1910]), 14). For a fuller discussion of the history of scholarship, see the article in preparation by Patricia Crone, "Jewish Christianity and the Qurʾān;" see also below, page 194, note 15. On the affinities between the Clementine Homilies and the Qurʾān regarding concern about "false Scriptures" in both texts, see also Gobillot, "Der Begriff Buch im Koran im Licht der pseudoklementinischen Schriften," 339–445; and Andrae, *Der Ursprung des Islams und das Christentum*, 198 (adducing Epiphanius *Panarion* 30:18, but not the Clementine Homilies); on the affinity between the Clementine literature and the Didascalia in this respect, see Kevin M. Vacarella, *Shaping Christian Identity: The False Scripture Argument in Early Christian Literature* (PhD, Florida State University, 2007), esp. 174–191. See also F. Stanley Jones, *Pseudoclementina Elchasaiticaque inter judaeochristiana: Collected Studies* (Leeuven: Peeters, 2012), 152–171.

carcasses" in general, as well as "animals caught by wild beasts" and "that which is divided (τμητοῦ)" in particular, furnishing us with a partial precedent to the Qurʾān's own list, which also included carrion, animals mangled by wild beasts, and divided (*mā … tastaqsimū*) meat.[5] The expansion in the Homilies of the definition of "strangled" meats stands neatly in the middle, with Acts and the Didascalia on the one side, and the Qurʾān on the other. If we were to trace the expansion and specification of the category of "suffocated" animals from Acts and the Didascalia, we might note that the Homilies already included "carrion" in general and that they specify that animals caught by wild beasts should specifically be named, likely in line with the parallel specification in the Hebrew Bible.

The Qurʾān affirms the entirety of the expanded list preserved by the Homilies very precisely and continues the legal development towards greater specificity by further including animals beaten to death, animals killed by falling, or by being gored. At the same time, the Qurʾān allows for exemptions, should one be "compelled by hunger, without inclining to sin" (Q5:3) and provides for the "purification" of animals that were mangled by a beast of prey, likely akin

---

[5] For a similar use of the same root to denote "dividing" see e.g. Q43:32; Q53:22; and Q54:28; the alternate meaning of "to take an oath" (e.g. Q5:53) seems not applicable here. See also below, page 119, note 56 on the affinity of the root with the Hebrew verb for "divining" [sic.]. See Clementine Homilies 7:8 and 8:19; see also *Recognitions* 6:10, see Georg Strecker: *Die Pseudoklementinen II: Rekognitionen in Rufins Übersetzung* (Berlin: Akademie Verlag, 1994), 193. See also Marmorstein, *Judaism and Christianity in the Middle of the Third Century*, 230 [8] and idem, *Religionsgeschichtliche Studien, 1: Die Bezeichnungen für Christen und Gnostiker im Talmud und Midras* (Skotschau: Marmorstein, 1910), 26–35.

to the procedure to "mention God's name over it" (Q5:4) that permits one to eat meat caught by hunting dogs.

At this point already, we can see how the Decree of the Apostles serves as a watershed between the Didascalia, on the one side, and, on the other side, those texts that continue to develop its ritual lawcode, such as the Clementine Homilies and the Qur'ān. I will now illustrate that the entirety of the enhanced Judaeo-Christian lawcode that we find in the Qur'ān – including the prohibition of pork, and the injunction to wash after intercourse and before prayer, as well as abstinence during the menses – was equally endorsed by Judaeo-Christians within the Didascalia's community, as well as by the gentile followers of Jesus in the Clementine Homilies.

The Didascalia's "Judaeo-Christians," the Clementine Homilies, and the Qur'ān

Legal culture establishes itself by either accepting or rejecting available legal options, and often by portraying divergent choices as devious, or as heretical.[6] Some spadework

[6] Already in antiquity the charges against heretics usually include legal transgressions, in addition, rabbis and church fathers alike often modified the law to widen the legal gulf between themselves and the Other; see below, page 82, note 7. For a muscular legal approach towards cultural difference see the references to Robert C. Post on page 19 above, note 29. One (of many) pertinent examples of a view starkly different from Post's is offered by Prakash Shah's analysis of the legislative and executive attempts of Britain to classify minorities; Shah traces the ensuing tension between any rigid definition and lived realities (see idem, *Legal Pluralism in Conflict: Coping with Cultural Diversity in Law* (London: Glass House Press, 2005), esp. 27–42). Conversely, Shah's work is helpful in reminding us to differentiate

in the Didascalia's heresiology lets us reconstruct a discourse that presupposes three parties among its audience, all three of which illuminate the Didascalia's continuities with the Qurʾān's legal culture and its changes.

We must be exceedingly careful not to equate the Didascalia's construction of its audience with its actual socio-historical circumstances. Groups are often invented, exaggerated or caricatured in heresiological discourse. The Didascalia employs the two traditional techniques of lumping together its adversaries and of inscribing them in a narrative about the history of legal codes.[7] Yet this does not preclude the possibility of assessing any historical group or practice behind the heresiology, namely through a careful reading of all the internal and external evidence. Portraying itself as stemming from apostolic times, the Didascalia describes what it sees as unorthodox as follows:

And again also through other false apostles (*šlyḥ'*)... was the enemy working. They all, however, had one law upon earth, that they should blaspheme against the Almighty God (*'lh' 'ḥyd kl*), and should not believe in the resurrection (*wbqymt'*). And again in other matters they were teaching and troubling the people. Indeed, many of them were teaching that a man should not take a wife, and were saying that if a man did not take a wife, this was holiness .... Again others of them taught that a man should not

between the historical realities of Late Antiquity on the one side and on the other the Qurʾān's own attempt at establishing a normative taxonomy of who the "people of the book" are and how they should behave (see my Conclusion).

[7] These techniques are used by heresiologists ranging from Irenaeus to Epiphanius, to the rabbis and also to the Clementine Literature, as illustrated by several of the contributions to the volume edited by Eduard Iricinschi and Holger Zellentin, *Heresy and Identity in Late Antiquity* (TSAJ 120; Tübingen: Mohr Siebeck, 2008).

eat flesh, and said that a man must not eat anything that has a soul in it. Others, however, said that one was bound to withhold from pork only (*dḥzyr' blḥwd*), but might eat those things which the Law pronounces pure (*dmdk'*), and that he should be circumcised according to the law .... Then we proceeded and preached the holy word of the catholic congregation rightly, and we returned again to come to the congregations, and found them seized by other opinions (*br'yn' 'ḥrn'*). For some, namely, were observing holiness [i.e. sexual abstinence], and some abstained from flesh and from wine (*ḥmr'*), and some from pork (*ḥzyr'*). And they were keeping (something) of all the bonds which are in the second legislation. (DA XXIII, 230.6–231.15)

This list of deviant ascetic and biblical observances does not contain any practices that would be surprising. Asceticism and vegetarianism were of course widespread in Late Antiquity. More pertinently, Christian and rabbinic heresiologists through the centuries have accused their opponents of observing similar practices in various configurations; the rabbis, especially, legislate against celibacy and asceticism.[8] Such Christian and rabbinic heresiologists, as in the passage above, trace back all heresies to the time of the apostles or to tannaitic times.

Heresiology should be taken, first and foremost, as evidence of religious discourse about invented and perceived enemies and, second, as a guide to the historical Late Antique religious landscape only when read with due suspicion and understanding of heresiological tropes.[9]

---

[8] For a summary of primary and secondary sources on Christian and rabbinic polemics against ascetic practices, especially in Epiphanius and Wayiqrah Rabbah, see Zellentin, *Rabbinic Parodies*, 52–94, see also pages 116–7 below.

[9] See Eduard Iricinschi and Holger Zellentin, "Making Selves and Marking Others: Identity and Late Antique Heresiologies," in: idem (eds.), *Heresy and Identity in Late Antiquity*, 1–27; cf. the dismissal

A closer look at the Didascalia, however, reveals quite a nuanced picture, yielding the impression that a subset of the practices it laments was observed not only in the time of the apostles, but also at the time of the Didascalia's Christian authors; and that these practices were observed not only by "heretical" groups at the margins of or even outside its own community, but by heterodox, and especially heteropractical, members squarely within it. We can read such complaints with much greater confidence in their historical relevance because such objections could have been verified by the historical audience. Moreover, these accusations suggest that the text's authority is not universally accepted – a state of affairs one is less likely to invent.[10]

Yet while the opinions and practices evoked by the Didascalia were likely observable at the time of writing, we should resist equating observances with groups. Thinking in terms of groups is exactly what the Didascalia's au-

---

of any rabbinic interaction of rabbis with the Christian Other by Adiel Schremer, *Brothers Estranged: Heresy, Christianity, and Jewish Identity in Late Antiquity* (Oxford: Oxford University Press, 2010). A study of the Qurʾān's heresiology remains an urgent desideratum; cf. Mohammad Ali Amir-Moezzi, "Heresy," in McAuliffe (ed.), *Encyclopaedia of the Qurʾān*, ad loc.

[10] The most important example for a similar scenario may again be John Chrysostom's *Adversus Judaeos* homilies, which castigate the Christian affinity for Jewish practice within John's community; see Robert L. Wilken, *John Chrysostom and the Jews: Rhetoric and Reality in the Late 4th Century* (Berkeley: University of California Press, 1983). Likewise, it is unlikely that rabbis would have entirely invented stories about Christian tendencies among rabbis; see Zellentin, *Rabbinic Parodies*, 137–232.

thors want their audience to do – establishing the existence of a schismatic group is the most fundamental aspect of heresiology and should never be accepted as evidence by the historian. We will never know if the Didascalia's Judaeo-Christians would have self-identified as an independent group within its broader Christian community. However, we can see continuity of practice and discourse between the Didascalia's Judaeo-Christians, the Clementine Homilies and the Qurʾān, which allows us to take the expanded Judaeo-Christian ritual lawcode – adding purity to the Didascalia's other laws – as one of the Qurʾān's legal points of departure.

In its concluding chapters, the Didascalia explicitly disentangles the named practices it rejects and previously has lumped together; here, it differentiates between two divergent groups. The Didascalia places itself as a "Christian" group in between a perceived group I will term the "antinomian ascetics," on the one hand, and, on the other hand, a perceived group observant of stricter purity rules, in addition to the ones the Didascalia itself commands. It is this latter group I will call the "Judaeo-Christian group." To a high degree at least, the practices and beliefs of the antinomian ascetic group are likely a heresiological construct, while the Judaeo-Christian group is described in such concrete terms and addressed at such length that it seems to reflect actual practices observed at the time of the Didascalia's composition. Whether the Didascalia describes or invents a social reality of Judaeo-Christianity within its community cannot be determined. A study of its discourse alone, however, is already rewarding, especially when it comes to sexual purity, food laws, the observance of Shabbat, and asceticism.

"Troubling the People:" Ritual Washing and Abstinence from Impure Meats

The Didascalia's starting point when describing the Judaeo-Christian group in more detail is a paraphrase of *Acts*:

> For also some days before, certain men had come down from Judaea and Antioch, and were teaching the brethren: If you do not circumcise and conduct yourselves according to the Law of Moses, and keep yourselves pure (*wmtdkyn*) from meats, and from the rest of all the other things, you cannot be saved, and they had much strife and debate ... (DA XXIV, 233.8–14)

This is more or less the famous passage from Acts 15:1, with the addition of the purity of meats, which does not appear there. The updating, as Fonrobert points out, "reinscribes that earlier conflict [of Acts] into [the Didascalia's] own contemporary conflict."[11] Here too, the Didascalia accuses the Judaeo-Christian group not of neglecting any commandments, but rather of taking ritual purity too far along the lines of the "Law of Moses." The Judaeo-Christian teachers enjoin circumcision, keeping "oneself pure from meats" and keeping oneself pure "from all the other things." The terminology of ritual purity here is precise: "keeping yourselves pure (*wmtdkyn*)" (DA XXIII 233.11) from meat does *not* mean abstinence from meat, which in

---

[11] Fonrobert, "The *Didascalia Apostolorum*," 490; Fonrobert here rightly argues against too definitive a reconstruction of groups; see also Marcus, "The *Testaments of the Twelve Patriarchs* and the *Didascalia Apostolorum*," 618. Charlotte Methuen, however, allows for two definable groups (see eadem, "Widows, Bishops, and the Struggle for Authority in the *Didascalia Apostolorum*," *JEH* 46 (1995): 204), a view that is defended, *pace* Fonrobert, by Stewart-Sykes: *The Didascalia Apostolorum*, 69–73.

the passages excerpted above is described not as a question of purity but as an issue of not eating *anything* that "has a soul in it." The Didascalia there also specifies that its opponents construct *purity* from meat as meaning that one must "withhold from pork only (*dḥzyr' blḥwd*), but might eat those things which the Law pronounces pure (*dmdk'*) (DA XXIII 230.19–231.1)." The Judaeo-Christian group, hence, allows for pure meat to be consumed.

The Didascalia uses the traditional voice of Acts to introduce the Judaeo-Christian group in ways comparable to other Christian heresiologists.[12] Still, the Didascalia seems concerned with contemporary practices rather than past ones, as we can see when it carefully describes and refutes those calling for purity from "meat" and "all the other things" in its concluding chapters. These chapters of the Didascalia, especially twenty-six, is addressed explicitly to those among his community "who have been converted (*d'tpnyw*) from the people (*'m'*)" (DA XXVI 241.9), i.e. the Jewish people; this is the Judaeo-Christian group in its congregation. While using stark language, the Didascalia never addresses these converts as "heretics" in its attempt to rein in their Jewish observances,

---

[12] See Anders Ekenberg, "Evidence for Jewish Believers in 'Church Orders' and Liturgical Texts," in: Oskar Skarsaune and Reidar Hvalvik (eds.), *Jewish Believers in Jesus: The Early Centuries* (Peabody, MA: Hendrickson, 2007), 649–653; Charlotte Elisheva Fonrobert, "Jewish Christians, Judaizers, and Christian anti-Judaism," in Virginia Burrus (ed.), *Late Ancient Christianity* (Minneapolis, MN: Fortress Press, 2005), 234–254; and A.F.J. Klijn and G.J. Reinink, *Patristic Evidence for Jewish-Christian Sects* (Leiden: Brill, 1973). For rabbinic polemics against Christian tendencies among rabbis and for Christian polemics against the observance of Israelite commandments, see, e.g., Zellentin, *Rabbinic Parodies*, 137–212.

in contrast to the words used to describe the antinomian ascetic "heretics" (*'rsywṭ'*, DA XXVI 254.25) I shall address momentarily.[13]

The Didascalia presents the Judaeo-Christian group as converts from Judaism to Christianity. This designation as "converts" may well be part of the Didascalia's heresiology, for it contrasts with the clear distinction between Jews and Jesus-believing gentiles we find in the Clementine Homilies. Whether the Didascalia's Judaeo-Christians would have seen themselves as "Israelites," as "Jews," as former Jews, as Christians, as Judaeo-Christians, or something quite distinct from all these notions is a complex question which we must bracket.[14] Yet while the ethnic classifica-

---

[13] Marcus notes that the Didascalia addresses the Torah-observers as "beloved brethren" (*'ḥ' ḥbyb'*) in DA XXVI, 241.12; see idem, "The *Testaments of the Twelve Patriarchs* and the *Didascalia Apostolorum*," 626, (the Jews are also called "brethren," *'ḥyn*, in DA XXI, 209.14 and DA XXVI 241.12). Marcus emphasizes the Didascalia's "eirenic attitude towards the Jews" (ibid., 608); he does not, however, note the difference between the Didascalia's treatment of antinomian ascetic "heretics" and those observant of Jewish rites. Instead, he claims that the Didascalia "views this Torah-observant group as heretical" (ibid.), a statement that should be attenuated. Note that elsewhere, the Didascalia explains the word "Jews" by means of the word "confession" (*mwdynwt'*), even though they do not "confess" (*mwdyn'*, DA XIII, 150.15–6) the killing of Christ; see below page 204, note 1.

[14] It is futile to speculate on whether or not the Didascalia's original authors, or its editors, were Jewish, gentile, or of mixed descent. As Marmorstein noted correctly, "it is not impossible that the writer of the Didascalia was a born Jew" (see idem, "Judaism and Christianity in the Middle of the Third Century," 233 [11]). Yet Marmorstein himself asks the more answerable question pertaining to the text's intimate familiarity with rabbinic culture at large, for which he adduces ample evidence (see ibid., esp. 231–33 [9–11]). Marmorstein's analysis needs to be evaluated in light of today's more precise dating of rabbinic sources, but it remains substantially unchallenged. On the

tion is fuzzy, the legal differences are clear: the Didascalia's Christian authors presuppose that these Judaeo-Christian members of their community agree with themselves on all the *aforementioned* commandments (discussed in Chapter One) and that they require *stricter* observances than the Didascalia's Christian group.

In addition to insisting on circumcision and abstaining from pork, the Didascalia's Christian authors construct the Judaeo-Christian group as requiring purification after sexual intercourse:

> Be thus minded therefore concerning everyone, concerning those who observe issues and the intercourse of marriage; indeed, all these observances are foolish and harmful. For if, when a man shall leave intercourse, or flux come out from him, he must be bathed, let him also wash his mattress – and he will have this travail and unceasing vexation: he will be bathing and he will be washing his clothes and his mattress, and he will not be able to do anything else ... on this account, beloved, flee and stay away from observances which are such. (DA XXVI, 259.8–261.1)

The Didascalia argues that purification after sexual intercourse is impractical, in effect an "unceasing vexation." Further, the Didascalia strongly rejects the notion current among members of its audience that menstruating women

question of the Didascalia's intimacy with rabbinic tradition, see also Marcus, "The *Testaments of the Twelve Patriarchs* and the *Didascalia Apostolorum*," 607. Marcus' assertion that "the composer of the [Didascalia] appears to be a Christian of Jewish birth" (ibid., 606) does not follow from the fact that the text addresses "those who converted from the Jewish people" in the first person plural. To the contrary, as Marcus himself notes, "the Jewish self-identification could simply be part of the fictional frame of composition by Jesus' original disciples" (ibid., 607). Cf. also Charlotte Elisheva Fonrobert, *Menstrual Purity: Rabbinic and Christian Reconstructions of Biblical Gender* (Stanford: Stanford University Press, 2000), 167 and 284, note 21.

should separate themselves from the community and that during the menstrual cycle the Holy Spirit would not inhabit a female Christian (see esp. XXVI, 256.3–259.17), as Fonrobert lucidly explains.[15] The Latin Didascalia follows the Syriac quite closely when it comes to denouncing ritual washing and withdrawal from the community.[16]

The Syriac Didascalia goes even so far as permitting sexual intercourse during the menstruation, which is remarkable, since the rabbis,[17] some pagan Roman sources,[18] and even some gentile Christians[19] all insist on abstinence from intercourse during menstruation. The Syriac Didascalia's legislation is all the more peculiar since it contradicts its own testimony earlier in the text. When quoting Ezekiel in the list excerpted in Chapter One, the Didascalia does

---

[15] See Fonrobert, *Menstrual Purity*, esp. 172–98.

[16] See Connolly, *Didascalia Apostolorum*, 249–251.

[17] See the tractates *Niddah* in the Mishna, Tosefta, and the Talmudim; the rabbis of course stipulate abstinence during the menses for Jews only, not for gentiles.

[18] See A. Richlin, "Pliny's Brassiere," in Laura K. McClure (ed.), *Sexuality and Gender in the Classical World: Readings and Sources* (Oxford: Blackwell, 2002), 231–3, as noted by Marcus in "The *Testaments of the Twelve Patriarchs* and the *Didascalia Apostolorum*," 622 note 72.

[19] Augustine argues that the commandments listed in Ezekiel 18.1–32 "are not to be taken in a metaphorical sense," and for Augustine this explicitly includes intercourse during a woman's menstruation (idem, *On Merit and the Forgiveness of Sins, and the Baptism of Infants* III.12 (21); see Roland Teske, *Augustine: Answer to the Pelagians*, (New York: New City Press, 1997), I:134). See also Fonrobert, *Menstrual Purity*, 160–209; and Shaye Cohen, "Menstruants and the Sacred in Judaism and Christianity," in Sarah. B. Pomeroy, *Women's History and Ancient History* (Chapel Hill: University of North Carolina Press, 1991), 273–99. See also Marmorstein, "Judaism and Christianity in the Middle of the Third Century," 230 [8] and idem, Religionsgeschichtliche Studien (Skotschau: Marmorstein, 1910), I, 26–35.

not state that any item on the list of transgressions, including the prohibition to approach (*ntqrb*, DA VI, 67.11) one's wife during her menses, would be affected by Jesus' abrogation of the law. Later, however, it explicitly exhorts husbands to "cleave" (*nqpyn*, XXVI, 262.13) to their wives during menstruation, using a term that denotes engaging in intercourse, as Marcus aptly notes.[20] Given the internal variance, and the fact that in this case the Syriac version of the Didascalia diverts from the Latin, we cannot exclude the possibility that the Syriac version contains a post-Qurʾānic alteration, and we should bracket the Christian authors' permission of intercourse during the menses.[21]

---

[20] Sokoloff, *A Syriac Dictionary*, 948, already noted by Marcus, "The *Testaments of the Twelve Patriarchs* and the *Didascalia Apostolorum*," 620. The manuscripts are homogenous at this place (only manuscript Paris Syr. 62 offers a slightly variant spelling, *nqypyn*), suggesting an early emendation of the Syriac Didascalia.

[21] The earlier, Latin version of the Didascalia forcefully confirms this prohibition stating that "itaque cum naturalia profluunt uxoribus uestris, nolite conuenire illis, sed sustinete eas et, scientes propria membra esse, diligite sicut proprias animas;" Connolly, *Didascalia Apostolorum*, 255. Vööbus states that a "look at the Latin with its strong prohibition … indicates that something is wrong with the Syriac text" (idem, *The Didascalia Apostolorum in Syriac* II, 244 note 229). For a discussion of the Syriac passage, see Marcus, "The *Testaments of the Twelve Patriarchs* and the *Didascalia Apostolorum*," 618–21, and Fonrobert, *Menstrual Purity*, 174–85. Marcus and Fonrobert seem to have missed the variant in the Latin Didascalia, as well as the reiteration of the prohibition of sex during the menses in Ezekiel, neither of which they address. Intriguingly, Vööbus claims that "a deliberate change [in the Syriac] cannot come into account here," a claim which he unfortunately does not sustain with any argument (idem, *The Didascalia Apostolorum in Syriac* II, 244 note 229). The same strict ruling against intercourse during the menses also informs the Apostolic Constitution, which follows the Latin Didascalia quite closely in this respect; see VI.28, Funk, *Didascalia et Constitutiones Apostolorum*,

What remains clear is that the Judaeo-Christian group is implied as having prohibited it.

The Didascalia's Judaeo-Christian group, in contrast to its Christian authors, insists on purification before the communal prayer for those who are in a state of ritual uncleanness – a purification practice the Didascalia also rejects:

> On this account, a woman (*'ntt'*) when she is in the way of women, and a man when an issue (*dwb'*) comes forth from him, and a man and his wife when they have intercourse and rise up one from another – without restraint, without bathing (*sḥyn*), let them assemble (*ntknšwn*) for they are pure (*ddkyn*)
>
> (DA XXVI, 262.21–263.2).

The Didascalia implies that the heteropractical part of its audience would not assemble and pray in a state of ritual impurity. (Here, the Latin and the Syriac again converge.[22])

---

volume I, 379. It seems, hence, that this passage has been changed at some point in the tradition of the Syriac Didascalia. This may or may not constitute evidence of a post-Islamic intervention in order to increase the gulf between Christian and Muslim ritual; see above page 42, note 50, and page 46, note 56. Further inquiry into this question is necessary; the issue however does not affect the overall analysis of the Didascalia's legal culture vis-à-vis the Qurʾān.

[22] The "assembling" in the Syriac is the "assembly of the congregation" on Sundays as specified in Chapter XIII. In this case, the Latin Didascalia fully endorses the Syriac version, reading: "Et mulier ergo cum in menstruis est, et uir cum in cursu seminis, et uir et mulier legibus ad nuptias conuenientes et ab alterutrum exurgentes, sine obseruatione et non loti orent, et mundi sunt" (Connolly, *Didascalia Apostolorum*, 255). As discussed by Dorothea Wendebourg, a position similar to that of the Didascalia, declaring that baptism leads to a state of perpetual purity, is endorsed, for example, by Clement of Alexandria (*Stromata* 3:12) and Methodius of Olympus (*De cibis* 5:3), cited by Wendebourg, "Die alttestamentlichen Reinheitsgesetze in der frühen Kirche," *Zeitschrift für Kirchengeschichte* 95 (1984): 149–170.

The women abstained from prayer during the menstrual cycle altogether, and the men and women bathed after sexual intercourse. Abstinence from the Eucharist or from visiting holy places under conditions of ritual impurity was not unheard of in Christianity, yet bathing after sexual intercourse was a much more confined practice.[23] As mentioned before, this and other practices the Didascalia names – abstinence from pork, circumcision, and ritual washing – are again all practices ascribed by Christian heresiologists to overly law-abiding sectarians.[24] In contrast

---

[23] See Cohen, "Menstruants and the Sacred in Judaism and Christianity," 287–90 and Wendebourg, "Die alttestamentlichen Reinheitsgesetze." As Sr. Vassa Larin perceptively notes, many of the canons endorsing abstinence from the Eucharist during the menses or after childbirth are of Egyptian origin, such as Canon 2 of Dionysius of Alexandria (264 C.E., see Charles Lett Feltoe (ed.), *The Letters and Other Remains of Dionysius of Alexandria* (Cambridge: University Press, 1904), 102–103) and Canon 6–7 of Timotheus of Alexandria (381 C.E., see Périclès-Pierre Joannou; *Discipline générale antique (IVe–IXes.)* (Grottaferratta-Rome: S. Nilo, 1964), volume 2, 243–244) and the Canons of Hippolytus (see Wilhelm Riedel ed. and trans., *Die Kirchenrechtsquellen des Patriarchats Alexandrien* (Leipzig: Deichert, 1900), 209); cited by Sr. Vassa Larin, "Ritual Impurity," *St Vladimir's Theological Quarterly* 52 (2008) 275–92. See also Peter J. Tomson, "Jewish Purity Laws as Viewed by the Church Fathers and by the Early Followers of Jesus," in Marcel J. H. M. Poorthuis and Joshua Schwartz (eds.), *Purity and Holiness: The Heritage of Leviticus* (Leiden: Brill, 2000), 73–91.

[24] In chapters 29 and 30 of his *Panarion* (see Williams, *The Panarion of Epiphanius of Salamis, Book I*, 112–151), Epiphanius constructs two prominent "Judaeo-Christian" groups, the "Nazoreans," and the "Ebionites," who allegedly use the Hebrew language, the Gospel of Matthew, and the Clementine Homilies; they reject parts of the Hebrew Bible; they hold Jesus to be of human parentage and see him as abolishing sacrifice; they equate Adam and Christ; they do not eat meat; they repudiate celibacy; they allow divorce and remarriage; they do not keep Passover; they are the Jews' enemies; and they observe

to the stereotypical straw men and remote groups of Irenaeus and Epiphanius, however, the Didascalia's argument with the Judaeo-Christian group seems to reflect a very concrete debate about ritual purity among its audience. Moreover, the corroborating testimony of the Clementine Homilies, which affirm a very similar list of practices from an *inside* perspective, is essential for relating the cognate legal culture to the Qurʾān. The relevant passage in the Clementine Homilies follows the previously quoted list of impure meats and deserves to be quoted in full:

> And this is the service He has appointed: To worship Him only, and believe only in the Prophet of truth, and to be baptized for the remission of sins, and thus by this pure baptism to be born again unto God by saving water; to abstain from the table of devils, that is, from food offered to idols, from dead carcasses, from animals that have been suffocated or caught by wild beasts, and from blood; not to live any longer impurely; to wash after intercourse; that the women on their part should keep the law of purification; that all should be sober-minded, given to good works, refraining from wrongdoing, looking for eternal life from the all-powerful God, and asking with prayer and continual supplication that they may win it.[25]

It has been noted that the language employed in this passage from the Clementine Homilies may be reflected in

---

purity and daily immersion, especially after intercourse. Epiphanius' description partially coincides with and partially contradicts practices attested by the Clementine Homilies and attributed by the Didascalia to its Judaeo-Christian group. This does not, however, allow us to give any *prima facie* historical value to Epiphanius' heresiologically tainted portrayal of these groups in terms of "Nazoreans" and "Ebionites." Heresiology resembles an archeological find that was looted – it is worth something only in as far as its original context can be established.

[25] Clementine Homilies 7:8.

the Qur'ān's prophetology; I hope to give the topic its due attention in the future.[26] The crucial point here is that the Clementine Homilies present a list of observances incumbent upon *gentiles* who seek salvation through Jesus. In addition to extending the list of impure meats, whose intermediate stage of development between the Didascalia and the Qur'ān we saw above, Jesus demands purity: women need to "keep the law of purification" which denotes abstinence from intercourse during menstruation as specified elsewhere in the text, and all members of its audience should bathe after intercourse.[27] The text also depicts the apostle Peter and his followers as bathing before praying; while Peter is Jewish the narrative emphasis remains noteworthy.[28]

All observances in question are of course again biblical, yet the Clementine Homilies attest to the same extension of a concrete subset of biblical observances to include gentiles which we saw ridiculed by the Didascalia. This allows us to corroborate the historicity of the Didascalia's description of such observances, which seems self-evident already from a literary and socio-historical point of view,

---

[26] See Pines, "Notes on Islam and on Arabic Christianity and Judaeo-Christianity," esp. 140–41. Joachim Gnilka has pointed out that the prophetology of the Qur'ān resembles that of the Clementine Homilies, which features Jesus as its culmination (see idem, *Die Nazarener und der Koran: Eine Spurensuche* (Freiburg/Basel/Wien: Herder, 2007) 109–10; he does not quote Pines' considerations; we should add the arguments of François de Blois, "Elchasai – Manes – Muḥammad," 44–6; Tor Andrae, *Der Ursprung des Islams und das Christentum*, 167, as well as Ignaz Goldziher, *Vorlesungen über den Islam*, 14).

[27] See Clementine Homilies 11:28.

[28] See Clementine Homilies 11:1.

by an *insider's* voice. While similar practices are largely attributed to groups such as the Nazoreans and deplored by the heresiologists of the fourth century such as John Chrysostom and Epiphanius, the evidence of the Clementine Homilies allows us to verify as accurate the specific ritual observances ascribed by the Didascalia to its Judaeo-Christian group.

If "Judaeo-Christian" legal culture, then, is alive and well in the fourth century, what should we conclude if similar practices are presupposed by the Qurʾān? The question partially surpasses the scope of the present inquiry. Suffice it to say that Christian heresiologists shift their focus towards other issues such as the Trinitarian debates, and pay little attention to Judaeo-Christian elements past the fourth century. While this could be taken as an argument from silence, indicating that the Jewish Jesus-movement miraculously disappeared, no evidence supports this. Rather, it is clear that the church fathers considered themselves as having parted ways with such believers: Epiphanius classified them as "mere Jews." Likewise, the anti-Jewish discourse of the Greek and Syriac church fathers, likewise, would have been at least partially addressed to believers in Jesus who were seen as observing too many Jewish observances as well.[29]

There is, then, a good chance that aspects of Judaeo-Christian practice remained part of the Jewish, as well as the Christian, world. Accordingly, at least in my opinion, the rabbis continue to discuss Jesus-belief amongst Jews

---

[29] *Panarion* II.9.1 (see Williams, *The Panarion of Epiphanius of Salamis, Book I*, 119). On anti-Judaism in the Greek and Syriac patristic literature see below, page 107, note 44.

and even among rabbis with *growing* intensity after the fourth century.[30] Moreover, the reception history of the Clementine Homilies speaks for the continuation of Judaeo-Christian elements: these texts were avidly read, copied, and translated in every century after the fourth without major emendations, and it is likely that the practices endorsed in them equally lived on.[31] More importantly, the recent work of Annette Reed and Pierluigi Piavonelli adduces much evidence of Judaeo-Christian literary activity past the fourth century; Reed especially points to the ways in which the "Christian" recensions of Judaeo-Christian works led to the spread of their ideas throughout broader Christian culture.[32]

---

[30] See page 87, note 12.

[31] The direct evidence of the continuing relevance of the Clementines, especially in the Syriac translation, past the fourth century, allows for a possible historical bridge between the fourth and the seventh century. See Anton de Lagarde, *The Pseudo-Clementine Recognitions and Homilies (10–14) in Syriac* (Gorgias Press, 2012 [1861]); and Stanley F. Jones, "Evaluating the Latin and Syriac Translations of the Pseudo-Clementine Recognitions," *Apocrypha* 3 (1992): 237–57, and the following note.

[32] See esp. Annette Y. Reed, "'Jewish-Christian' Apocrypha and the History of Jewish/Christian Relations," in Pierluigi Piovanelli (ed.) *Christian Apocryphal Texts for the New Millennium: Achievements, Prospects, and Challenges* (forthcoming); eadem, "Rabbis, Jewish Christians and Other Late Antique Jews: Reflections on the Fate of Judaism(s) after 70 CE," in Ian H. Henderson, Gerbern S. Oegema, et al. (eds.), *The Changing Face of Judaism, Christianity and Other Greco-Roman Religions in Antiquity* (Gütersloh: Gütersloher Verlagshaus, 2005), 323–46); Pierliuigi Piovanelli, "The Book of the Cock and the Rediscovery of Ancient Jewish-Christian traditions in Fifth-Century Palestine," in Henderson and Oegema (eds.), *The Changing Face of Judaism*, 308–322; and idem, "Exploring the Ethiopic Book of the Cock, an Apocryphal Passion Gospel from Late Antiquity," *Harvard Theological Review* 96 (2003): 427–54.

Hence, there is no positive evidence for the disappearance of Judaeo-Christian practice, and only evidence from silence against it. The burden of proof must thus be on those who want to stipulate the convenient disappearance of Judaeo-Christianity. In my view, aspects of Judaeo-Christianity lived on among believers in Jesus, if not in a distinct group, then at least as discrete practices within other Jewish and Christian groups – the very scenario the Didascalia and the rabbis deplore. The Qurʾān's own continuity with a Judaeo-Christian legal culture, corroborated by its affinity for, as well as by its explicit departure from, specific cognate practices of its time, leaves no doubt about the persistence of Judaeo-Christian *practice* in seventh-century Arabia, and perhaps in adjacent territories as well.

The Qurʾān requires of its audience a catalogue of purity rules similar to that of the Clementine Homilies and of the Didascalia's Judaeo-Christian group, in addition to the previously named commandments also shared by the Christian group. To begin with, we saw that the Didascalia's Judaeo-Christian group seems not to obey the entire biblical catalogue of *kashrut*, but rather wants to "keep pure (*wmtdkyn*) from meats," which is specified as the abstinence from "pork alone" (*ḥzyrʾ blḥwd*, DA XXIII, 230.19, see also DA XXIV 231.14), in addition to the prohibitions of the Decree of the Apostles. Likewise, the Qurʾān extends its list of impure meats to include pork (*ḫinzīr*) as well, not requiring the avoidance of any other meats if they are properly slaughtered or from anything "which you may purify" (*ḏakkaytum*). Again, the Qurʾān uses concepts and lexemes cognate to those of the Didascalia.[33]

[33] The Latin reads: "a sola porcina carne debere se abstinere, ea

Likewise, swine are prohibited for Jews in the Clementine Homilies as part of their general observance of the Torah – Jews will gain salvation through the law of Moses, as discussed in the Introduction – yet the Homilies seem to discourage pork consumption for gentiles as well. In the Homilies, "tasting dead flesh, or filling themselves with that which is torn of beasts, or that which is divided, or that which is strangled, or anything else at all that is unclean" is prohibited to all of humanity, Jew and gentile alike.[34] What could the term "anything else at all that is unclean" (ἄλλου τινὸς ἀκαθάρτου ἐμπιπλάμενος) denote in addition to the meats listed explicitly?

The question can partially be answered by considering the narrative background of the Homilies' gentile *nomos*. The key to the purity laws of the Clementine Homilies is the avoidance of "unclean spirits" (ἀκάθαρτα πνεύματα, Clementine Homilies 11:15). As I will discuss in more detail below, the Homilies warn that demons are allowed to enter any person who consumes impure meat. The concept that impurity attracts demons forms the very center of the Homilies' ritual food laws. There is no discussion of the extent to which this category would include the unclean animals of Leviticus, such as the camel, the hare, and the rock badger, yet pork stands out in this list. Pork is first called "impure," also in Leviticus 11:7 (ἀκάθαρτα in the Septuagint). Throughout Late Antiquity, moreover, Jews

uero quae in lege sunt munda debere manducare ...," Connolly, *Didascalia Apostolerum*, 203. Note that Hans Joachim Schoeps has already observed that the Didascalia's prohibition of pork might be pertinent to understanding the Qurʾān in idem, *Theologie und Geschichte des Judenchristentums* (Tübingen: Mohr Siebeck, 1949), 341.

[34] Clementine Homilies 8:19.

and non-Jews alike perceived pork as the epitome of the Israelite notion of impurity; pork functions as a central symbol in many Jewish and non-Jewish texts.[35]

More concretely, the Clementine Homilies develop the theme of Matthew 8:28–33 and warn those who act irrationally that "becoming like swine (χοῖροι), you become the desire of demons (δαιμόνων αἰτήματα ἐγένεσθε)." For Matthew, this formulation went along with abstinence from pork as part of the Gospel's observance of scriptural law. The Homilies' demonology, in turn, makes the avoidance of impurity an especially urgent issue, as we will see. In the Homilies, moreover, becoming like swine functions in contrast to the humanity one receives through "the law of God (τοῦ θεοῦ νόμον)."[36] While calling somebody a pig in itself would not exclude the permissibility of consuming pork, the association of swine and demons, juxtaposed to "the law of God," doubly evokes the impurity of pork and the danger of attracting demons. Such language, comparable to the imagery that the Clementine Homilies uses for wine (on which more below), certainly discourages the consumption of pork even if the text as we have it does not

---

[35] The association of Jewish rules of uncleanness and pork hardly needs to be emphasized. It is simply listed as one of the impure animals in the Torah (see e.g. Leviticus 11:7 and Deuteronomy 14:8), yet invoked already as a symbol of impurity in Isaiah (65:4, 66:3 and 17); it is presented as such in 1 Maccabees 1:47 and the refusal to eat pork symbolizes the law-abidance of the martyrs in 2 Maccabees 7 and in 4 Maccabees 5 and 6. For a perceptive overview of the ample symbolic uses of pork in Greco-Roman and rabbinic discourse on Jewishness, see Jordan D. Rosenblum, "'Why Do You Refuse to Eat Pork?' Jews, Food, and Identity in Roman Palestine," *Jewish Quarterly Review* 100 (2010): 95–110.

[36] Clementine Homilies 10:6 see also 19:14. On the law-observance of Matthew see below, page 129, note 3.

go as far as the Qurʾān and the Didascalia's Judaeo-Christian group, which both posit an outright prohibition.

Regarding its marital purity laws, the Qurʾān instructs its audience as follows:

So keep away from women (*nisāʾ*) during the menses,
And do not approach them (*taqrabūhunna*) till they are pure (*taṭahharna*) (Q2:222).

Given how widely abstinence from intercourse during the menstruation was practiced, it is of little surprise that the Qurʾān shares this practice with the Didascalia's Judaeo-Christian group and with the Clementine Homilies – the fear of demons looms large for the Judaeo-Christians, as we saw above. Despite the widespread practice of abstinence during the menses, however, we should note the lexical affinity between the Arabic and the Syriac for "approaching" (*ntqrb* / *taqrabūhunna*) and the explicit emphasis on the women's ritual purity in both texts (the Qurʾān here uses a term cognate to rabbinic *ṭhr*). The Qurʾān's legal code, finally, portrays ritual purity quite centrally in ways reminiscent of the Didascalia's Judaeo-Christian group:

O you who have faith!
When you stand up for prayer,
Wash your faces
And your hands up to the elbows,
And wipe a part of your heads and your feet,
Up to the ankles.
If you are (ritually) impure, purify (*fa-ṭ-ṭahharū*) yourselves.
But if you are sick, or on a journey,
Or any of you has come from the privy,
Or you have touched women,
And you cannot find water,
Then make ablutions with good ground (*ṣaʿīdan ṭayyiban*)

And wipe a part of your faces and your hands with it.
God does not require
To put you to hardship,
But He desires to purify (*yuṭahhirakum*) you,
And to complete His blessings upon you
So that you may give thanks.
Remember God's blessing upon you
And His covenant with which He has bound you
When you said, 'We hear and obey' (*samiʿnā wa-ʾaṭaʿnā*)
(Q5:6–7).

The Qurʾān concurs with the Didascalia's Judaeo-Christian "group" that purification after sexual intercourse and before prayer is required by God, two practices we saw equally endorsed by the Clementine Homilies. While the Didascalia goes far in rejecting precisely these practices found in part of its audience, the Qurʾān and the Clementine Homilies insist that "God desires to purify you" and that "purification" is part of the "worship of God." The Qurʾān in this respect reminds its audience that this is part of "the covenant with which He has bound you," evoking the Israelite covenant;[37] whereas the Clementine Homilies states, "for so the law of God commands."[38] The Didascalia, by contrast, defines ritual washing as among those practices abrogated by Jesus – a concept of which the Clementine Homilies and the Qurʾān conceive more narrowly.

Intriguingly, the Qurʾān's and the Didascalia's formulations for and against the requirements for purity read almost as if they were reasoning against each other – only

[37] The "Israelite" resonances of this verse become clear when comparing the concluding line of Q5:7 with Q4:46 and Q2:93, but see also Q2:285.

[38] See Clementine Homilies 11:28.

the Latin parallels to the Syriac text (indicated above) assure us that the Didascalia does not respond to the Qur'ān. The Didascalia seeks to reduce purity requirements ad absurdum by arguing that such ritual observance would lead to "unceasing vexation;" whereas the Qur'ān asserts that God does not require hardship and concedes that purity cannot always be attained, but then insists that purity should always be striven for.[39] The proximity between the practices of the Didascalia's Judaeo-Christian group and the Clementine Homilies and with the Qur'ān allows us to reconstruct the ritual catalogue of Judaeo-Christians that remained stable from the time of the fourth or fifth through the seventh centuries (and beyond), corroborated by the conceptual and lexical continuities between the three texts.

The following picture now emerges. The Didascalia seeks to establish that a form of Judaeo-Christianity exists in between the self-declared orthodoxies of rabbinic Judaism, on the one side, and, on the other, its own form of Syriac Christianity. The Jewish-leaning form of Christianity endorsed by the Didascalia's authorial voice takes law seriously as a prerequisite to salvation and, as we will see in Chapter Three, constructs Jesus more as a law-giver than as the sacrificial victim of typical Christian discourse. The Qur'ān shares much of its legal culture with this group,

---

[39] See page 90, note 16 for a reference to the Latin text. Pregill points to the affinity between the requirement for purity when touching the Qur'ān, expressed in Q56:77–79, and the Qur'ānic conception of the Aaronite priesthood; see idem, *The Living Calf of Sinai*, chapter seven. Note that the Talmud suggests a rather practical reason behind the prohibition to touch the Torah in a state of ritual impurity: the matter led to some dispute, and one "Amora in the West" suggested that the prohibition prevents the sages from visiting their wives "like roosters" (Bavli *Berakhot* 20b).

but this overlap may be coincidental to the Qurʾān's much more immediate proximity to the Judaeo-Christian law practiced within the Didascalia's community, allegedly by the Judaeo-Christian group. This group, or at least the individuals classified as a group by the Didascalia's Christian authors, shares most of its laws, and specifically most of its ritual laws, with the Qurʾān: the Judaeo-Christian ritual lawcode.

I do not claim that the affinity between the laws of the Qurʾān and the laws of the Didascalia's Judaeo-Christian group would offer a comprehensive background of the legal culture of either text and, to the contrary, will offer one more example illustrative of the complexity of the Qurʾān's laws. Just as we saw in the case of impure meats, the Qurʾān develops aspects of an established Judaeo-Christian legal culture that it largely accepts. Indeed, the Qurʾān specifies a ritual of purification more clearly than the Didascalia by indicating that hands, feet, and part of the face need to be washed, and by allowing for exemptions in the case of travel, disease, or when no water is available. As was the case in the Qurʾān's catalogue of impure meats, continuing the tradition of Acts, the Didascalia, and the Clementine Homilies, the details of washing constitute the extension of another specific tradition, in the present instance likely a rabbinic one.

The early rabbis, for example, in line with Exodus 30:20–1, insist on the washing of hands and feet before entering the Sanctuary (see e.g. Mishna *Kelim* 1:9), whereas later rabbinic tradition emphasizes the washing of hands, feet, and face, just like the Qurʾān (see e.g. Bavli *Shabbat* 25b). Most importantly, as Joseph Witztum reminds me, the Babylonian Talmud upholds a reported Palestinian tradition that after relieving oneself, washing of hands is sufficient before reciting the Shema, and "if one has no water (*mym*) for washing his hands, he can rub (*mqnḥ ydyw*) his hands with earth or with a pebble or with sawdust (*b'pr wbṣrwr wbqsmyt*) (Bavli *Berakhot* 15a)." The Qur'ān may or may not share a specific tradition of practice with the Talmud insofar as both texts conceptualize washing as the cleaning of hands, feet, and face – a widespread practice indeed. Yet more concretely, the dispensation in both texts from washing one's hands before prayer with *water* after the use of the privy and allowing for washing with *sand* instead suggests a specific shared legal practice. Here, the Qur'ān accepts what seems to be a rabbinic practice, which it also develops by insisting on using "good", i.e. "pure" ground (*ṣaʿīdan ṭayyiban*) and by including the feet and the face in addition to the hands.[40] Hence, both in the cases of impure meat and of washing before prayer, the Qur'ān both continues and modifies established practice, be it Judaeo-Christian or rabbinic.

Circumcision and Shabbat

In the texts here discussed, circumcision is not as central of a topic as it used to be in the Greek context of the first or second century, e.g. in the Acts of the Apostles (which rejects circumcision for gentiles, but in turn depicts Paul as having Timothy circumcised "because of the Jews," see Acts 16:3). The Didascalia simply rejects it by pointing to its spiritual dimension, termed in the prophetic tradition the "circumcision of the heart" (DA XXIV, 232.16–21,

[40] On the meaning of ṭayyib, "good," as "pure," see pages 144–5.

see also DA XXVI, 243.18–244.8). The Didascalia's Judaeo-Christian group is portrayed as endorsing the practice (DA XXIV, 233.10, see also DA XXIII, 231.2). The Clementine Homilies remain silent on the topic.[41]

Since circumcision was common among most inhabitants of Arabia in the seventh-century C.E.,[42] it does not seem to be far-fetched to stipulate that the Qurʾān assumes the practice as well, even if it mentions, like the Didascalia, the practice's spiritual dimension, in this case, the "uncircumcision of the heart" (see Q2:88 and Q4:155).[43] Yet neither the Qurʾān nor the Clementine Homilies anywhere suggest that the practice would be required of gentile believers. No matter whether the practice was assumed or not in the milieu of both texts, the circumcision of the flesh, unlike that of the heart, may or may not have been a central issue. In order to avoid an argument from silence, however, I will exclude the practice from our deliberations. We still can summarize that regarding the consumption of impure

[41] Note that the "Letter of Peter to James," a document often attached to the Clementine Homilies, states that the document should only be given to those who are circumcised (4:1 = *Diamartyria* 1.1 in Rehm, *Die Pseudoklementinen*, 3).

[42] Cohen, *The Beginnings of Jewishness*, 39–49. See also Jacob M. Sasson, "Circumcision in the Ancient Near East," *Journal of Biblical Literature* 85 (1966): 473–6; and Zdzislaw Zmygrider-Konopka, "Les Romains et la circoncision de juifs," *Eos* 33 (1931): 334–50.

[43] The Qurʾān would have expected at least part of its audience to grasp the phrase "circumcision of the heart," when stating that the Israelites once said that "our hearts are uncircumcised (*qulūbunā ġulfun*)" (Q2:88). Here, the Qurʾān shares the Didascalia's own insistence on the "circumcision of the heart (*dlb'*)," which the Didascalia's Christian group, in contrast to its perceived Judaeo-Christian group, considers as sufficient (see DA XXVI, 232.14–21 and Reynolds' lucid explanation in idem, *The Qurʾān and Its Biblical Subtext* (London: Routledge, 2010), 147–55).

meats, among them pork, abstinence from sex during the menses, and washing after intercourse and before prayer, the Qurʾān seems to adhere to the longer list of ritual laws the Didascalia ascribes to its Judaeo-Christian group – yet only insofar as it can be corroborated by the Clementine Homilies' specification of gentile commandments.

This is also the case regarding Shabbat. While struggles about the Shabbat are likely as old as the institution itself and feature prominently in Christian anti-Jewish polemics, it still makes sense to establish the precise way the Didascalia, the Qurʾān, and the Clementine Homilies relate to its observance.[44] The Didascalia's Christian authors associate Shabbat with the passion and with mourning (DA XXI.215.1–218.1), elaborately rejecting Shabbat along with other commandments associated with the Judaeo-Christian group. The text's authors begin by designating it a Jewish practice (DA XIII, 150.10) and go on to call for an "assembly of rest (*dnyḥʾ*)" on Sunday (DA XV, 160.19); finally, they address their "Jewish" constituents as follows:

> Be quiet, beloved brethren, you who from among the people have believed (*dhymnw*), and [yet] wish to be bound with the bonds, and say that the Shabbat is prior to the first day of the week ... on this account, brethren, every day is of the Lord .... But this [Shabbat] has been given as a type for the times ... However, the Lord

[44] On Christian anti-Jewish polemics more generally, see e.g. Miriam S. Taylor, *Anti-Judaism and Early Christian Identity: A Critique of the Scholarly Consensus* (Brill: Leiden, 1995); Ora Limor and Guy Stroumsa, *Contra Iudaeos: Ancient and Medieval Polemics between Christians and Jews* (Tübingen: Mohr Siebeck, 1996); A. P. Hayman, "The Image of the Jew in Syriac Anti-Jewish Polemical Literature," in Jacob Neusner and E. S. Frerichs (eds.), "*To See Ourselves as Others See Us:*" *Christians, Jews, and "Others" in Late Antiquity* (Chico: Scholars Press, 1985), 423–41.

our Savior, when He came, fulfilled the similes and explained the parables, and He showed those things that are life-giving, and those that cannot help He abolished, and those that cannot give life He abrogated (*šr'*). (DA XXVI, 251.11–253.13)

Given that the Didascalia modifies the stereotypical Christian rejection of Shabbat with such insistence and with a complex argument (only a small part of which I excerpt here), the text may well address a dispute over practice of its own time. In line with the broader attitude towards biblical observances, the Didascalia's Judaeo-Christian group is portrayed as having held that Shabbat is indeed "prior," i.e. more meaningful, to the first day of the week, and that the requirement of rest on that day is still valid.[45]

Shabbat, however, is conspicuously absent from the Clementine Homilies. Its Jewish heroes are not explicitly portrayed as keeping it. The fact that the Jews would observe it, of course, seems very likely, given the general validity of the Torah for Jews. Moreover, Peter once refers to the Israelites as the "sons of the new moons and the Sabbaths" (Clementine Homilies, 19:22) in a difficult passage, which nevertheless clearly endorses the divine appointment of calendrical cycles. The only other reference to the term Shabbat occurs in the alleged eleven-day Shabbat cycle of the devious opponent Simon (Clementine

[45] As Wilson B. Bishai has noted, Shabbat observance is being required in addition to Sunday by the Ethiopic and Arabic versions, but not by the Syriac and Greek versions of the Apostolic Constitutions; see idem, "Sabbath Observance from Coptic Sources," *Andrews University Seminary Studies* 1 (1963): 25–31; see also Werner Vyhmeister, "The Sabbath in Asia" and "The Sabbath in Egypt and Ethiopia," in Kenneth A. Strand and Daniel A. Augsburger (eds.), *Sabbath in Scripture and History* (Washington, DC: Review and Herald Publishing Association, 1982), 151–168 and 169–189.

Homilies 2:35). Even without fully grasping the Homilies' calendrical heresiology, we can see that the doubly negative association of moral and calendrical deviancy in turn suggests the expected endorsement of Shabbat as a *Jewish* practice. The Homilies, however, do not impose Shabbat on the gentiles who seek salvation through Jesus rather than through Moses. Rather, its ritual law for gentiles only focuses on purity, not on calendrical observances.

While an argument from silence, as in the case of circumcision, should ultimately be bracketed, we can again entertain the possibility that the Qurʾān's view of Shabbat observance seems at least broadly similar to that of the Clementine Homilies. Like the Clementine Homilies, it chooses not to impose the Shabbat on its gentile audience, while seeing its observance as incumbent on the Jews, who are punished in various ways for *failing* to keep it (Q2:65, Q7:163).

We need not necessarily read the Qurʾān's point of view as an endorsement of a previous legal position. As with all other laws, the choice between extending Jewish observances to gentiles is limited to two options only – to keep, or not to keep them. Yet despite the vagaries, we can situate the Qurʾān's likely imposition of Shabbat on Jews but not on gentiles in the middle of a sliding scale, along with the Clementine Homilies, in between the Didascalia's Christian group, who abolish Shabbat entirely, and the Didascalia's "Jewish" believers, who seem simply to observe it. Moreover, the divergence itself may illustrate the Qurʾān's intriguing statement:

The Sabbath was only prescribed
For those who differed (*iḫtalafū*) about it
Your Lord will indeed judge between them

On the Day of the Resurrection
Concerning that about which they used to differ (*yaḫtalifūna*)
(Q16:124).

According to Andrew Rippin, the Qurʾān here possibly "reflects earlier Jewish-Christian debates over the proper day of worship."[46] I would extend Rippin's position to suggest the Qurʾān may well reflect the divergence over views on Shabbat in a Christian-Judaeo-Christian-Jewish debate, which can vaguely be sketched based on the views in the Didascalia and the Clementine Homilies. The Qurʾān's postponemet of a final judgment on the issue of Shabbat among its contemporaries, in turn, points to its view that Shabbat has not yet been abrogated for the Jews.[47]

Wine, Swine, and Demons in the Clementine Homilies and in the Qurʾān

In addition to its Judaeo-Christian group, the Didascalia is also concerned about a group it describes in more sinister terms, as "heretics" – as I mentioned before, this is a term it never applies to those whose observance goes further than its own. Accordingly, these antinomian "heretics," the Didascalia emphasizes already in the quote above, are portrayed as rejecting the law altogether, employing con-

---

[46] See also Andrew Rippin, "Sabbath," in McAuliffe (ed.), *Encyclopaedia of the Qurʾān*, ad loc.

[47] Other passages addressing Shabbat include Q2:65, Q4:47, Q4:154, Q7:163 and 166, and Q16:124. On the formulation that God will judge between Jews and Christians "on the Day of the Resurrection, concerning that about which they used to differ (*yaḫtalifūna*)," see also Q2:113 below, page 185–6.

cepts and words which may again furnish us with a helpful background for reading the Qurʾān. Just like the "circumcision party," in the Didascalia's paraphrase of Acts, it describes the heretics as a phenomenon from the time of the apostles. The charge of antinomianism in association with abstinence from wine again conforms to traditional Christian, and to a certain extent also to rabbinic, heresiology.[48] In a very brief passage in its final chapter, addressed to its constituents, the Didascalia describes the perceived sins of the heretics for a second time in more detail:

> Therefore keep away from all heretics who follow not the Law and the prophets; and the Almighty God (*'lh' 'ḥyd kl*), not only do they not obey him (*mštmʿyn*), but are His enemies; who keep away (*mtrḥqyn*) from meats, and forbid to marry (*lmzdwwgw*), and believe not in the resurrection (*wbqymt'*) of the body; but who moreover will not eat and drink, but are willing to rise (as) demons, empty spirits, who shall be condemned forever (*lʿlm*) and tormented in unquenchable fire (*bnwr' dl' dʿk'*). Flee and keep away from them, therefore, that you may not perish with them. (DA XXVI, 254.25–255.7)

These "heretics" within the Didascalia's community, in contrast to the Christian and the alleged Judaeo-Christian parties, do not observe any of the Didascalia's aforementioned catalogue of commandments summarized as the "the Law and the prophets." In addition, the Didascalia accuses this ascetic antinomian group of prohibiting the consumption of meat, depicting them as "keeping away" (*mtrḥqyn*) from meats. As already discussed above, the legal vocabulary is precise: the Didascalia carefully differentiates between the Judaeo-Christian group who simply "remain pure" (*mtdkyn*) from impure meats, but consume

[48] See Zellentin, *Rabbinic Parodies*, 79–94.

what the law permits, and the antinomian group who "keep away" (*mtrḥqyn*) from meat, avoiding it altogether. The formulation that they "will not eat and drink" – perhaps in the next world as Joseph Witztum suggested to me – parallels the previous citation that accuses them of abstaining from meat and wine (*ḥmr'*) in this world. The heretics are portrayed as prohibiting marriage, as denying the resurrection of the body, and instead as believing that they will stand up as spirits, here portrayed as demonic ones.

This passage concerning the heretical group shows that the Didascalia's initial lumping together of deviant behavior, be it too Jewish or too ascetic, was preparatory rhetoric for its engagement of each of its constructed groups individually. The depiction of the ascetic antinomian group in turn reinforces the distinct character of the alleged Judaeo-Christian group. In contrast to its engagement with the Judaeo-Christian group, however, the Didascalia's polemical tone, its lack of argument, and the brevity of information makes the question of how far a distinct ascetic antinomian group actually constituted part of the Didascalia's community even more difficult to answer.[49] For the present purposes, however, it suffices to point out that the Qurʾān's heresiology takes a point of departure very similar to that of the Didascalia's Christian authors – but then sides again with the Clementine Homilies regarding

[49] There is of course no shortage of other texts that portray the heretics in similar terms. In the Clementine Homilies, for example, Simon, the archenemy, is also accused of doubting the resurrection (see 2:22). On the Clementine Homilies' own heresiology, see the fundamental study by Annette Y. Reed, "Heresiology and the (Jewish-) Christian Novel: Narrativized Polemics in the Pseudo-Clementines," in Eduard Iricinschi and Holger Zellentin (eds.), *Heresy and Identity in Late Antiquity*, 273–98.

wine. For as we saw in the case of Shabbat, the Clementine Homilies, which discourage the consumption of wine, may help explain the background against which to appreciate the Qurʾān's *internally* shifting attitude towards wine. As in all aspects of ritual law, the Qurʾān's continuity with the Didascalia's ritual law only applies to instances in which the Clementine Homilies extend the ritual law to gentiles, as it does in the case of wine. This suggests that "Judaeo-Christianity," the fusion of Jewish and gentile ritual law, may well have been a concept employed by the Didascalia to distort and discredit the actual practices of some members of its community. At the same time, the discourse shared between the Qurʾān and the Didascalia can be meaningful regardless of the questions when and whether any anti-nomian "heresy" ever actually existed in the community of the Didascalia or of the Qurʾān.

Before turning to the issue of wine, I will offer a few brief examples of how the Qurʾān and the Didascalia share some of the widespread stereotypical depiction of heretics. The Didascalia names the heretics "the enemies of God" and promises their physical and eternal punishment after the Day of Judgment in the "Gehenna of fire" (*ghn' dnwr'*, DA V, 60.5). Likewise, in the Qurʾān, the fires of Gehenna (*nār ǧahannam*, 9:35) are "the requital of the enemies of God – the Fire (*an-nār*) – in it they will have an everlasting abode" (Q41:28, see also Q2:80, Q3:24).[50] Such language

[50] Note that in Q3:89, those who repent (*allaḏīna tābū*) may be forgiven, yet those who "turn faithless after their faith" will have a "painful punishment" (Q3:90–1). Likewise, the Didascalia states that "whosoever does evil after baptism, the same is already condemned to the Gehenna of fire" (DA V, 60.5 see already *Hebrews* 10:26). Note also the prominence of the theme of repentance in both the Qurʾān

is, of course, part of the Jewish and Christian Late Antique Near East generally, so the conceptual and lexical affinities in the depiction of the enemies could be seen as evidence only of a general continuity of discourse.

More specific than the negative echo of a shared heresiology, however, is how the Qurʾān and the Didascalia both promulgate positive commandments in a way that makes them seem to be a direct *response* to the position the Didascalia ascribes to its heretics. In both texts, the heretics become a negative foil against which central religious tenets are emphasized. In effect, the Didascalia explicitly describes itself as written by the twelve apostles convening in Jerusalem in response to the teaching it associates with the heretics:

[This work is written]… for the confirmation (*lšwrr'*) of you all. And we have confirmed (*wšrryn*) and constituted (*wsmnn*) that you all worship (*dtsgdwn*) God Almighty (*l'lh' 'ḥyd kl*) and Jesus the Messiah (*wlyšwʿ mšyḥ'*) and the Holy Spirit (*wlrwḥ' qdyš'*),

---

and the Didascalia, as well as the affinity of terms (*tawba* in the Arabic, *twb* in the Syriac, e.g. DA V, 62.3). Likewise, the Didascalia's language of moral perversion which is used to describe the heretics as not following the law and not obeying God, even if a commonplace in Late Antique discourse in general, may have a more specific echo in the Qurʾān's description of a group that is usually translated as "hypocrites" (*munāfiqūn*) who "bid what is wrong and forbid what is right" (Q9:67), and are also destined to the everlasting fire. Arthur Jefferey has sought to establish that the Qurʾānic term for hypocrites, *munāfiqūn*, is derived from the cognate term used for the translation of "heretics" in the Ethiopic "Didascalia," see idem, *The Foreign Vocabulary of the Qurʾān* (Leiden: Brill, 2007 [1938]), 272. While the possibility is intriguing, no Ethiopic text of the "Didascalia," i.e. the Apostolic Constitutions, can be dated prior to the 14th century – the Ethiopic "Didascalia" may as well have taken over an Arabic term from the Qurʾān. One the Ethiopic Didascalia see also above, page 49, note 59.

> that you be ministered to by the holy Scriptures (*bktbʾ qdyšʾ*) and believe (*wthymnwn*) in the resurrection (*bqymtʾ*) of the dead, and that you make use of all His creatures with thanksgiving, and (that you) take a wife. (DA XXIV, 232.4–9)

Both the commandments and the language used here in the Didascalia are again part of the broader Late Antique Biblical culture and would have been familiar to the Qurʾān's audience as well (albeit partially objectionable when it comes to worshipping Jesus; the Latin is sadly missing). The Qurʾān itself institutes that one must "worship" God (*li-llāhi yasǧudu*, Q13:15); for the Qurʾān, the Messiah Jesus (*masīḥa ʿīsa*, 4:157), the Holy Spirit (*rūḥ al-qudus*, Q2:87), and Scripture (*al-kitāb*, Q2:87) are as essential as the day of the resurrection (*yawm al-qiyāma*, Q2:174). The Didascalia equates lack of belief in the resurrection with "denying God" (*dkpryn bʾlhʾ*, DA XX, 197.9–10), just as the Qurʾān laments that the "deniers," or "unbelievers" (*allaḏīna kafarū*), say that "they will not be raised" (Q64:7, see also Q6:29; Q11:7, Q13:5 etc.). Unsurprisingly, the lexical and conceptual overlaps between the Didascalia's Syriac and the Qurʾān's Arabic are closest where commonplace theological concepts are conveyed. What is noteworthy, however, is not the heresiology, but how this heresiology gives rise to the formulation of two specific commandments in both texts.

The Qurʾān indeed sides with the Didascalia regarding the precepts here mentioned, and it affirms them as if to respond to a similarly constructed group of heretics. Akin to the Didascalia's statement "that you make use of all His creatures with thanksgiving," the Qurʾān states that "you are permitted [the consumption of] animals of grazing livestock, except what is announced to you" (Q5:1), denying any wholesale prohibition of meat such as is called for by the Didascalia's heretics. Likewise, just like the Didascalia encourages its constituent that you "take a wife," dismissing the widespread ideal of celibacy in ascetic strands of Christianity, also the Qur'ān admonishes its adherents to "marry off those who are single among you" (Q24:32). In other words, the Didascalia and the Qur'ān address an audience that expects clarification on these matters and, for this reason, both specifically allow marriage and meat. We can therefore assume that abstinence from both were options within the cultural memory of both texts. While both texts react to this memory with law affirmative of marriage, we should note that the Qur'ān's respective legislation goes far beyond that of the Didascalia, marking an important aspect of the independence of the former from the latter.[51]

Needless to say, similar prohibitions of asceticism can be found in rabbinic Judaism and Christianity. For example, the prohibition of abstaining from marriage and wine in response to the destruction of the Temple is found in

[51] The intricate legislation the Qur'ān puts forward in regards to matters of marriage, divorce, and inheritance, most often introduced as God's boundaries (*ḥudūd*)," are not at all addressed in the Didascalia, which remains remarkably coy regarding such matters, but see the denunciation of remarrying more than once in DA XIV, 155.3–12. The consistency and coherence of the Qur'ānic language, along with its departure from tradition, suggests either legal innovation in the Qur'ān (as suggested e.g. by Q2:187) or its engagement with a different legal corpus than the Didascalia at this point. The Qur'ān's prohibition of close relations (Q4:22–3), however, has close affinities not only with Leviticus (18:7–16), but also with the Didascalia (DA III, 50.6–51.19) in its recasting (in most manuscripts) of a collection of various legal traditions. On the Didascalia's Third Chapter, see above, page 43, note 51.

Tosefta *Sotah* 15:11 and repeated in Bavli *Bava Batra* 60b. Similarly, disdain of marriage is explicitly prohibited in Canon I of the Synod of Gangra – and of course marriage is endorsed in the Clementine Homilies.[52] To reiterate, few aspects shared by the Qurʾān and the Didascalia would not have other parallels elsewhere, yet the continuity between Biblical Late Antiquity and the Qurʾān can be established especially well through its affinity with the legal culture of the Didascalia, as corroborated by the Clementine Homilies.

In several cases now, we have seen that the Qurʾān shares the practices promulgated by the Didascalia's Judaeo-Christian group, to the extent that they can be corroborated by the Clementine Homilies. And again, the Clementine Homilies may allow us to reconstruct the Qurʾān's shifting attitude towards wine. The consumption of wine, to begin with, was of course endorsed in Jewish and Christian legal culture: the consumption of wine was part of Shabbat and the Eucharist.[53] Yet allowing wine is usually paired with a clear warning against the dangers of excess.[54] At one point, the Qurʾān clearly shares this bal-

---

[52] On the synod of Gangra see Migne, *Dionysii Exigui justi, facundi opera omnia. Patrologia Latina* 67, 55–6. The Clementine Homilies endorse marriage in their very narrative structure, and explicitly e.g. in 3:26 and 58.

[53] Needless to say, Shabbat and the Eucharist are central rites of Jewish and Christian communities respectively; the Didascalia emphasizes the Eucharist in chapters DA I, DA IX, DA XI and especially DA XXVI; see also Stewart-Sykes, *The Didascalia apostolorum*, 77–81 and below, page 122, note 62.

[54] On the finely calibrated attitude towards wine in rabbinic and Christian literature and the dangers of drinking too much or too little, see Zellentin, *Rabbinic Parodies*, 51–94.

anced view, even when gravitating toward a negative view, when stating that

They ask you concerning wine (*al-ḫamr*) and *al-maysir*,
Say, "There is great sin in both of them,
and some profits for the people,
but their sinfulness outweighs their profit." (Q2:219)

The Qurʾān consents to the general Late Antique openness concerning wine consumption (shared by the Didascalia), admitting the limited profits that people have by consuming wine. Ultimately, though, the Qurʾān restricts wine consumption. In a passage that became tantamount to the notion of Qurʾānic self-abrogation, the Qurʾān's language regarding wine is much stronger:

Oh you who have faith!
Indeed wine (*al-ḫamr*) and *al-maysir*
and idols and the arrows (*al-ʾazlām*)
Are abominations of Satan's doing,
So avoid them, so that you may be felicitous. (Q5:90)

The Qurʾān at one point prohibits wine in a nuanced manner and at another point more strictly, giving rise to a discourse about inner-Qurʾānic abrogation on which the current inquiry may ultimately bear.[55] Intriguingly, however, the Qurʾān prohibits wine by associating it with three other temptations depicted as satanic: idols and a practice called *maysir*, which in turn is associated with the arrows. These arrows, as we have seen, are used to divide the animal in Q5:3. The context there is the expansion of the prohibition to consume meat improperly slaughtered,

---

[55] On inner-Qurʾānic abrogation, see most recently Sinai, "The Qurʾān as Process," 409 and above, page 3, note 5, and page 18, note 27.

as well as idol meat. In Q5:90, however, the Qurʾān associates the same arrows not only with forbidden meats, but also more immediately with satanic practices. While the meaning of the verse is far from clear – knowledge of local Arabian practice is likely assumed – the traditional reading of the passage as pertaining to divination seems correct.[56]

[56] The Qurʾānic association of arrows and divining may go back to the association of the two in the Hebrew Bible, as Simi Chavel suggested to me in an oral communication. In Ezekiel, for example, the king of Babylon "stands at the parting of the way, at the fork in the two roads, to use divination (*lqsm qsm*); he shakes the arrows (*ḥṣym*), he consults the gods, he looks at the liver" (Ezekiel 21:21, cf. 2 Kings 13:14–19). More research needs to be done on this question, yet tentatively, the homophony of the Arabic and the Hebrew root *qsm*, which denote "dividing," and "divining" respectively, suggests that the arrows dividing (forbidden) meat in Q5:3 and 90 likely have mantic functions. For traditional readings of the prohibition of *maisir* in the Qurʾān, see cf. T. Fahd, "Foretelling in the Qurʾān," in McAuliffe (ed.), *Encyclopaedia of the Qurʾān*, ad loc. Regarding lots in Ancient Near Eastern and Islamic culture see Patricia Crone and Adam Silverstein, "The Ancient Near East and Islam: The Case of Lot-Casting," *Journal of Semitic Studies* 55 (2010): 423–50. Regarding the prohibition of divining in the Didascalia, see DA III, 33.15, DA III 35.17–36.4 and DA III.44.12–45.3; regarding the prohibition of magic more broadly, see also DA VII and DA XXIII; no arrows appear here. Gambling, often associated with divining, does not appear in the Didascalia, and it is unclear how categorically the Qurʾān would have prohibited it. Other ancient church orders that have incorporated parts of the Didascalia, such as the Apostolic Constitution, prohibit gambling; see also *The Ecclesiastical Canons of the Same Holy Apostles* 41 and 42; see Heinz Ohme, "Sources of the Greek Canon Law to the Quinisext Council (691/2)," 30. The rabbis, to the contrary, were much more lenient towards gambling; see Joshua Schwartz, "Jews at the Dice Table: Gambling in Ancient Jewish Society Revisited," in Raʿanan Boustan et. al. (eds.), *Envisioning Judaism*, Volume 1, 129–146; Joshua Schwartz, "Gambling in Ancient Jewish Society and in the Greco-Roman World," in Martin Goodman (ed.), *Jews in the Graeco-Roman World* (Oxford, 1998), 145–65.

The Qurʾān's association of wine, idols, and divination with satanic practices, in turn, can be read in light of the view of the Clementine Homilies on wine, demons, divination – and swine.

Indeed, as mentioned above, in order to understand the Clementine Homilies' attitude towards wine and swine, one needs to understand its demonology. While this central and complex matter requires further study, it is well summarized by the following passage.[57] God instructs the demons to keep away from humans, first addressing the former, then the latter:

> "unless any one of his own accord subject himself to you, worshipping you (sc. the demons), and sacrificing and pouring libations, and partaking of your table, or accomplishing anything else that they ought not, or shedding blood, or tasting dead flesh, or filling themselves with that which is torn of beasts, or that which is divided (τμητοῦ), or that which is strangled, or anything else that is unclean (ἀκαθάρτου)... but if any of those who worship me go astray, either committing adultery, or practicing magic, or living impurely (ἀκαθάρτως), or doing any other of the things which are not well-pleasing to me, then they will have to suffer something at your (sc. the demon's) hands or those of others, according to my order. But upon them, when they repent, I, judging of their repentance, whether it be worthy of pardon or not, shall give sentence" .... But you (sc. the believers) ought to know that the demons have no power over anyone, unless first he be their table-companion; since not even their chief can do anything contrary to the law imposed upon them by God.[58]

The entirety of the Clementine Homilies' purity laws, hence, rests on its demonology. The reason to stay pure is that God has allowed demons to attack humans only if they

[57] Joseph Verheyden, "The Demonization of the Opponent," is a good starting point; see above, page 10, note 16.

[58] Clementine Homilies 8:19–20.

become impure by engaging in illicit action: demons are attracted to blood, and blood is the significant component of illicit meats. The worst one can do is to consume meat sacrificed to idols or libations (3:26; 9:7; 10:23; 11:15), which in the Greco-Roman world usually consisted of wine.[59]

The theory behind the demonology is as follows: Demons (δαίμονας), being the products of the union between angelic and human beings, desire meat and (alcoholic) drink (βρωτὰ καὶ ποτὰ), like humans. They cannot fulfill their wants, since they are spiritual beings (πνεύματα), and therefore enter the bodies of humans in order to use them for their pleasure. The best way to avoid demons, hence, is to deprive them through "want of means" (ἔνδεια), "fasting" (νηστεία), and "ascetic practices" (κακουχία); abstinence from wine and impure meats will cause the demons to leave.[60] It is for this reason that the consumption of wine is explicitly discouraged.

The Homilies' association of wine and meat with demons, however, does not amount to the wholesale prohibition of meat and wine (such as ascribed by the Didascalia to the antinomian ascetics). As we saw above, meats are permitted with the exception of impure meats: "food offered to idols, dead carcasses, animals that have been suffocated or caught by wild beasts, and blood," as well as

---

[59] Wine is very much a ritual drink per se in Greek religion, and wine and sacrifice are more often than not conceived of as co-dependent from the times of Homer to that of the Greek Novels. See Walter Burkert, *Greek Religion* (Cambridge, MA: Harvard University Press, 1985 [1977]), 72–3.

[60] Clementine Homilies 9:10. "Drink," of course, designates alcoholic beverages in this context; drinking of non-alcoholic beverages, and "giving drink to the thirsty," is endorsed by the Clementine Homilies; see e.g. 3:36, 3:69, and 11:4.

"divided" meat.[61] Likewise, wine as such is not explicitly prohibited. Yet just as we saw in the case of swine, wine is associated repeatedly with the demonic desires and its consumption is *thereby* discouraged. Unsurprisingly, then, do the Clementine Homilies depict the Eucharist solely in terms of breaking bread.[62]

In the Clementine Homilies, the demons are attracted to human beings precisely when they drink too much wine; as soon as they drink any wine offered to idols or eat any divided meat, they and their chief receive authority over human beings. Moreover, the demons in the Homilies are in turn responsible for the practice of divination.[63] The Qurʾān, likewise, prohibits wine as an "abomination of Satan's doing," and names it along with "idols" and "arrows" (*ʾazlām*, Q5:90), which are used to divide meat according to Q5:3. It hence associates wine with apparent divining practices in Q5:90. It seems quite likely that here the Qurʾān not only continues a development of specific ritual laws in its Arabian context that we already saw in its expansion of impure meats, but also seems to continue the association of impurity with demons such as we find in the Didascalia. There is no need to posit any textual influence

[61] Clementine Homilies 7:8, see above, page 79–81.

[62] When depicting the Eucharist, the Clementine Homilies only speak of "breaking the bread for the Eucharist" (τὸν ἄρτον ἐπ' εὐχαριστίᾳ κλάσας, Clementine Homilies 14:1); in another formulation the text even speaks of "having broken the Eucharist" (καὶ εὐχαριστίαν κλάσας, Clementine Homilies 11:36). The association of "breaking" and the Eucharist (an echo perhaps of the Peshitta of Acts 2:42) suggests that bread alone completes the ritual. While the language of breaking the bread is that of Matthew 26:26, the absence of wine in the Homilies is noteworthy at least; see also below, page 133.

[63] See Clementine Homilies 9:14–18.

to explain this continuous development; rather, practice and oral discourse seem to have informed what the texts presuppose.

A summary overview will help to visualize the sliding scale of the increasing affinity between the ritual law applied to gentiles, which we find among the Didascalia's Christian authors, the Didascalia's Judaeo-Christians, the Clementine Homilies, and the Qurʾān. Blanks in the following table indicate lack of information, while parentheses indicate discouragement in place of prohibition:

Ritual Law for Gentiles	Didascalia (Christian Believers)	Didascalia (Judaeo-Christian group)	Clementine Homilies	Qurʾān
I. Marital purity				
No intercourse during menses	No	Yes	Yes	Yes
Purification after sexual intercourse	No	Yes	Yes	Yes
Washing before worship	No	Yes	Yes	Yes
II. Food purity				
No consumption of wine	No		(Yes)	Yes
No consumption of pork	No	Yes	(Yes)	Yes
No consumption of blood	Yes	Yes	Yes	Yes
No consumption of animals strangled	Yes	Yes	Yes	Yes

Ritual Law for Gentiles	Didascalia (Christian Believers)	Didascalia (Judaeo-Christian group)	Clementine Homilies	Qurʾān
No consumption of idol meat	Yes	Yes	Yes	Yes
No consumption of animals sacrificed on stone altars	Yes (hewn stone)		Yes	Yes
No consumption of carrion			Yes	Yes
No consumption of divided meat			Yes	Yes (by arrows)
No consumption of animals mangled			Yes	Yes
No consumption of animals fallen				Yes
No consumption of animals gored				Yes
No consumption of animals beaten to death				Yes

When it comes to ritual purity, then, the Qurʾān shares the Judaeo-Christian ritual lawcode of the Clementine Homilies, which in turn corroborates the ritual observances of the Didascalia, including most of the observances the Didascalia attributes to its Judaeo-Christian group. At the same time, the Qurʾān is not bound by precedent. It continues the development of the definition of impure meats, based on the Decree of the Apostles, which we saw had already begun in the Clementine Homilies. Likewise, the Qurʾān specifies the washing ritual in conversation with rabbinic practice. It would therefore be wrong to conceive of the Qurʾān's ritual code as a literary continuation of any one text. Rather, the continuity of practice suggests interaction of living communities.

In Chapter One, I discussed the prevailing commonalities between the general lawcodes of the Qurʾān and the Didascalia, more specifically the additions of both texts to the Ten Commandments. The present chapter illustrates the commonalities between the ritual lawcodes of the Didascalia's Judaeo-Christians, the Clementine Homilies, and the Qurʾān. In the next chapters, I will explore the many ways in which the Qurʾān and the Didascalia share legal narratives. I will then conclude that the majority of the Christians among the Qurʾān's audience do not live by the Judaeo-Christian lawcode. I will suggest that the Christian and perhaps the rabbinic communities with which the Qurʾān's audience was familiar contained individual Judaeo-Christians within theirs midst, but that the majority of Jews and Christians in the time of the Qurʾān's composition would stand closer to the Didascalia and the Talmud than to the Judaeo-Christian tradition.

Chapter Three

Narratives of Law in the Didascalia and in the Qurʾān

The Didascalia, we have seen in Chapters One and Two, allows us better to understand certain practices and beliefs endorsed in common by the Qurʾān. In the case of the "Decalogue" and the added "judgments" or "elaborations," we also saw how the continuity and change that marks the relationship between the Didascalia's and the Qurʾān's *nomos* is complemented by similarly continuous and changing elements of *narrative*. Along with the commonly shared story of Moses and the tablets, we have seen the specific laws about giving one's kinsman his due, not slaying one's children because of poverty, and trading correctly and fairly; we have also seen the continuity and abrogation inherent in the Qurʾān's rulings on alms, prayer, and fasting. While the Didascalia presents its legal narratives in a systematic way to an audience, some of whose members are implied to be unfamiliar with them, the opposite is the case in the Qurʾān. Rather, the Qurʾān expects its audience to know what it never spells out, a feature that makes the Qurʾān often so difficult to grasp. Nevertheless, based on the narratives we find spelled out in the Didascalia and alluded to in the Qurʾān, we can tentatively establish a coherent and similar theoretical legal framework within which both texts operate. We now can turn to the Qurʾān's broader theory of law, for the appreciation of which the Didascalia once more constitutes an important background.

Jesus and the Law in the Didascalia and in the Qurʾān

The central narrative of law in the Qurʾān is the affirmation of the "Torah and the Gospel" (*tawrāta wa-l-ʾinǧīla*, Q3:3). The Qurʾān's narrative of a broad "Decalogue," the story of *Mūsā* and the Torah, should be addressed in conjunction with the story of *ʿĪsā* and the Gospel. The role of Jesus in the Qurʾān has received much scholarly attention, the work of Pines being once more pertinent for the present purpose.[1] Yet the role of Jesus can be more fully understood by taking the Didascalia's "Jewish" leaning view of Jesus as a lawgiver as the point of departure. Namely, the Didascalia presents Jesus' role in the history of law as follows:

[1] Stories such as Maryam under the palm tree, the talking baby Jesus, and the boy Jesus' creation of clay birds that fly, in the surahs *Āl ʿImrān*, *Nisāʾ*, *Māʾidah*, and *Maryam*, are told in a way that assumes and corrects the audience's familiarity with these narratives. See e.g. Q3:33–64; Q4:156 and Q5:17–19; as well as Samir Khalil Samir, "The Theological Christian Influence on the Qur'an: A Reflection," in Reynolds (ed.), *The Qurʾān in its Historical Context*, 141–162; Suleiman A. Mourad, "Mary in the Qur'an: A Reexamination of Her Presentation," in Reynolds (ed.), ibid., 163–174; and the responses to the two articles by Michael Marx, "Glimpses of a Mariology in the Qur'an: From Hagiography to Theology via Religious-Political Debate," in Neuwirth et al. (eds.), *The Qurʾān in Context*, 533–63, and by Reynolds, *The Qurʾān and Its Biblical Subtext*, 130–46. The Qurʾān assumes familiarity with Jesus traditions while emphasizing difference from what at least part of its audience has heard: it narrates Jesus' miracles mostly in order to point out persistently that they all occurred with God's specific permission. Jesus is put in his place perhaps the most strongly in Q5:110. Here, God is portrayed as addressing Jesus directly and as recounting four of Jesus' miracles; after each of them the Qurʾān has God insist that they occurred "with my leave" (*bi-ʾiḏnī*). The Qurʾān here leaves no doubt about Jesus' subservient status in relation to God. See also Angelika Neuwirth, "The House of Abraham and the House of Amram" in eadem et al. (eds.), *The Qurʾān in Context*, 499–532.

Indeed, [Jesus] said thus: "I am not come to abrogate (*d'šr'*) the Law (*nmws'*) nor the prophets, but to fulfill (*d'ml'*) them. The Law (*nmws'*) therefore is not abrogated (*mštr'*), but the second legislation (*tnyn nmws'*) is temporary (*dzbn'*), and is abrogated (*wmštr'*)... Indeed, it is in the second legislation that sacrifices (*dbḥ'*) are written. (DA XXVI, 242.21–243.1 and 247.21 22)[2]

Based on a rephrasing of Matthew 5:17, the Didascalia advocates the abrogation of sacrifice and of many other practices along with the continuity of the Torah.[3] In a broad

---

[2] The phrase, "and abrogated," is missing in the Latin, which simply states: "lex ergo est indestructibilis, secundatio autem legis temporalis" (Connolly, *Didascalia Apostolorum*, 219). The Syriac version's apparent emendation of the original fits well with its revisions that turn away from purity laws indicated above. Note that the Didascalia's term for "law" is the common Syriac term *nmws'*, a loanword from Greek *nomos*. Intriguingly, the Didascalia uses the term *'wryt'*, "Torah," only once, namely in its defense of the "Torah and the Prophets" against the antinomian ascetic "heretics" in DA XXIII, 230.9. By contrast, when seeking to limit purity observance, the Didascalia speaks of "the Law and the Prophets" (*nmws' wnby'*), e.g. DA XXVI, 243.9.

[3] The Didascalia quotes Matthew's well known exhortation not to abrogate, but to fulfill, the Torah as long as heaven and earth do not pass away (5:17–18), a statement that in the original context may well mean what it says: that all the Laws of the Torah are obligatory for Matthew's community, and that Jesus takes issue only with Pharisaic additions to them; see Zellentin, "Jesus and the Tradition of the Elders: Originalism and Traditionalism in Early Judean Legal Theory," Menahem Kister, "Law, Morality, and Rhetoric in Some Sayings of Jesus," in James L. Kugel (ed.), *Studies in Ancient Midrash* (Cambridge, MA: Harvard University Press, 2001), 150–4; Anthony J. Saldarini, *Matthew's Christian-Jewish Community* (Chicago: The University of Chicago Press, 1994), e.g. 5, 74, 143, and Marcus, "The *Testaments of the Twelve Patriarchs* and the *Didascalia Apostolorum*," 604 (note 28) and 608. For a well-argued dissenting view see Roland Deines, *Die Gerechtigkeit der Tora im Reich des Messias: Mt 5,13–20 als Schlüsseltext der matthäischen Theologie* (WUNT 177; Tübingen: Mohr Siebeck, 2005). Greek and Syriac patristic tradition in general

sense, the Didascalia's emphasis on the enduring general validity of "the Law" amidst its partial abrogation, i.e. the differentiation between an enduring and temporal aspect of the Mosaic Law, is shared with strands of early patristic (and, to a degree, even rabbinic) literature.[4] Likewise, the Didascalia seems to reflect broadly the Christian view of Jesus as abrogating the Torah, or at least parts thereof, which was well-known throughout Antiquity – even to the Babylonian rabbis.[5] In the Didascalia, however, the emphasis on legal continuity is almost as strong as the emphasis on the partial abrogation; this is the key to appreciating the "Jewish" tendency of the Didascalia's legal narrative. Most importantly, only the Didascalia introduces a specific concept of a "primary" and a "secondary" law. On the one

---

have understood Matthew in their own supercessionist context as meaning that *all* of the Torah is abrogated as a means of salvation; the resulting tension between the Matthean passage and its Christian readers was noticed and gleefully exploited even by the Babylonian rabbis; see Zellentin, *Rabbinic Parodies*, 160–62.

[4] For the continuity of law, see for example, Tertullian, *Adversus Judaeos* VI (Geoffrey Dunn, *Tertullian* (London/New York: Routledge, 2004), 78); Justin Martyr, *Dialogue with Trypho* XI, XII, XLVI–VII, and CXVII (A. Lukyn Williams, *Justin Martyr: The Dialogue with Trypho* (New York: Macmillan, 1930), 22–25, 90–5, and 240–3, see also below, page 143, note 19). The church fathers generally emphasize the "newness" of the new covenant more than the Didascalia does, which introduces "newness" only with respect to the new fasting rules (DA XXI, 208.14–5, see page 63-4 above) or in the context of the confirmation of the enduring law. See also Willem Cornelis van Unnik, "The Significance of Moses' Law for the Churches of Christ according to the Syriac Didascalia," in idem, *Sparsa Collecta. Part 3: Patristica–Gnostica–Liturgica*, (Leiden: Brill, 1983), 7–39. For rabbinic views of abrogation of the Torah (or parts of it), see e.g. Bavli *Berakhot* 63a, *Menachot* 99b, and *Avodah Zarah* 36a.

[5] See Zellentin, *Rabbinic Parodies*, 160–62.

hand, the enduringly valid "primary" law corresponds to the commandments spelled out in Chapter One; on the other hand, the ritual part of the law that the Didascalia portrays as abrogated, including sacrifice and the additional ritual code of the Judaeo Christian group, corresponds to the "secondary" law.

In addition to rabbinic literature, there are two Late Antique texts whose emphasis on the continuity of the law given to the Israelites is as strong as that of the Didascalia; these are the Clementine Homilies and the Qur'ān. First, in the Clementine Homilies, we encounter a view of Jesus closely related to, though markedly different from that of the Didascalia:

> And also that [Jesus] said, "I am not come to destroy the law," and yet that he appeared to be destroying it, is the part of one intimating that the things which he destroyed did not belong to the law. And [Jesus'] saying, "The heaven and the earth shall pass away, but one jot or one tittle shall not pass from the law," intimated that the things which pass away before the heaven and the earth do not belong to the law in reality.[6]

While the abrogation in the Didascalia pertained to the entirety of the Torah's ritual law, including sacrifice, in the Clementine Homilies, the abrogated part of the Torah pertains almost exclusively to sacrifice. The simple argument here is that since sacrifice was factually abrogated by the destruction of the Temple, it cannot have been part of God's enduring law. Other than that, Moses' Law is still incumbent upon Jews (see Clementine Homilies 8:5–7) and a concise part of its ritual observances are incumbent

---

[6] Clementine Homilies 3:51. See also 3:52, ibid., 76. The Clementine *Letter of Peter to James* 2:3–5 (see Rehm, *Die Pseudoklementinen*), 2, also understands Matthew's saying in 5:17 in a law-affirming sense.

upon gentiles, as we have seen. Such a view could easily have been held by the Didascalia's Judaeo-Christian group as well, yet this is a question that has to be bracketed for lack of evidence. The saying's rendering in the Clementine Homilies, regardless, shows that the *very partial* abrogation of the Torah could be advocated by a person who fully endorses, in principle, the centrality and enduring validity of the laws God gave to the Israelites as well as those given to the gentiles, as the Clementine Homilies emphatically do.

The second text that emphasizes the continuity of the laws given to the Israelites is the Qurʾān. To be sure, the Qurʾān does not repeat the Didascalia's concepts of "primary" and "secondary" Torah; rather, it has a more direct relationship with biblical law than either the Didascalia or the Clementine Homilies. For example, as I mentioned earlier, the Qurʾān goes straight back to the biblical *leges talionis*, along with their Matthean updating which emphasizes compassion, when excluding the killing of a murderer from the prohibition of taking a life.[7] Likewise, when it comes to sacrifice, the Qurʾān combines the Hebrew Bible's concomitant endorsement and criticism of sacrifice.

Indeed, the Qurʾān shares the criticism of sacrifice that is so prominent in the Bible's prophetical books and that is emphasized by Christian and Judaeo-Christian tradition. Ritual slaughter does not effectuate salvation: rather, the Qurʾān states, "it is not the [slaughtered camel's] flesh or its blood that reaches God, rather it is your Godwariness (*at-taqwā*) that reaches Him (Q22:37, see also Q5:27). Accordingly, in the Jewish and Christian, and especially

[7] See page 70, note 16.

Judaeo-Christian, traditions (as we have seen in the Didascalia and in the Clementine Homilies), sacrifice is essentially seen as abrogated and replaced respectively with prayer or the Eucharist.[8]

The Qurʾān, however, also emphasizes that the slaughter of camels in the context of the Hajj is a "symbol (*šaʿāʾir*) of God" (Q22:36). The word for "symbol" is a difficult one, the Arabic root *šʿr* ranges in its denotation from "poets" (Q26:224) to "perceiving" (Q2:154). Yet the Qurʾān's symbolic ritual discourse regardless remains firmly tethered to a practical reality since it effectively maintains sacrifice within its ritual code.[9] The Qurʾān's notion of

---

[8] The rabbis' daily prayer schedule based on the three daily temple sacrifices, as well as the Syriac term for Eucharist, *qwrbn'*, based on the Biblical Hebrew term for "sacrifice," may suffice as illustrations of this complex issue of the replacements of sacrifice; see e.g. the aforementioned passage specifying washing in Bavli *Berakhot* (15a), where Hiyya bar Abba states, in the name of Rabbi Yohanan, that "the one who eases himself and washes his hands and puts on Tephilin and reads the Shema and prays – scripture accounts it for him as if he built an altar and sacrificed a sacrifice, as it is written: I will wash my hands in cleanliness (*bnqywn*, literally 'innocence') and I will circle Your altar, oh God! (Psalms 26:6, see also Bavli *Yoma* 30a);" and Sokoloff, *A Syriac Dictionary* 1343. The Didascalia uses *'wkrysṭi'* for Eucharist (DA IX 115.1) and *qwrbn'* for sacrifice (DA VIII 95.17); for the Clementine Homilies' Eucharist, see 11:36 and 14:1. Accordingly, the Eucharist in the Homilies is depicted as the breaking of bread only, not the consumption of wine; see below, page 122, note 62.

[9] "Symbols" are equally emphasized in Q2:158 and Q5:2, in addition to Q22:32 and 36. Neuwirth agrees that sacrifice is not entirely dis-empowered, yet also emphasizes that the spiritual state defines the valid outcome of the sacrifice; see eadem, *Der Koran: Handkommentar mit Übersetzung. Band 1: Poetische Prophetie. Frühmekkanische Suren*, 554–7. The fact that sacrifice must be performed in the proper ethical context, of course, is a trope known from the biblical prophetic discourse as well and became a Late Antique common place; see Ron

"abrogation" of the Torah actually seems to emphasize the immediate continuity with the Torah more than the Christian tradition in general would. In some ways the Qurʾān emphasizes this continuity even more than the Didascalia (with the possible exception of the latter's Judaeo-Christian group) and the Clementine Homilies. Still, an implicit partition of law into enduring commandments and temporary ones abrogated by Jesus, similar to the one presented in those texts, may indeed form the point of departure of the Qurʾān's following statement:

> [God] will teach [Jesus] the Book and the wisdom, and [he will be] an apostle to the Sons of Israel ... and [I, Jesus, shall come] to confirm (*wa-muṣaddiqan*) that which is before me of the Torah (*li-mā bayna yadayya mina-t-tawrāti*), and to make lawful for you (*wa-li-ʾuḥilla lakum*) some (*baʿḍa*) of the things that were forbidden (*ḥurrima ʿalaykum*) to you. (Q3:48–50)

Christian traditions generally did not equate the coming of Jesus with complete lawlessness. Yet the specific positive emphasis that Jesus made lawful *some* (*baʿḍa*) of the things that were hitherto forbidden, implying that many others remained forbidden, is again a nuance that points to the affinity between the views expressed in Didascalia, the Clementine Homilies, and the Qurʾān. These three texts indeed can be placed on a sliding scale depicting how far Jesus' abrogations of Israelite law reached: according to the Didascalia's Christian authors, all of the ritual and sacrificial code is abrogated for Jews and gentiles alike; in the

---

Hendel, "Away from Ritual: The Prophetic Critique," in Saul M. Olyan (ed.), *Social Theory and The Study Of Israelite Religion: Essays in Retrospect and Prospect* (Atlanta: Society of Biblical Literature, 2012), 59–80; and Guy Stroumsa, *The End of Sacrifice: Religious Transformations in Late Antiquity* (Chicago: Chicago University Press, 2009).

Clementine Homilies, the ritual code is fully maintained for Jews and partially maintained for gentiles, while sacrifice of animals is fully abrogated; in the Qurʾān, "some things" that used to be forbidden are abrogated for Jews, while a partial ritual code, including elements of animal sacrifice, is also maintained for gentiles. From a legal point of view, the Didascalia's alleged Judaeo-Christian group seems most closely related to the Qurʾān's view of Jewish law, as we shall see; for the Qurʾān's own ritual law applicable to its gentile community, the Clementine Homilies are the most closely related.

Jesus' role for divine law in all three texts informs a view of Jesus that lacks any expiatory understanding of the crucifixion.[10] As Joseph Witztum points out to me, such a concept could easily be read into the Didascalia, yet its absence remains noteworthy. Even if we should be careful when arguing from silence, a comparison with the Qurʾānic view of Jesus here guides us to appreciate the Didascalia's depiction of Jesus not as sacrificial lamb, but as the one to confirm and to abrogate the Torah. What exactly may be the result, legally speaking, of the Qurʾān's partial

[10] The Didascalia persistently speaks about baptism, prayer, and repentance as the means of forgiveness, e.g. in chapters DA XX–XXI. Note that Jesus' suffering is central to the interceding power of prayer and the cross itself is discussed in chapter DA XIX, yet no staurology proper appears in the Didascalia. The Qurʾān diminishes Jesus' interceding power even more by denouncing those who say "these are our intercessors with God" as committing *shirk* ("associationism," Q10:18, see below, page 190–1, note 8). More pointedly, some of those who have been given the book will regret it or repent on judgment day and state that "our Lord's apostles had certainly brought the truth. If only we had some intercessors to intercede for us" (Q7:53), emphasizing their vain hope in Jesus' alleged power – if one reads the Qurʾān with an assumed knowledge of Jesus' role as expressed in the Didascalia.

abrogation of the laws given to the Israelites? A close reading of several Qurʾānic passages in light of – though not determined by – the Didascalia's views of Jesus' abrogation of Israelite law may clarify Jesus' role in the Qurʾān, allowing us further to appreciate Muhammad's cognate role as well. For the proximity of law and narrative in the Didascalia's and in the Qurʾān's concepts of Jesus goes beyond his role as partially abrogating the Israelite law.

In the Qurʾān, Jesus is initially sent to the Israelites (see Q3:49, Q61:6 and 14), but then he functions as a "sign for the nations" (*ʾāyatan li-l-ʿālamīna*, Q21:91). This is quite in line with the general Christian narrative: the Gospel is salvation "to the Jew first, and also to the Greek," Paul writes (Romans 1:16). Yet the Qurʾān, in my view, displays the more *ongoing* immediateness of Jesus' relationship with "the Jews" that we also find in the Didascalia. When the Didascalia discusses the abrogation of parts of the Torah, it specifies that Jesus "did not say [that the second legislation is abrogated] to the gentiles, but He said it to us, His disciples from among the Jews (*ywdyʾ*), and brought us out from burdens and the heavy load" (DA XXVI, 248.8). Its foundation narrative, its very raison d'être, is that it is the task of the apostles to bring the message to the gentiles. In the way the Qurʾān depicts Jesus as the "apostle to the Sons of Israel" first, and to the gentiles only indirectly, it constructs a view similar to that put forth by Christian literature more broadly, especially as expressed in the Didascalia. Both texts then present themselves as showing Jesus' relevance for their non-Jewish *and* their Jewish audiences in similar ways – which form the basis of the Qurʾān's independent development of Jesus' tasks in the role it plays itself in the history of divine law.

The Didascalia simultaneously sees Jesus and itself as affirming tradition. It states that "indeed, in the Gospel (*b'wnglywn*) [Jesus] renewed and fulfilled and confirmed (*wšrr*) the Law ... Truly it was to this end, indeed, that [Jesus] came, that the Law be confirmed (*dnšrr*), and that the second legislation be abrogated" (DA XXVI, 246.21–4).[11] Presenting its own writing as a confirmation of previous teachings, the Didascalia states that "those things which were said before (*mnqdym*), hear also now" (DA IX, 103.3–4). Affirmation here occurs amidst alteration of current practice; its implied apostolic authors portray the correction of heretical teachings by stating that "we had established (*'tqnn*) and confirmed (*wšrrnn*) and set down (*wsmnn*) [the Didascalia] (DA XXV 240.6)."[12]

[11] The Syriac verb for "confirmation," *šrr*, ranges in its meaning from "establishing," to "fulfilling," "guarding," and "strengthening;" see Sokoloff, *A Syriac Dictionary*, 1612.

[12] The object of the sentence is missing; the Latin Didascalia explicates what is obvious in the Syriac: the apostles confirmed *haec statuentes* (Connolly, *Didascalia Apostolorum*, 215). The *afel* form of the verb *tqn*, used by the Didascalia here to denote the "establishing" of tradition, can also denote "fixing" or "repairing;" see Sokoloff, *A Syriac Dictionary*, 1662. The theme of the correction of corrupted tradition (highlighted by Gobillot in the Clementine Homilies and in the Qur'ān, and by Vaccarella in the case of the Clementine Homilies and the Didascalia; see above, page 79, note 4) is further developed in the Qur'ān by extending the discourse to include self-corrections outside of the scope of corruption: "For any word that We abrogate, or remove from memories, We bring another which is better than it, or similar to it. Do you not know that God has power over all things?" (Q2:106, see also Q16:101, Q45:29). We may now be well-advised to read these verses as illuminating the Qur'ān's engagement with narrative or legal variance both with previous tradition as well as within its own time. See John Burton, *The Sources of Islamic Law: Islamic Theories of Abrogation* (Edinburgh: Edinburgh University Press, 1990), 1–28. See also page 3, note 5.

The parallelism between Jesus and Muhammad in the Qurʾān has most recently been emphasized by Joseph Witztum, whose fundamental contribution to the question will be discussed in chapter four and in the conclusion. I suggest that the Qurʾān also repeats and emphasizes a view on "confirmation" and "affirmation" of previous law which further develops concepts akin to the Didascalia's, with words that are lexically distinct. As we have seen in the passage above, Jesus also came "to confirm that which is before me of the Torah" (*wa-muṣaddiqan li-mā bayna yadayya mina-t'-tawrāti*, Q3:50). This language of Jesus' "confirmation" of the Torah in *Sūrat ʾĀl ʿImrān* not only affirms the Didascalia's wording, it moreover mirrors precisely the language the Qurʾān uses to describe its own role: in *Sūrat al-Māʾidah*, for example, the Qurʾān likewise portrays itself as "confirming what was before it from the book" (*muṣaddiqan li-mā bayna yadayhi mina'l-kitābi*, Q5:48). In this passage, the Qurʾān uses the same terms to portray its own role that it uses to designate Jesus' and the Gospel's confirmation of law given to the Israelites previously. However, Jesus only confirms the Torah, whereas the Qurʾān confirms the entirety of the heavenly book. The Qurʾān's "confirmation," its simultaneous affirmation and alteration of previous law through Jesus and itself, indeed constitutes the apex of its central legal narrative: the affirmation and alteration of previous legal culture. It seems that central elements of the specific legal culture the Qurʾān seeks to preserve may equally have been recorded by the Didascalia.[13]

---

[13] On the Qurʾān's "confirming that which is with you" or "what was before it" (literally: "what is in his hands"), see also Q2:41, 89, 91,

In the Didascalia, accordingly, we learned that "even before [Jesus'] coming, [God] foretold [Jesus'] coming through the prophets" and that Jesus is the one who "brought us out from burdens and the heavy load" (DA XXVI, 248.8–9). The Qur'ān's own apostle is likewise presented as the one "whose mention they find written with them in the Torah and the Gospel," and as the one who "relieves them of their burdens and shackles that were upon them" (Q7:157), an affinity stressed by Witztum.[14] Both texts, hence, see Jesus as having partially abrogated the food laws of the Israelites, with similar results according to the Didascalia's Judaeo-Christian group. The Qur'ān takes the additional step of presenting Muhammad in a role comparable to that of Jesus.

97, 101, Q3:3, 81; Q4:47; Q6:92; Q10:37; Q12:111; Q35:31; Q37:37 ("confirmation of the apostles," *ṣaddaqa'-l-mursalīna*); Q46:12 and 30. The Qur'ān is also called an "elaboration of the book" (*tafṣīla l-kitābi*, Q10:37), indicating further elucidation of a culture shared with a broader audience; see above, page 57, note 3. Notably, the same language of "confirmation" is used to describe John (Q3:39), Jesus (Q3:50, Q5:46, Q61:6) and Mary (Q66:12) "confirming" what was before. On the Arabic root *ṣdq* and its Aramaic and Syriac cognates, see above, pages 59–60, note 5.

[14] Witztum, *The Syriac Milieu of the Quran*, 275–6. For a recent useful attempt to assess aspects of the Qur'ānic legal paradigms, see Joseph E. Lowry, "When Less is More: Law and Commandment in *Sūrat al-An'ām*," *Journal of Qur'ānic Studies* 9 (2007), 22–42. Lowry's emphasis on the presence of legal simplification in the Qur'ān suggests a basic outlook shared with the Didascalia's concept of the simplicity of its legal requirements as spelled out in chapters I and XXVI, and its rejection of "Jewish" observances. See also Brannon M. Wheeler, "Israel and the Torah of Muḥammad," in John C. Reeves (ed.), *Bible and Qur'ān: Essays in Scriptural Intertextuality* (Atlanta: Society of Biblical Literature, 2003), 61–85, and the fundamental study by Ze'ev Maghen, *After Hardship Cometh Ease: The Jews as Backdrop for Muslim Moderation* (Berlin: DeGruyter, 2006).

The commonalities as well as the discrepancies between the broad narratives of the confirmation of the law amidst partial abrogation correspond in both texts to the overlap and differences between their actual legal codes. This will become even clearer when considering the shared legal narrative about the origins of the part of the law that Jesus abrogates as divine punishment for the Israelite's sins, as we will now do. In Chapter Four, a comparison of these shared legal narratives will then allow us to re-evaluate the Qurʾān's statements about food laws shared between its own community, the Jews, and the *naṣārā*, the Christians – and the relationship of that last group to the Didascalia's Christian and Judaeo-Christian group.

Sin and the Law in the Didascalia and in the Qurʾān

Several scholars, most recently Witztum, note that the Qurʾān, "following the Christian tradition, ... describes [the Jewish law] as a load and as fetters which will be removed by Muhammad ... and is understood to have been imposed as a consequence of sin ..."[15] "Sin," of course, is a broad category, but the history of the "Golden Calf" proves to be a linchpin for understanding both the Qurʾān's and the Didascalia's views of Judaism and of the Torah, as Michael Pregill also argues in a publication in

[15] Witztum, *The Syriac Milieu of the Quran*, 275–6; Witztum gives a short summary of research. Previous scholars who have remarked upon this connection include: Andrae, *Der Ursprung des Islams und das Christentum*, 198; Horovitz, *Koranische Untersuchungen* (Berlin: de Gruyter, 1926), 38; Ahrens, "Christliches im Qoran," 158; Pines, "Notes on Islam and on Arabic Christianity and Judaeo-Christianity," 140–41; and Wheeler, "Israel and the Torah of Muḥammad," 82.

preparation.[16] The Golden Calf is central to the Didascalia, which often reiterates that the "Secondary Law" was a punishment for the Golden Calf incident and for other sins and that it is only this part of the law that Jesus came to abrogate. The Didascalia explicates this idea in its meandering sequel to the passage already cited in which it details Jesus' partial abrogation of the law. The gist of the argument can be abbreviated as follows:

> The Law thus consists of the Ten Words and the judgments (*wdyn'*), to which Jesus bore witness (*d'shd*) ...., these which God spoke before that the people made the calf and worshipped idols .... So then the Law is easy and light ... But when the people denied (*kpr*) God .... who set up the Law for them in the mount (*bṭwr'*) – Him they denied (*kprw*) and said: "We have no God to go before us"; and they made them a molten calf (*'gl'*) and worshipped it (*sgdw*) and sacrificed (*wdbḥw*) to a graven image. Therefore the Lord became angry, and in the heat of His anger – yet with the mercy (*rḥm'*) of His goodness – He bound them with the second legislation, and laid heavy burdens upon them and a hard yoke upon their neck ... Therefore He laid upon them continual burnt offerings as a necessity and commanded them to depart (*'prq*) from meats (*m'klt'*) through distinction (*byd pwršn'*) of meats .... For because of the multitude of their sins there were laid upon them customs (*'yd'*) not describable. Yet in not one of them did they abide, but they again provoked the Lord to anger. On this account He yet added to them by the second legislation a blindness worthy of their works ... This people's heart (*lbh*) is hardened (*'t'by*)... (DA XXVI, 243.1–246.9).[17]

Here, the Didascalia specifies that the temporary part of the law was given to the Israelites as a punishment for the

[16] See Pregill, *The Living Calf of Sinai*, Chapter One.

[17] The Didascalia introduces the topic of the Golden Calf in chapter II and explains its point of view at great length and with elaborate exegesis in Chapter XXVI.

Golden Calf (as related in Exodus 32), for idolatry, and for "a multitude of sins." Rather than annihilating the Israelites, as one would expect, God *in his mercy* merely punished them relatively mildly – with additional laws. Yet immediately the Israelites neglected these as well, so God blinded them (in a metaphorical sense). The Didascalia's reading hearkens back to Ezekiel, who states that because the Israelites violated God's ordinances, namely the Shabbat, and because they committed idolatry, God gave them "statutes that were not good and ordinances by which they could not live" (Ezekiel 20:25). According to the Didascalia, these "laws which are not good" (*dyn' dl' špyryn*) are the "second legislation" (DA XXVI, 250.17–20) as opposed to the first good and enduring law given on Sinai.

For the Didascalia, indeed, the entirety of the Torah revealed before the Golden Calf ("the Ten Words and the judgments") is enduring, with only the ritual laws revealed thereafter being abrogated by Jesus. The Didascalia spells out in great detail what "the judgments" are, namely the enduring parts of the law in addition to the Ten Commandments – the entirety of the laws discussed in detail in Chapter One that it considers as enduringly valid.[18]

[18] Joel Marcus sees the secondary legislation as encompassing "practically everything in the Torah except the Decalogue," (idem, "The *Testaments of the Twelve Patriarchs* and the *Didascalia Apostolorum*," 606), while the "judgments" to be followed are laws "associated" with the Decalogue (ibid., 616). This may not be entirely untrue, though Marcus vastly underestimates the Didascalia's commitment to the biblical laws and established tradition when it comes to fair measures, the prohibition of cheating, the prohibition of usury and other laws discussed in Chapter One. Charlotte Elisheva Fonrobert seeks to explain the "secondary legislation" in terms of rabbinic *halakha* (see eadem, "The Didascalia Apostolorum: A Mishnah for

The Didascalia's teaching of laws as punishment, which is fiercely rejected by the rabbis, is not unheard of in the Christian tradition.[19] In this sense, we encounter a ge-

---

the Disciples of Jesus," 483–511). Elsewhere, however, she emphasizes the Christianized nature of purity laws to which the Didascalia's Judaeo-Christian group adheres; see above, page 90, note 15.

[19] While some church fathers have related "the Law" to the Golden Calf in various ways, the Didascalia's concept of the primary law departs quite markedly from Christian supercessionism by emphasizing the law's enduring validity as a means to gain salvation. On comparable patristic views, see e.g. Tertullian, *Adversus Judaeos*, esp. I–II (Dunn, *Tertullian*, 68–72) and Justin Martyr, *Dialogue with Trypho*, XXI–II, and XXVII (Williams, *Justin Martyr*, 42–7 and 53–5); see also above, page 130, note 4. Likewise, as Witztum noted, Aphrahat, in *Demonstrations* XV.3, explains the dietary laws as a result of the Israelites' worship of Egyptian idols (see Jean Parisot, "Aphraatis Sapientis Persae Demonstrationes," in René Graffin et al (eds.), *Patrologia Syriaca* (Paris: Firmin-Didot, 1894), I:736, cited by Witztum, *The Syriac Milieu of the Qur'ān*, 276–7). For a contextualization of the Didascalia in Patristic discourse, see also van Unnik, "The Significance of Moses' Law for the Churches of Christ," 7–39; see also Vaccarella, *Shaping Christian Identity*, 81–118; and Marcel Simon, *Verus Israel: A Study of the Relations Between Christians and Jews in the Roman Empire, AD 135–425* (trans. H. McKeating) (Oxford: Oxford University Press, 1986), 88–91. Marmorstein discusses the rabbinic responses to the idea that the commandments were a punishment for the Golden Calf and summarizes that "[i]t cannot be denied that Christian fanatic polemics lurk behind these [rabbinic apologetic] sayings" (idem, *Judaism and Christianity in the Middle of the Third Century*, 246–7 [24–5]; see also 241–47 [19–25]). The most remarkable rabbinic doctrine that may need to be understood against such polemics may be Resh Lakish's teaching that the *entirety* of the written and the oral Torah were already given at Sinai, including "Scripture, Mishnah, Halakhot, Talmud, Toseftot, Aggadot, and even what a distinguished disciple would in the future say in the presence of his teacher (Wayiqra Rabbah 22.1, Yerushalmi Hagiga 1.8 (76d, 32–7), and Bavli *Berakhot* 5a, mentioned previously when hinting at the possibility that the Qur'ān shares this view, see above, page 57, note 3). The claim for a Sinaitic origin of the Oral Torah as a whole is

ometrical difficulty in the comparison of narratives that is parallel to the one we saw in the comparison of the Didascalia's and the Qurʾān's actual commandments. Everything these two texts share, they also share with other Jewish and Christian sources, such that the kinship of their legal narratives has to be contrasted constantly with general Late Antique discourse. The role the Golden Calf occupies in the Qurʾān, moreover, is not as easily understood as the legal narratives discussed to this point. Nevertheless, a reading of the Qurʾān's presentation of the Golden Calf narrative in light of the story's role in the Didascalia allows us better to appreciate the Qurʾān's narrative outset. For a story similar to the one recorded in the Didascalia may be what the Qurʾān assumes its audience to know, as a close reading illustrates.

For the Qurʾān, just as for the Didascalia, some of its laws were given to the Israelites as a punishment for sin, as can be seen most fully in the following passage:

Due to the wrongdoing (*ẓulmin*) of the Jews,
We prohibited them (*ḥarramnā*) good things (*ṭayyibātin*)
That were permitted (*ʾuḥillat lahum*) to them earlier.
And for their barring many from the way of God,
And for their taking usury
– though they had been forbidden from it –
And for eating up the wealth of the people wrongfully.
(Q4:160–1)

---

not attested earlier than in the the post-Mishnaic tractate *Pirqe Avoth* (1:1, not necessarily much earlier than Wayiqra Rabbah). While the continuity of some aspects of rabbinic tradition and the written Torah is an early rabbinic concept (see e.g. Sifra *Tsav* 11:6, see also *Behuqotai* 2:3 and 13:8), the development and emphasis of this rabbinic view may now be understood as a response to the Christian attempt to differentiate between a primary and a secondary law, as recorded in the Didascalia, as I argue in a study in preparation.

Just as the Didascalia presents the secondary law as a punishment for "the multitude of their sins," the Qurʾān indicates that the *ẓulm*, "the wrongdoing" of the Jews, and their additional alleged financial transgressions – likely along with other crimes listed elsewhere, such as murder, expulsion (Q2:85), and the killing of prophets (Q2:61) – lead to the prohibition of *ṭayyibāt*, "good things." "Good things" is a term the Qurʾān strictly employs for permitted nourishment,[20] echoing the Didascalia's description that the "Judaeo-Christian" group "might eat those things which the Law pronounces pure" (*dmdk'*, DA XXIII, 231.1). For the Judaeo-Christians, pork remains barred as in the Qurʾān. The list of punishments for the Israelites in the Didascalia uses food laws as *pars pro toto* for the broader ritual laws given as punishment ("customs unspeakable"), which is the case in the Qurʾān as well; yet food laws also remain a distinct category of ritual law.

In the Didascalia, likewise, we saw that the list of Israelite transgressions that led to the punishment uses a specific "wrongdoing" as *pars pro toto* for all crimes: the Golden Calf. Pines alleges that the Qurʾān does not "set forth the view that the sin for which the Children of Israel were punished ... was the worship of the Golden Calf," yet a closer reading of the corresponding Qurʾānic passages on

[20] In Q2:57, Q7:160, and Q20:81, the Israelites are enjoined to eat the "good things," as is the Qurʾān's audience, e.g. in Q2:172, Q7:32, Q5:87, and Q23:51. See also Q2:267, Q7:19, Q8:26. The association of the lexeme *ṭayyib* with purity can be seen in the use of "good" soil for ritual ablution in Q4:43 and Q5:6 (as discussed above on pages 104–5).

their own and in light of the Didascalia suggests that Pines erred on this point.[21]

The Qurʾān, in Q4:153–5, introduces the Golden Calf, thereby opening the long passage that discusses the Israelites' *ẓulm* (their "wrongdoing") and leads to the climax that the law *was* given as punishment for these sins in Q4:160:

The People of the Book ask *you*
To bring down for them a Book from the sky.
Certainly they asked Moses
For (something) greater than that,
For they said, "Show us God visibly,"
Whereat a thunderbolt[22] seized them for their wrongdoing (*ẓulmihim*).
Yet [the Israelites] took up the calf (*al-ʿiǧl*)
After all the manifest proof that had come to them
Yet We excused that
And we gave Moses a manifest authority.
And We raised the Mount above them
For their covenant (*bi-mīṯāqihim*)
And We said to them, "Enter the gate prostrating"[23]
And We said to them, "Do not violate the Sabbath,"
And We took from them a solemn covenant.

---

[21] Pines, "Notes on Islam and on Arabic Christianity and Judaeo-Christianity," 141; cf. Witztum, *The Syriac Milieu of the Quran*, 276.

[22] The "thunder" is a punishment associated with the people of Thamud in the Qurʾān; e.g. Q51:44. Note that thunder also appears in the context of the giving of the law in Exodus 20:18, yet here not as punishment. The Bible uses thunder as punishment mostly in the context of Egypt; see Exodus 19 and Psalms 78:48.

[23] On prostrating before the gate, see Q2:58 and Gobillot, "Der Begriff Buch im Koran," 425–30. Gobillot's reading of the surah in light of Numbers 31:1–20 does leave some questions open, but is more persuasive than the one suggested by Uri Rubin, who places the passage in the context of Judges 12:5–6 (see idem, *Between Bible and Qur'an: The Children of Israel and the Islamic Self-Image* (Princeton: The Darwin Press, 1999), 83–99).

Then because of their breaking their covenant
Their defiance of God's signs,
Their killing of the prophets unjustly
And for saying, "Our hearts are uncircumcised
(*qulūbunā ġulfun*)."
Rather Allah has set a seal (*ṭabaʿa*) on them for their denial
(*bi-kufrihim*),
So they do not have faith except a few. (Q4:155)[24]

A few conceptual and lexical correspondences already evoke a broad sense of proximity between this Qur'ānic passage and the Didascalia. The Qur'ān here insists that the Israelites broke their covenant and committed various other crimes, explicating their uncircumcision of their hearts (*qulūb*), whereupon God "put a seal" (*ṭabaʿa*) on the Israelites – likely on their heart – for their denial (*kufr*).[25] We saw that the Didascalia, also in the context of discussing the Golden Calf, states that the Israelites did not keep the commandments and denied (*kpr*) God (DA XXVI 244.10) and that God therefore added to them "a blindness worthy of their works ... This people's heart (*lbh*) is hardened" (*'t'by*, DA XXVI, 245.17–246.9).[26] The

[24] The verse is closely paralleled by Q2:51–56 and 83–93.

[25] Q4:155, see also Q2:88. The formulation evokes the Qur'ān's formula against unbelievers that God will "cast veils on their hearts, lest they should understand, and a deafness into their ears" (Q17:46; see also Q18:57 and Q45:23). On the root *kpr*, see also below, page 162, note 6.

[26] The Didascalia cites the formulation of a "hardened heart and shut ears" twice, first as it appears in Isaiah 6:10, and then as it appears in Matthew 13:14–15. The Qur'ānic language here is shared not only by the Didascalia, but also, as Reynolds has pointed out, by parts of the Syriac Christian anti-Jewish polemics (see idem, "On the Qur'ānic Accusation of Scriptural Falsification (taḥrīf) and Christian anti-Jewish Polemic," *Journal of the American Oriental Society* 130 (2010): 198).

conceptual and lexical proximity – unbelief is punished with the impairment of the senses – is of course biblical, speaking for a shared general discourse. While the differences in wording exclude literary influence, a closer reading of the Qurʾān will point to a more specific correspondence of the narratives themselves.[27]

[27] Both the Qurʾān and the Didascalia connect the sins ensuing from the Golden Calf with Jesus' crucifixion. At the same time, however, both texts clear the Jews from the charge of having participated in the crucifixion, yet in starkly different ways. The Didascalia, on the one hand, states that because of the Golden Calf and the ensuing punishment, i.e. the Secondary Legislation, "when Christ should come [the Jews] might not be able to assist him," since they were prohibited from helping a man hanging from a tree (DA XXVI, 245.17–246.2, see Deuteronomy 21:22–23 and Galatians 3:13). The Didascalia, in its occasional openness toward Jews, assumes that the Jewish population naturally would have helped Jesus, had God not prevented them! On the other hand, however, the Didascalia makes it very clear that the "chiefs of the people" asked Jesus "from Pilate to be put to death (*lqṭl'*). And they hung (*wzqpwh*) him … and those hours wherein our Lord was crucified (*'ṣṭlb*) were reckoned a day" (DA XXI, 207.1–4, but see also page 204, note 1 on the Jews' lack of confession to have killed the Messiah). The Qurʾān, by contrast, asserts, just after relating the Golden Calf incident, that the Jews "did not kill (*wa-mā qatalūhu*), nor did they crucify (*wa-mā ṣalabūhu*)" Jesus, yet charges them with boasting to have done so (Q4:157). Hence, in neither text did "the Jews" actually put Jesus to death. In both texts, he seems to have died, or at least left the world. In the Qurʾān, however, the death is likely not violent, in line with Griffith's argument that, according to the Qurʾān's consistent prophetology, God always helps his prophets. The Qurʾān may rather react to the rabbinic claim that the Jews, not the Romans, killed Jesus, which it strongly censors. See Peter Schäfer, *Jesus in the Talmud* (Princeton, NJ: Princeton University Press, 2007), 63–74; Sidney Griffith, *The Bible in Arabic*, 37–8; idem, "*Al-Naṣārā* in the Qurʾān: a Hermeneutical Reflection," in Reynolds (ed.), *New Perspectives on the Qurʾān*, 318; and Todd Lawson, *The Crucifixion and the Qur'an: A Study in the History of Muslim Thought* (Oxford: Oneworld, 2009), 26–42.

In apparent distinction from the Didascalia, however, the Golden Calf incident in the Qurʾān seems to be twofold: a request to see God visibly, *and* the creation of the Golden Calf. Yet these two offenses, which appear intertwined, are actually identical, as a closer reading reveals.[28] The Qurʾān *first* designates the Israelite's request to see God visibly with the (quite common) term "their wrongdoing" (*ẓulmihim*), which is then immediately *followed* by the Golden Calf incident, suggesting two separate offenses.[29] In the parallel account in *Sūrat al-Baqarah*, however, the same lexemes are employed to describe the two events in inverse order: in Q2:51, the Qurʾān first presents the Golden Calf, accusing the Israelites to be *ẓālimūn* or "wrongdoers," who have *ẓalamtum ʾanfusakum*, "wronged yourselves," by taking the calf for worship (Q2:54). The passage *then* specifies the Israelites' demand to "see God visibly" (Q2:55), whereupon a "thunderbolt" seized them. The inversion of order, together with a coherent terminology, suggests that the Qurʾān sees the two acts as two *aspects* of the same sin – the sin of the calf, in other words, *was* an attempt to make God visible.

The Qurʾān indeed describes the Golden Calf of the Israelites with the words: "this is your god, and the god of Moses" (Q20:88), explaining that the Golden Calf is by no means a deity different from God, but merely a (no less

---

[28] On the Golden Calf in the Qurʾān, see also Q2:51, 54, 92, 93; Q4:153; Q7:148–57; and Q20:83–98.

[29] The term *ẓulm* designates very many forms of "wrongdoing" in the Qurʾān (see e.g. Adam's sin in Q2:35 and the denial of Muhammad in Q17:47), yet we should note that it very often designates specifically Israelite wrongdoings (see e.g. Q2:145, Q6:21). In effect, the extent of sinfulness attributed to the Israelites in the Qurʾān is paralleled only in the Hebrew Bible.

sinful) representation of the Israelite God. This, of course, is also the way the Golden Calf is presented in the Hebrew Bible, as Pregill shows, and once more we can see how the Qurʾān engages the Hebrew Bible directly, "bypassing," as it were, even the Didascalia and the broader exegetical tradition of Late Antiquity.[30] The sin of the Golden Calf, hence, is not twofold after all in the Qurʾān. Rather, the Qurʾān's view is distinct from the Didascalia's only in as far as the former in this instance reads the Hebrew Bible more closely than the latter.

In recognition of the Qurʾān's dialogue with a large variety of traditions – including its occasionally immediate

---

[30] The Bible's depiction of the calf seems to oscillate between the view that the one calf represents a plurality, or at least a duality of the God of Israel, and the view that the calf is actually meant to represent God – which still is a transgression. The first view is foregrounded when Aaron states about the calf that "these are your gods (*'lhyk*), Israel" (Exodus 32:4), clearly a plural implying polytheism – yet, this passage employs the *plurale tantum*, which usually designates the one God of Israel in a grammatical construct also found elsewhere to designate the real "God of Israel" (Micah 4:12). In the sequel, however, Aaron seems to understand the calf not as a separate divinity, but as a visible symbol for the *one* God: after Aaron produces the calf, he orders it to be honored in a festival "to the Lord" (*ḥg lyhwh*, Exodus 32:5). Here, the Tetragrammaton is used, the second central name of God in the Hebrew Bible, in a construction that is singular, implying God's oneness. By contrast, in the Didascalia, as well as more broadly in the rabbinic and patristic traditions, the Golden Calf is often represented in terms of idolatry proper, as a deity distinct from God, a tradition the Qurʾān bypasses. The fact that the Qurʾān can sometimes engage the Biblical "text" directly, in whatever form and not "filtered" through any known previous exegesis, has already been argued by Neuwirth, for example in eadem, "Qur'anic Readings of the Psalms," in eadem et al. (eds.), *The Qurʾān in Context*, 733–78, and is reiterated forcefully by Pregill in *The Living Calf of Sinai*, Chapter One.

access to the Hebrew Bible – we must resist reading too much of the Didascalia into the Qurʾān – unless, of course, it invites us to do so. Let us consider the Qurʾān's own testimony on the centrality of the Golden Calf as the one prototypical sin – followed by many others – that leads to the giving of *additional* laws. For the previous passage can now be read as already explicating this idea in the following terms:

Yet We excused that [sin of the Golden Calf]
And we gave Moses a manifest authority (*sulṭānan mubīnan*).
And We raised the Mount above them
For their covenant (*mīṯāq*, Q4:153–4).

Just as in the Didascalia, where God's anger was mixed with *rḥmʾ* ("mercy," DA XXVI 245.2) and where the expected death sentence for the entire people was commuted into an extra set of laws, God in the Qurʾān likewise *forgave* the *ẓulm*, the "wrongdoing," and instead gave Moses authority (*sulṭān*). The very necessity for this authority, accepted under the threatening mountain raised above the head, implies that this passage assumes *another* covenant in addition to the original one – this covenant *is* God's expression of his forgiveness. Both texts clearly differentiate between the two laws given in close succession, the first one before the Golden Calf, the second one thereafter, both designated with the same term *mīṯāq* in the Qurʾān (Q2:83 and Q4:162, see Chapter One). Both the Didascalia and the Qurʾān positively depict God's first interaction with Moses "on the Mount" (*bṭwrʾ*, DA XXVI 244.22), or "from the side of the mount" (*min ğānibi ṭ-ṭūri*, Q19:52, Q20:80, Q28:29 and 46). Both texts then negatively depict a second set of laws, associated with the "second legislation" in the Didascalia and with the "raising" of Mount Sinai over the reluctant Israelites in the Qurʾān (Q2:63 and 93, Q4:154).

Affinity with the Didascalia again does not preclude the Qurʾān's innovative dialogue with another tradition. Indeed, the Qurʾān here skillfully expands on the narrative shared with the Didascalia by employing the rabbis' own weapons in order to depict Jewish sinfulness: the raised Mount is a Talmudic image originally employed to dramatize the Israelites' reluctance to accept the Torah. The Qurʾān employs this image to highlight its notion, in contrast with widespread rabbinic views, that parts of the law are by no means a boon.[31] A few verses later, the Qurʾān then reiterates what still rings in the audience's ear, stating that "due to the wrongdoing (*ẓulmin*) of the Jews, We prohibited them (*ḥarramnā lahum*) good things (*ṭayyibātin*)," in addition to instituting the Shabbat and other observances. Additional laws, then, were given as a punishment for the Golden Calf and other sins in both texts. The "mercy" and the "forgiveness" of which both texts speak is the giving of the second covenant in place of annihilation, and even this mild punishment later abrogated by Jesus and Muhammad.

Despite the different emphases on a partial abrogation of the law, the Qurʾān therefore takes the narrative shared with the Didascalia as its point of departure for another aspect of its legal culture: the cognate narrative that part of the Torah was given as a punishment for the Israelite's

[31] On the image of the mountain hovering over the Israelites see Bavli *Avodah Zarah* 2b and Bavli *Shabbat* 88a. On the rabbis' positive views of the law see above, page 57, note 3, and page 143, note 19.

wrongdoing and that the prototypical wrongdoing was the Golden Calf. Though the use of the word *ẓulm* in Q4:153 in itself may not yet justify reading the same word *ẓulm* in Q4:160 as designating the Golden Calf alone, the Golden Calf inversely symbolizes the worst of all wrongdoings of the Israelites in the Qur'ān.[32] This, of course, was already the Didascalia's view, which depicts the making of the calf as the epitome of the "multitude" of the Israelites' sins.

Again, despite the many narrative and lexical commonalities, the way in which the Qur'ān puts forward its depiction of the events on and under Mount Sinai shows its structural integrity as much as its interpretive independence from the narrative recorded in the Didascalia. The Qur'ān elaborates upon the version of the narrative preserved in the Didascalia and occasionally hearkens back to the Hebrew Bible and the Talmud more directly, equally reflecting a milieu of orality. The key to understanding the Qur'ān's simultaneous affirmation and alteration of previous oral discourse, akin to the oral discourse similarly preserved in the Didascalia, is not to join the two texts too closely. At no point should we forget that the affinities between them are nothing but a scholarly tool concocted to grasp the faint written echo of a vivid oral culture that remains incrementally approachable, but ultimately beyond our full grasp. The Qur'ān's direct engagement of the Hebrew Bible and the rabbinic tradition, moreover, shows the multi-voiced reality of this discourse, which may easily be forgotten in light of my necessarily simplistic focus on two or three witnesses alone (as I will illustrate in the

[32] The Qur'ān hence later repeats that "you took up the calf in his presence, and you were wrongdoers" (*ẓālimūna*, Q2:92).

Epilogue). We will now return to the realm of law proper, assessing in Chapter Four the interplay between the food laws for Jews and for gentiles according to the Qur'ān and to the Didascalia's alleged Judaeo-Christian group. I will then conclude by considering the Judaeo-Christian continuities between the audiences of both texts.

Chapter Four

Jesus, Muhammad, and Judaeo-Christian Food Laws

Its particular take on salvation history, discussed in Chapter Three, prepares the ground for the role the Didascalia attributes to Jesus: Christ came to abrogate the second legislation, which in turn was given as the punishment for the Israelites' sins, especially that of the Golden Calf:

> Indeed the second legislation was imposed for the making of the calf and for idolatry .... Indeed, in the Gospel (*b'wnglywn*) He renewed and fulfilled and confirmed (*wšrr*) the Law ... Truly it was to this end, indeed, that [Jesus] came, that the Law be confirmed (*dnšrr*), and that the second legislation be abrogated ... and to demonstrate the resurrection of the dead (*wqymt' dmyt'*). Indeed, even before [Jesus'] coming, [God] foretold [Jesus'] coming through the prophets ... (DA XXVI, 246.18–247.1)

The key role of Jesus in the Didascalia is not the forgiveness of sins, but to demonstrate the resurrection of the dead and the abrogation of the secondary laws. The concepts presented in this passage of the Didascalia may again help us understand the Qurʾān more precisely – in its own terms.

The Qurʾān implicitly connects Jesus' abrogation of the second legislation with the laws given after the Golden Calf, as reading its inner-textual references in conversation with the legal narrative of the Didascalia allows us to understand. Namely, both *Sūrat al-Nisāʾ* and *ʾĀl ʿImrān* employ the same language when explaining how God nullifies His earlier decree through Jesus: after the Golden Calf, God says about the Israelites: "We prohibited them (*ḥarramnā lahum*) good things (*ṭayyibātin*) that were permitted (*ʾuḥillat lahum*) to them earlier" (Q4:160); then Jesus comes "to make lawful for you (*li-ʾuḥilla lakum*) some of the things that were forbidden (*ḥurrima ʿalaykum*) to you" (Q3:50). When reading both surahs together, the Qurʾān's likely assumption – expressed through conceptual and lexical consistency – becomes evident that the *good things* now *permitted* to the *Israelites* are those previously *prohibited* to them after the Golden Calf. "Good things" (*ṭayyibātin*), we saw above, clearly means pure food.[1] Some of these foods, even though they are essentially pure, were prohibited to the Israelites after the Golden Calf; Jesus permits them again without changing the definition of purity. The simple reading of both passages together, hence, suggests that the Qurʾān's Jesus abrogated mainly Jewish *food* laws – the rest of the Torah may remain valid for Jews, just as the Judaeo-Christian ritual lawcode remains valid for gentiles.

This contextual reading of two Qurʾānic surahs, up to this point, is rather conjectural. If we were to rely only on the two adduced Qurʾānic passages, we should exercise great caution. Given the wide use of the lexemes *ḥrm* and *ḥll* in the Qurʾān, we cannot yet be certain that the essentially pure things Jesus allows were those prohibited after the Golden Calf, such as the ones specified in Q6:146: animals with undivided hoofs, fat of oxen and sheep not connected to tissue or bones. The evidence, however, accumulates, if we read nomos alongside narrative, and even more so if we

[1] See pages 104–5 and 145.

take the next step and read the Qurʾān in dialogue with the tradition preserved in the Didascalia: both the Didascalia and the Qurʾān tell very similar legal stories and, in both texts, according to the Didascalia's Judaeo-Christian group, the result of Jesus' repeal of those laws which were given after the Golden Calf is that the *same* foods are prohibited: pork, carrion of various forms, and idol meat. The Clementine Homilies corroborate this Judaeo-Christian lawcode, as we saw in Chapter Three. It is the previously established conceptual, stylistic, lexical, and most of all, legal similarities between the three texts that now allows us to explore more fully the Qurʾān's teaching on the role of Jesus as abrogating those Israelite *food* laws that were given after the Golden Calf. The affinity allows us, moreover, to see how the food laws of the Didascalia's Judaeo-Christians, its "believing Jews," are equally applied to gentiles in the Clementine Homilies – as well as in the Qurʾān.

Jesus and Muhammad

As mentioned above, Witztum points to the fact that the Qurʾān mirrors its own language describing Jesus' abrogation of the Torah when confirming abrogation in its own times. In the sequel of the passage quoted above, the Qurʾān broadens the concept (also known from the Didascalia) of the messenger predicted in Scripture who will ease the burden of the law to include not only Jesus, the prophet to the people of the book, but also Muhammad, the "unlettered prophet," or perhaps better the "prophet to the gentile nations" (*an-nabiyya'l-ʾummiyya*, Q7:157).[2]

[2] The term *ʾummī* is often rendered as "unlettered," following the

Here, we learn that Muhammad, like Jesus, "makes lawful to them (*wa-yuḥillu lahumu*, i.e. to the Qurʾān's audience) the good things (*ṭayyibāti*) and forbids them (*yuḥarrimu ʿalayhimu*) all the impure things (*ḫabāʾiṯ*)" (Q7:157).[3] Likewise, just before the passage in *Sūrat al-Māʾidah* that institutes many of the very purity laws discussed above, we read:

---

definition of Q2:78: "and among them are *ʾummiyyūna* who do not know the Book (*lā yaʿlamūna l-kitāba*)." While "unlettered" is not an incorrect rendering, it is clear that the term designates being lettered in the heavenly Book, not in all books, as Q3:20 makes clear when differentiating between "those who received the Book" (*allaḏīna ʾūtu l-kitāba*) and the *ʾummiyyīna*, and especially in Q3:75, where the "people of the book" (*ʾahli l-kitāb*) are accused of cheating on the *ʾummiyyīna*. The charge that lettered people cheat on analphabets would presuppose the involvement of written documents here, which is not mentioned – more is at stake, namely cheating regarding the Heavenly Book. Finally, in Q62:2, Muhammad is depicted as being sent to the *ʾummiyyīna* as "an apostle from among them." If we read the term "unlettered" in a broad sense, not a single lettered person would have been among the prophet's tribe! Hence, while Muhammad is depicted as being "unlettered" in as far as he is not a writer or reciter of common books in Q29:47–8, the term *ʾummī* must hence denote those "unlettered ones" who were not yet given any part of the Heavenly Book, that is, the gentile nations. This is in line with the term's common Hebrew cognate "people of the world" (*'mwt hʿwlm*) and with the Qurʾān's self-designation as gentile (see above, page 10, note 17). See the excellent summary by Sebastian Günther, "Illiteracy," and idem, "Ummī," in McAuliffe (ed.), *Encyclopaedia of the Qurʾān*, ad loc, based on idem, "Muḥammad, the Illiterate Prophet: An Islamic Creed in the Qurʾān and Qurʾānic Exegesis," *Journal of Qur'anic Studies* 4 (2002): 1–26; see also above, page 139, note 13, and below, page 164.

[3] The term *ḫabāʾiṯa* denotes moral and ritual impurity, such as the acts of the people of Lot designated by the same term in Q21:74. The prequel of the verse Q7:157, however, focuses on morality, suggesting that we read the cited passage not as merely repeating itself but as addressing ritual purity as well.

Today I have perfected your religion for you
And I have completed my blessings upon you
And I have approved *al-islām* as your religion
They ask you as to what is lawful to them (*ʾuḥilla lahum*).
Say, "lawful for you (*ʾuḥilla lakumu*) are the good things (*aṭ-ṭayy-ibātu*)."
As for what you have taught hunting dogs [to catch]
Teaching them out of what God has taught you,
Eat of what they catch for you
And mention God's name over it,
And be wary of God.
Indeed, God is swift at reckoning.
Today, lawful for you (*ʾuḥilla lakumu*) are the good things (*aṭ-ṭayyibātu*),
the food of those who were given the Book is lawful to you (*ḥillun lakum*),
and your food is lawful to them (*ḥillun lahum*) (Q5:3–5)

The Qurʾān here suggests that the *food* law of its own audience are continuous with those God has decreed upon "those who were given the book." The sameness of "Muslim" and "Israelite" food laws is certainly no trivial matter. This remarkable statement can now be understood in the context of the Qurʾān's suggested teaching that the sameness of Israelite and gentile food laws prevails *after* Jesus' abrogation of the additional food laws previously given to the Israelites as a result of the Golden Calf and other early sins. Again, a closer reading is necessary in order to appreciate the Qurʾān's legal, conceptual, and lexical consistency, throughout its surahs and, to a degree, with the Judaeo-Christian tradition of its times.

First, the cited surah again uses the same terminology ("forbidden" / "lawful for you" / "good things") that it uses to describe the initial establishment of the food laws for the Israelites after the Golden Calf and their abrogation through Jesus in *Sūrat al-Nisāʾ* (Q4:160) and *ʾĀl ʿImrān* (Q3:50).[4] Likewise, the passage from *Sūrat al-Māʾidah*, after allowing for a specific exemption in line with its liberal legal tendency in matters of purity – the game procured through hunting dogs can be made permissible – explicates, surprisingly, that there should be full continuity between its own food laws and the food laws of "those who were given the Book." This has led to considerable scholarly debate, since we are faced with an apparent conundrum. On the one hand, the rabbinic food laws of the Qurʾān's time go far beyond those retained by the Qurʾān; on the other hand, if "those who were given the book" include Christians, this would stand in tension with the fact that Christian views of permissible food are far less restrictive than those of the Qurʾān, allowing for example the consumption of pork.[5] How then can the Qurʾān allege

[4] See pages 134–5.

[5] Based on the Qurʾān's view that "the food of those who were given the Book is lawful to you" in Q3:50, de Blois concludes that such a diet would exclude pork and that the people in question cannot have been "Christians who are notorious for their porcophagy" (see idem, "Naṣrānī (Ναζωραῖος) and ḥanīf (ἐθνικός)," 16). Griffith countered that in this context "those who were given the book" may actually be only the Jews, arguing that the notion "those who were given the Book" elsewhere designates only the Christians, and not the Jews (idem, "Al-Naṣārā in the Qurʾān," 315–16). In other words, if it were only one party there, it may only be the other party here. Both insights are valuable, though both must now be amended. Pace de Blois, I do not agree that Christians could not be meant here since we cannot deduce actual practice from legal injunction. Pace Griffith, "those who were given the book" in the two verses he adduces, namely in Q4:171 and Q5:77, actually includes the Jews. Q4:171 does of course contain a polemic against the Trinity, yet it is preceded by an address to the Jews that extends until Q4:170. The exhortation not to "exceed the bounds in your religion" in Q4:171 is therefore directed

full overlap of food laws for Jews, Christians, and for its own community?

The Qurʾān, in effect, does not allege, it decrees, and the problem can be partially resolved when studying the Qurʾān's legal injunctions closely – and with the help of the Didascalia. In the following, I will suggest that the Qurʾān sees Jesus first and foremost as a prophet to the Israelites; in the Conclusion, I will speculate what this may mean for its use of the term "people of the book," "people of the Gospel," and the Christians, the *naṣārā*. Yet already now we can establish that, as we saw above, in both the Didascalia and in the Qurʾān, Jesus is an apostle to the Sons of Israel first, and to the nations later. While many of "the Jews" portrayed in the Qurʾān (and in the Didascalia) certainly reject Jesus, we should also note that this rejection would of course not annul God's decree to remove part of the Israelite food laws; moreover, the rejection of Jesus does not pertain to all children of Israel.

To the contrary, according to the Qurʾān, some of the Jews believed in Jesus, and thereby in Jesus' partial abrogation of the food laws, allowing for the likely continuity of food laws between "Israelites" and the Qurʾān's own community. The Qurʾān indicates that "among the people of Moses is a community (*ʾummatun*) that guides by the truth and does justice thereby" (Q7:159), a statement that

---

towards the Jews as much as towards the Christians. Likewise, the similar formulation in Q5:77 not to "unduly exceed the bounds in your religion" is followed by a specification that "the Children of Israel were cursed on the tongue of David and Jesus son of Mary." As I argue in the Conclusion, the Qurʾān conceptualizes the people of the book as *one* people, regardless of the internal division of this people into Jews and Christians.

coheres with an intriguing portrayal of "believing" Israelites elsewhere, to which Pines has drawn our attention:

Jesus son of Mary said to the disciples,
"Who will be my helpers for God's sake?"
The Disciples said "we will be God's helpers (*ʾanṣāru llāhi*)!"
So a group of the Children of Israel believed (*fa-ʾāmanat*),
and a group disbelieved (*kafarat*),
Then We strengthened the faithful against their enemies,
and they became the dominant ones. (Q61:14)

In the words of Pines, "according to this verse the Children of Israel were divided into two conflicting parties, one of which believed in Jesus and one that did not. The text makes it clear that the former was in the right."[6] Reynolds quite correctly reads the dominant party with reference to the Christian apostles, and he sees their dominance in terms of the "Christian idea of the triumph of the Cross."[7]

---

[6] Pines, "Notes on Islam and on Arabic Christianity and Judaeo-Christianity," 135. A similar idea may stand behind Q3:55, where we learn that God will set those who follow Jesus "above the faithless until the Day of Resurrection." The Qurʾān's differentiation between "believing" and "unbelieving" Israelites employed here, of course, evokes an early "Christian" way of describing Jewish followers of Jesus, which Pines rightly points out to be preserved nowhere as prominently as in the Clementine tradition – and in the Qurʾān. It is denoted in both texts by the lexemes *hmn*/*āmn* and *kpr*; see Pines, "Notes on Islam and on Arabic Christianity and Judaeo-Christianity," 135–8, 144. Pines notes that possibly Q43:65 "also contains an allusion to the conflict between these two groups" of believing and unbelieving Israelites; ibid. 137. According to Nöldeke's chronology of the Qurʾān, this surah is middle-Meccan. Such an allusion would therefore constitute a very early reflection of the inner-Jewish schism. Overall, the evidence for reading this surah in terms of an inner-Jewish schism rather than as a schism between Jews and Christians ignores the fact that for the Qurʾān, Christians are Israelites, see below, page 164.

[7] Gabriel Said Reynolds, "The Quran and the Apostles of Jesus," *Bulletin of the School of Oriental and African Studies* 76 (2013): 224.

This "triumph" should of course be seen not only in theological, but also in political, terms. It seems to me that the "dominance" of the believing Israelites in the time of the Qurʾān is that of the church over the synagogue more broadly, a prominent theme in patristic literature and a fact reflected in the political realities of the Byzantine Empire and its allied states. Are the Christians then Israelites for the Qurʾān, like the Jews? The answer, in my view, is affirmative.

Before turning to the socio-historical implications of this issue, we should note the ethnic implications. In the Qurʾān's view, then, Jesus' disciples are Israelites, who in the Qurʾān's time had become more prominent than those Jews who reject Jesus, among whose number we should certainly place the rabbinic Jews. Likewise, the believers in Jesus are presented as Israelites in ethnic terms. This need not mean that the Qurʾān excludes gentile Jesus-believers here – to the contrary, the pre-Constantinian Christian churches had long defined themselves in ethnic terms and most later churches saw themselves as the "true Israel."[8] In post-biblical literature, the "Israelite" nature of Jesus-belief may nowhere have been formulated as immediately as in the Didascalia, whose laws (even in its Christian iteration, and even more so in its "Judaeo-Christian" iteration shared with the Clementine Homilies) are closer to the Qurʾān's than those of any other Jewish and Christian group. Likewise, both texts present both Jews and Christians fully as part of Israel, "the people."

---

[8] See Denise Kimber Buell, *Why This New Race: Ethnic Reasoning in Early Christianity* (New York: Columbia University Press, 2005) and Simon, *Verus Israel.*

The Christian outlook of the Didascalia does not complicate matters by juxtaposing the "spiritual" with the "carnal" Israel, as many other Late Antique Christians did: its community simply constitutes the one true Israel, usually addressed as *'m'*, as "the people" (see e.g. DA IV 56:12, 57:5). Indeed, it uses the same term, *'m'*, to designate the people of Israel and the church; the term occurs, with either meaning, over 160 times. The "carnal" continuity with Scriptural Israel, in addition to the lexical one, becomes clear when understanding that the one Israelite people is made up, in evocative alliteration, of members from the *'m'* and from the *'mm'*, from the one Jewish people and from the many gentile peoples (e.g. DA XV, 159.1 and 14, see also DA XXV and DA XXVI). The nation and the nations together constitute *the* nation of Israel, that is, the church. There is then no reason why the Qurʾān *would* exclude those Christians who follow the Didascalia, whom I see as constituting part of its audience, from its definition of Israel. For both texts, both the Christians and the Jews are part of Israel.

In turn, if the food of the Qurʾān's audience "is lawful to them (*ḥillun lahum*)," that is, to the people of the book, we can deduce a few of the "Israelite" food laws that according to the Qurʾān *were* abrogated for the Jews. Namely, all the Israelite food laws that do not apply to the Qurʾān's own audience were abrogated for the Israelites as well. Yet only a few of them are explicated, such as the ones specified in Q6:146: animals with undivided hoofs, fat of oxen and sheep not connected to tissue or bones. A full list of the other food laws that have been abrogated for the Israelites cannot be determined. The Qurʾān does not further specify which additional food laws had been imposed on the Israelites *after* the Golden Calf incident; given their abrogation by Jesus (and/or Muhammad) and their merely "historical" value, the silence is not surprising. Moreover, the fact that the rabbis did not accept this abrogation matters as little as the fact that most Greek and Syriac church fathers saw the abrogation as going much further: the Qurʾān, to reiterate, does not describe common practice, but decrees its conception on all "sons of Israel." It is noteworthy in this respect that the Qurʾān instructs not to "prohibit (*tuḥarrimu*) the good things (*ṭayyibāti*) that God has made lawful for you (*ʾaḥalla llāhu lakum*)" (Q5:87), once again employing the same terminology we saw earlier in the same surah, addressed to opponents, likely rabbinic, who insist on stricter purity rules. Likewise, it accuses the Christians, since they "forgot (or "neglected," *nasū*) a part of what they had been reminded," namely, they forgot a part of their own "covenant" (*mīṯāq*, Q5:14). I suggest that the food laws that the Qurʾān sees as incumbent on the entire people of the book, the food laws it shares with the Didascalia's Judaeo-Christian group and with the Clementine Homilies, are among the things that it accuses the *naṣārā*, the Christians, of having forgotten.

Stages of Ritual Law in the Qurʾān and in the Didascalia

The Qurʾān's view of the food laws before the giving of the Torah seems clear. The broader aspects of law, spanning all true religions and finding their final iteration in the Qurʾān, are evoked, for example, in the famous passage Q30:30, defining the *fiṭra*, roughly translatable as the "original conception."[9] A similar presupposition pertaining to laws that are in place for more than one community becomes apparent when the Qurʾān specifies that "prescribed for you is fasting, as it was prescribed for those who were before you (*ʿalā-llaḏīna min qablikum*), so that you may be Godwary" (Q2:183). As discussed in Chapter One, it seems that the Qurʾān conceptualizes the "covenant" laws God gave to Moses on Sinai as universal and as applying to both Israelites and to its own community, while parts of the laws given to Moses after the Golden Calf are portrayed as temporary and as applying only to the Israelites. Likewise, the Qurʾān considers *part* of the Jewish laws as abrogated by Jesus and by Muhammad; with respect to food laws and ritual purity more broadly, it is this simplified lawcode that the Qurʾān equally applies to its gentile community – the Judaeo-Christian ritual lawcode.

Despite its concept of *fiṭra*, however, the Qurʾān does not stipulate any sense of "natural" *ritual* law that would be self-evident to humans apart from any revelation; there was no Israelite purity law before the giving of the Torah. When it comes to food laws, for example, the Qurʾān states that "all food was lawful to the Children of Israel, except what Israel [i.e. Jacob] had forbidden himself, before the Torah was sent down" (Q3:93). Jacob, Isaac, Ishmael and Abraham did not operate under any external

[9] On "original law" in the Qurʾān and in later Muslim tradition, see esp. Geneviève Gobillot, *La conception originelle, ses interprétations et fonctions chez les penseurs musulmans: la fiṭra* (Cairo: Institut Français d'Archéologie Orientale, 2000), esp. 7–14 on the Semitic roots of the word *fiṭra*. For the earlier development of the concept of universal law, see also Zellentin, "Jesus and the Tradition of the Elders: Originalism and Traditionalism in Early Judean Legal Theory" (forthcoming).

ritual restraint when partaking of food. The Qurʾān positions itself between cognate patristic and rabbinic tendencies on this issue.

To reiterate, the church fathers insisted on the fact that the patriarchs did not obey *kashrut*, as Joseph Witztum reminds us, while the rabbis insisted that they obeyed much of it. For according to the rabbis, the patriarchs kept "all the Torah" (*kl htwrh*, Mishna *Qiddushin* 4:14); and the rabbis especially insisted that the patriarchs kept kosher and observed the Shabbat (see e.g. Bereshit Rabbah 48:14 and 79.6, and Bavli *Bava Metsia* 86b). The Qurʾān, in turn, emphasizes that at least one of the patriarchs – "Israel" – imposed *some* food laws on himself voluntarily *avant la lettre*, occupying a middle position on the matter that neatly dovetails with Jesus' cognate permission of *some* of the previously prohibited foods in Q3:50. One can only speculate what these voluntary restrictions of "Israel" may have been. I would not suggest, however, that the Qurʾān wants us to imagine Abraham or his grandson partaking of pork, blood, carrion, or idol meat.

Witztum reads Q3:93 to indicate the Qurʾān's view that "no dietary restrictions (except for one) existed before the Torah was revealed," pointing to cognate Christian statements that the Bible's food laws were not kept by the patriarchs. Witztum also adduces previous readings that this single prohibition may have been either the sciatic tendon or the meat and milk of camels.[10] There is, however, no mention of a *single* prohibition in the Qurʾān. Moreover,

---

[10] See Witztum, *The Syriac Milieu of the Quran*, 277. Witztum's own view, as argued in a publication in preparation, is that the sciatic tendon, according to the Qurʾān, is the most likely prohibition observed by Jacob.

the Qurʾān's argument is predicated on the notion that "since Abraham did not follow these rules [of the Torah], neither should the Muslims," as Witztum correctly states.[11] In light of the suggested continuity between the legal cultures of the Didascalia and the Qurʾān, a similar logic likely pertains to Shabbat: the Didascalia states that Abraham did not keep it (DA XXVI, 252.22–253.6); the Didascalia – as well as the Qurʾān and likely the Clementine Homilies – accordingly rejects it as incumbent upon gentiles.

Regarding food laws, however, reading the Qurʾānic *nomos* along with the narrative makes on aspect of Witztum's conclusion here problematic: if the Qurʾān's audience is not to eat pork or carrion or meat sacrificed to idols, surely Abraham or Jacob would not have eaten these foods either – Abraham's rejection of idol worship suggests at least a rejection of idol meat! The Qurʾān's catalogue of forbidden foods for its own community is already commensurate with the Israelite code after Jesus' abrogations. It may well be that we should also associate this code with what "Israel forbade himself." If so, the Qurʾān stands in between the *Christian* notion that the patriarchs kept none of the later ritual law and the *rabbinic* notion that the patriarchs kept "all the Torah."

Despite the fact that much is left implicit in both the Didascalia and the Qurʾān, we can tentatively hazard the assertion that there are four stages that both the Qurʾān and the Didascalia see in the history of ritual food laws, which can be roughly sketched as follows:[12]

---

[11] See Witztum, *The Syriac Milieu of the Quran*, 277.

[12] My position here has developed from a previous claim and reflects the criticism that Joseph Witztum kindly shared with me, as well my wrestling with his own reading as summarized above.

- Stage one, before the giving of the Torah, when no ritual law was given at all and its observation is anticipated only by the patriarchs.
- Stage two, after the initial giving to the Israelites of the original Torah, which includes the prohibition of blood, carrion of various kinds, and idol meat, as well as pork according to the Judaeo-Christian group of the Didascalia and the Qurʾān (equally at least discouraged by the Clementine Homilies) – the Judaeo-Christian ritual lawcode.
- Stage three, after the Golden Calf, when additional laws are given to the Israelites as punishment for the Golden Calf and other sins, such as avoiding animals with undivided hoofs, fat of oxen and sheep not connected to tissue or bones (Q6:146).
- Stage four, when Jesus abrogates additional laws given to the Israelites in stage three, allowing a return to stage two for Israelite food laws. Jesus, as a "sign to the nations," extends these laws of stage two to apply to all gentiles – again, the Judaeo-Christian ritual law code. The Qurʾān presents Muhammad, the "unlettered" or "gentile" prophet (*an-nabiyya l-ʾummiyya*), as reconfirming and possibly extending stage four. It further turns the Judaeo-Christian discouragement of wine consumption as seen in the Clementine Homilies into law at this stage.[13]

[13] Since the Qurʾān does not specify which food laws exactly Jesus abrogated, we do not know if this implies that any further laws are abrogated by Muhammad, or if he simply affirmed Jesus' abrogation – since many Israelites rejected Jesus, the latter option is more likely, though the former is conceivable as well. As is the case with the exact food laws before the Golden Calf, the Didascalia cannot guide

This sketch is of course necessarily simplistic and will need to be tested in future studies that will continue the comparison of legal codes such as those – among others – of the Didascalia's Judaeo-Christian group, of the Clementine Homilies, and of the Qur'ān. What is more certain already now, however, is that this comparison corroborates the conceptual overlap of food laws the Qur'ān stipulates: the food that is permitted to its gentile audience and the food that is permitted by God to the Israelites ever since Jesus abrogated part of the Jewish food laws is the same. The fact that the rabbis reject the abrogation, and that the Christians forget part of their covenant, does not change the force of divine law.

Simply put, the actual food laws of the Didascalia's Judaeo-Christian group and those of the Qur'ān are largely similar; at the same time, the Qur'ān takes the Didascalia's narrative establishing a legal salvation history as one of its points of departure. The Qur'ān explicates such an overlap by stating that "the food of those who were given the Book is lawful to you" (Q5:5). In no way, of course, does the Qur'ān stipulate *actual* overlap of practice between its own community and the people of the book. The Qur'ān only states that God has revoked the food laws given as punishment, not that the rabbis agree with this view. Likewise, it is important to note that the overlap of food laws does not extend to the conflation of other laws – the Jews seem still to be held to observe Shabbat, and God will judge between those who disagree about it, as we saw in Chapter Three.

---

us towards understanding exactly which food laws were in place for the Israelites in the time between Jesus and Muhammad.

In the Qur'ān, God has appointed "a code of law and a custom" (*šir'atan wa-minhāǧan*) to each "community" (*'umma*, Q5:48). To reiterate, the conflation of food laws does *not* lead to the full conflation of law, let alone religions.[14] The Didascalia, by contrast, suggests that the various lawcodes of different religions are temporally distinct rather than given to different communities:

"for every age (*zbn'*), there is a just (*dzdq'*) law (*nmws'*). Now while you have the Gospel ..., the renewal of the law and the seal (*wḥwtm'*), seek nothing else, (anything) more than the Law and the prophets" (*nmws' wnby'*). (DA XXVI, 254.14–7)

Both texts, the Qur'ān and the Didascalia, share the sense of different divine lawcodes valid in different circumstances, yet the Didascalia presents itself as the "seal" of all legislations. The Qur'ān, on the one hand, presents Muhammad as the "seal of the prophets" (*ḫātam n-nabiyyīna*, Q33:40), applying a concept cognate to that of the Didascalia's "seal" of revelations to the last messenger thereof.[15] On the other hand, however, unlike the Didascalia's Christian authors, who (along with the general Christian view) abrogate the Jewish law, the Qur'ān allows for the ongoing validity of various lawcodes at the *same* time, enabling an

---

[14] As Hallaq aptly notes, the Qur'ān repeatedly stresses "that believers must judge by what was revealed to them .... It is noteworthy here that the 'normative way' is represented by the term *minhāj*, a cognate of the Hebraic word *minhāg* [custom]. The creation of an Islamic parallel here speaks for itself" (idem, *The Origins and Evolution of Islamic Law*, 21).

[15] On the notion of the "seal of the prophets," see also François de Blois, "Elchasai – Manes – Muḥammad," 44–6; cf. also Hartmut Bobzin, "The 'Seal of the Prophets': Towards and Understanding of Muhammad's Prophethood," in Neuwirth et al., *The Qur'ān in Context*, 565–584.

ecumenical co-existence of various religious communities side-by-side – not unlike the Clementine Homilies' view presented in the Introduction.

If we take the three documents here discussed as representative of three points of view, we can summarize the Qurʾān's grand synthesis as follows. The Didascalia's Christian authors see Jesus as abrogating *all* ritual law except for the Decree of the Apostles, by extension abrogating Judaism as a whole. The Clementine Homilies in turn insist that the Jews have *no* need of Jesus at all, stipulating the full validity of Mosaic law for Jews and the validity of the Judaeo-Christian lawcode for gentiles. The Qurʾān yet again puts forward a view that engages and develops aspects preserved in *both* of the other documents: it accepts the Judaeo-Christian lawcode as incumbent upon gentiles and it allows Jews to remain Jews, albeit with partially abrogated food laws. I submit for further consideration that the Qurʾān's criticism of other forms of Christianity and Judaism with which it was equally conversant may best be understood based on its synthesis of the two legal points of view closest to its own tradition: first, Christianity affirmative of law as envisioned by the Didascalia and, second, Judaeo-Christianity affirmative of ritual purity as envisioned, perhaps, by the Didascalia's Jewish believers and by the Clementine Homilies. These two documents are the only preserved witnesses of a much richer oral tradition and legal culture, but they allow us at least an incremental approach to access the Qurʾān and what is known about its first audience.

The special status of food laws within community formation has recently begun to receive due scholarly attention in the study of Judaism and Christianity; it should indeed not be surprising to find that the Qur᾿ān would treat food laws differently from other laws.[16] For the Qur᾿ān, then, the Jews are to judge by the Torah (Q5:44), but to eat by the law of Jesus and Muhammad. Likewise, the "people of the Gospel" (*᾿ahl al-᾿inǧīl*, Q5:47) are expected to judge by their own scripture by which they are defined.[17] According to the Qur᾿ān, however, in the Gospel, Jesus only abrogates part of the food laws.

In light of the statement that "the food of those who were given the Book is lawful to you (*ḥillun lakum*)," that is, to the Qur᾿ān's own gentile audience, it seems that the Qur᾿ān sees the same food laws as incumbent on the people of the Gospel as well. For part of these laws, this is not a surprise at all, given that the Qur᾿ān fully shares the Christian list of forbidden meats in Acts, in the Decree of the Apostles. Yet the Qur᾿ān, as we saw, prohibits pork and continues to develop the definition of "strangled" meat and blood to include many other forms of carrion. In this sense it takes the list of the Clementine Homilies and the Didascalia's Judaeo-Christian group, which goes far beyond Christian tradition and especially Christian practice, as one of its points of departure.

---

[16] See, for example, David M. Freidenreich, *Foreigners and Their Food: Constructing Otherness in Jewish, Christian, and Islamic Law* (Berkeley, CA: University of California Press, 2011); Jordan D. Rosenblum, *Food and Identity in Early Rabbinic Judaism* (Cambridge: Cambridge University Press, 2010), and my review of Rosenblum (touching on Freidenreich) in the *Journal for the Study of Judaism* 44 (2013): 123–5; see also Dennis Smith, *From Symposium to Eucharist: The Banquet in the Early Christian World* (Minneapolis, MN: Fortress Press, 2003).

[17] This passage is analyzed in detail by Goitein, "The Birth-Hour of Muslim Law," 125–9.

The Qur'ān's endorsement of the Judaeo-Christian ritual lawcode does not allow us to deduce what a possible historical "people of the Gospel" in the Hijaz of the seventh century really would have eaten – all we learn is that according to the Qurʾān, those who follow "the Gospel" *should* eat according to what is written in this Gospel. Yet on this question of what the Gospel teaches to eat there is significant overlap between the Qurʾān, the Didascalia's Judaeo-Christian group, and the Clementine Homilies. Both in its narrative and in its *nomos*, the Didascalia provides a concrete historical background that allows us to appreciate aspects of the Qurʾān's legal culture. I conclude, then, by considering whether the Qurʾān may show an awareness of Judaeo-Christian members of the Christian community who actually did endorse the Judaeo-Christian ritual lawcode. For it seems unlikely that there were none.

Conclusion

Judaeo-Christian Legal Culture as a Point of Departure for the Qurʾān

Rather than looking at the Didascalia as the textual source of the Qurʾān, we should see both documents as evidence of Judaeo-Christian legal culture, corroborated by the Clementine Homilies, that had emerged by the third or fourth century C.E. at the latest, and that persisted at least until the seventh. This legal culture was never necessarily embodied in an independent social entity. The Didascalia, despite its Judaeo-Christian elements, sees itself as Christian, and in its own evidence presents the Judaeo-Christian group as firmly embedded in the midst of its community; there is no reason, then, to posit independent Judaeo-Christian churches. Similarly, the rabbinic tendency to conceptualize Jewish Jesus-belief mainly in rabbinic terms does not suggest an independent network of Judaeo-Christian synagogues. While we should not exclude this possibility in the Near and Middle East, there is no evidence to confirm it. We have clear evidence for Judaeo-Christian texts and tenets, yet these likely have been preserved within or in emulation of other forms of Judaism and Christianity. The way in which contemporary movements such as "Messianic Jews" or "Hebrew Christians" see themselves and are seen by others alternatively as Jews or as Christians may be a helpful comparison.[1] The

[1] Notably, some Jesus-believing groups seek to emulate rabbinic

invention of "Judaeo-Christianity" as a means of religious classification may be the result of the church fathers' and the rabbis' joint effort of establishing a difference between Judaism and Christianity. Our difficulty in grasping texts such as the Clementine Homilies and the Qur'ān may largely originate from these texts' refusal to accept this difference as unbridgeable.

How the demonstrable Judaeo-Christian legal culture relates to parts of the earlier Jesus movement – in continuity, though with clear differences, in my view – and how it fared after the establishment of the Caliphates – either by being at least partially absorbed into Islam, by being suppressed, or by morphing into Judaism or Christianity – cannot be addressed here.[2] Yet how Ju-

practice; see the fine discussion by Dan Cohn-Sherbok, "Modern Hebrew Christians and Messianic Judaism," in Peter J. Tomson and Doris Lambers-Petry (eds.), *The Image of the Judaeo-Christians in Ancient Jewish and Christian Literature* (Tübingen: Mohr Siebeck, 2003), 287–98.

[2] Seeking to understand the earlier tradition would include an inquiry into the reception history of Matthew, the Didache, and possibly earlier versions of the Clementine Homilies (the so-called "Grundschrift," see Stanley F. Jones, "The Pseudo-Clementines: a History of Research, Part I" *The Second Century* 2 (1982): 14–33) and above, page 97, note 32; likewise, one could explore the possibility of earlier redactions of the Didascalia, see Stewart-Sykes, *The Didascalia Apostolorum*, 22–44 and above, pages 43–4, note 52. The question of what happened to Judaeo-Christian legal culture after the establishment of the Caliphates has not received sufficient attention; my view is that it was likely absorbed into Islam in Arabia and Mesopotamia, but may well have persisted in various forms in Ethiopia. Pines repeatedly argues that part of the later Muslim anti-Christian polemic is inspired by Judaeo-Christian texts or movements, a notion that has largely been dismissed; see idem, "Gospel Quotations and Cognate Topics in Abd al-Jabbar's *Tathbit* in Relation to Early Christian and Judaeo-Christian Readings and Traditions," *Jerusalem Studies*

daeo-Christian legal culture developed from the fourth to the seventh century – in dialogue with the broader Jewish and Christian traditions, yet demonstrably distinct from it – is a question that we can only answer in light of the Qur'ān itself. The necessary circularity of an attempt to read the Qur'ān in light of its continuity with a concrete

in Arabic and Islam 9 (1987): 195–278, idem, "Notes on Islam and on Arabic Christianity and Judaeo-Christianity," 145–52; idem and Shaul Shaked, "Fragment of a Jewish-Christian Composition from the Cairo Geniza," in M. Sharon (ed.), Studies in Islamic History and Civilization in Honour of Professor David Ayalon (Leiden: Brill, 1986), 307–318; Shlomo Pines, "Judaeo-Christian Materials in an Arabic Jewish Treatise," *Proceedings of the American Academy for Jewish Research* 35 (1967): 187–217; and idem, *The Jewish Christians of the Early Centuries of Christianity According to a New Source* (Jerusalem: Israel Academy of Sciences and Humanities, 1966); all of Pines' publications have been reprinted in *The Collected Works of Shlomo Pines* (Jerusalem: Magnes Press, 1979–1996). Pines' suggestions regarding the post-Qur'ānic materials have generally been criticized; see Gabriel Reynolds, *A Muslim Theologian in a Sectarian Milieu: 'Abd al-Jabbār and the Critique of Christian Origins* (Leiden: Brill, 2004), 1–18; Daniel J. Lasker, "The Jewish Critique of Christianity under Islam in the Middle Ages," *Proceedings of the American Academy for Jewish Research* 57 (1990–1991), esp. 126–7; Nicholas R.M. de Lange, "A Fragment of Byzantine Anti-Christian Polemic," *Journal of Jewish Studies* 41 (1990): 92–100; S.M. Stern, "'Abd al-Jabbār's Account of How Christ's Religion was Falsified by the Adoption of Roman Customs," *The Journal of Theological Studies* 19 (1968): 128–185. A study affirmative of Pines' general tendencies, adducing much additional material is Patricia Crone, "Islam, Judeo-Christianity and Byzantine iconoclasm," in eadem, *From Kavād to al-Ghazālī: Religion, Law, and Political Thought in the Near East, c. 600–c. 1100* (Aldershot: Ashgate, 2005 [1980]), 59–96. For a full bibliography on 'Abd al-Jabbār, see Gabriel Reynolds, "*Tathbīt dalā'il al-nubuwwa,* 'The confirmation of the proofs of prophethood'; '*Tathbīt*,' 'The confirmation,'" in Thomas et al. (eds.), *Christian-Muslim Relations. A Bibliographical History.* Volume 2 (900–1050) (Leiden: Brill, 2010), 604–9.

Judaeo-Christian legal culture at the same time as using it as evidence for this culture is attenuated by the breadth of evidence. This evidence, we can summarize, includes aspects of shared law we would classify as civil, criminal, and, most prominently, as ethical and ritual, embraced by the Didascalia's Judaeo-Christian group and by the Qurʾān, and the Qurʾān's many explicit and implicit references to its legal points of departure.

In detail, the Qurʾān endorses the distinct selection of (mostly biblical) laws also promulgated by the Didascalia, as well as the ritual law of the Didascalia's Judaeo-Christian group in as far as this law is corroborated by the Clementine Homilies. From among the Biblical obligations beyond the Ten Commandments, both the Qurʾān and the Didascalia highlight the giving of alms, care for orphans, prayer, fasting, and festivals, and both add covering for women. Both forbid manslaughter and especially the killing of children, as well as boasting, vain talk, falsifying measures, usury, and divining. Both reject abstinence from marriage and from the consumption of meat, but endorse the dietary restrictions of the Decree of the Apostles: the meat of strangled animals, meat offered to idols, and blood. Both texts posit that their list of observances constitutes the law given by God on Mount Sinai, to which observances were added after the sin of the Golden Calf. It was Jesus' role to take away these added observances and to restore the leaner, originally revealed law, a task which in the Qurʾān is completed by Muhammad. In the many cases in which the Qurʾān departs from previous practice, as it does for example when it comes to the direction of prayer and the nature of the festivals, it does so by indicating its departure from previous observance explicitly.

In addition, the Qur'ān endorses the Judaeo-Christian lawcode of the Clementine Homilies, largely shared by the Didascalia's Judaeo-Christian group: the prohibition of carrion, divided animals, and mangled ones, as well as swine and wine, the two items regarding which the Clementine Homilies fall short of a full prohibition. Likewise, the Qur'ān also follows the Judaeo-Christian prohibition of intercourse during the menses and purification after sexual intercourse and before worship. A shared legal culture can therefore be attributed to the audience of the Qur'ān and that of the Didascalia, and even more so to the latter's alleged Judaeo-Christian party, whose purity rules are largely corroborated by the Clementine Homilies.

To reiterate, the nomos of this shared culture is largely comprised of biblical observances, apart from a few exceptions – veiling of women, for example, does not appear in the Hebrew Bible and is present in the New Testament only in cultic contexts. Parts of this culture's cognate legal narratives are also shared by rabbis and church fathers. Yet the choice of precepts and the emphases of its legal narrative that marks this legal culture are distinct from other known Jewish and Christian models. Whether the members of the Didascalia's community whom it casts as Judaeo-Christians saw themselves as Jews, as Christians, or as something in the middle cannot be decided – yet no matter what they called themselves, their practice does not coincide with rabbinic Judaism or with known forms of Christianity. The Clementine Homilies equally participate in this Judaeo-Christian legal culture, which expands part of the Bible's ritual lawcode in regard to *gentiles* – people who should occupy a position, according to Epiphanius, in between the church and the synagogue (*Panarion* 30.1.4), but were more likely at home in both. Whereas Epiphanius saw these people' station as an evil one, the Qurʾān emancipates its own emerging "middle nation" (*ʾummatan wasaṭan*, Q2:143) from rabbinic and Episcopal authority (as I will briefly illustrate in the epilogue).

Judaeo-Christian Legal Culture as Confirmed by the Qurʾān

The triangle of texts – Qurʾān, Clementine Homilies, and Didascalia – makes it all but certain that the lawcode of the Judaeo-Christians is *not* a heresiological invention by the Didascalia's Christian authors, a possibility I rejected already above. Rather, the Judaeo-Christians were part of the Didascalia's community and constitute a trend within Christian or Jewish groups of which but three *concrete* snapshots were preserved: the close outsider's description by the Jewish-leaning, yet fully Christian authors of the Didascalia; the insider's view of the Clementine Homilies; and then the very different outsider's perspective of the Qurʾān, which defines itself through its emancipation from its legal precedents. The extant rabbinic and patristic heresiological portrayals of Judaeo-Christians should be re-evaluated against these three perspectives.

The Qurʾān's legal fabric points to the historical accuracy of at least one of its central legal claims: in light of the evidence provided by the Didascalia, the Qurʾān's position that it is "confirming what was before it from the book" (*muṣaddiqan li-mā bayna yadayhi mina l-kitābi*, Q5:48) seems plausible, at least from the point of view of the Judaeo-Christian legal culture from the fourth century onwards. Moreover, the Qurʾān's legal, conceptual, and stylistic alterations are often explicitly marked as alterations vis-à-vis previous practice (and that includes its use of the Arabic tongue). Therefore, we must not reduce the Qurʾān to what it affirms and alters. Rather than conceiving of the Muslim Scripture as the mechanical result of an ill-informed prophet's dabbling in Christian heresies (a still widespread notion), we should read the Qurʾān's dialogue with an established oral culture as intentionally establishing its own independence from that culture. We can appreciate the Qurʾān's legal culture in a threefold way. It endorses a specific legal tradition of understanding the Gospel that also found expression in the Didascalia. Second, it endorses a ritual lawcode imposed upon gentiles that continues the development of the Decree of the Apostles already attested to in the Clementine Homilies, a lawcode distinct from the fuller Jewish observances of the Torah. And, third, it endorses a form of worship akin to Judaeo-Christianity, situated squarely within the Judaism and Christianity of its time.

The Upright Nation and the naṣārā *among the People of the Book*

To reiterate, the Qurʾān shares much of the Judaeo-Christian legal culture and, when departing therefrom, it generally lets its audience know. We can turn to the question of how the Qurʾān may have perceived people who observed the Judaeo-Christian lawcode, either as a discrete group, as has been suggested, or as members of other groups, as I believe is more likely. Given the Qurʾān's endorsement of their lawcode, we should expect some sort of acknowledgment of an independent Judaeo-Christian group or subgroup, should it have existed. Yet the Qur'ān only acknowledges Jewish and Christian piety in general terms, never in terms of a distinct set of ritual observances.

A good starting point is the following Qur'ānic statement about those who are "believers" (*mu'minūna*, Q3:110) among the people of the book, in which we may now hear an echo of the Didascalia's instructions for fasting:

Yet they are not all alike.
Among the people of the book (*'ahli l-kitābi*) there is an upright nation (*'ummatun qā'imatun*)
They recite God's words in the watches of the night (*al-layl*)
And prostrate (*yasǧudūna*)
They believe in God (*yu'minūna bi-llāhi*) and the Last Day (*al-yawmi l-'āḫiri*)
And bid what is right
And forbid what is wrong
And are active in good deeds.
They are among the righteous. (Q3:113–114)

Daniel Madigan has drawn our attention to elements this passage shares with the broader Syriac ascetic tradition and he is undoubtedly right that the practices evoked in the Qur'ān were widespread.[3] Yet the Qur'ān emphasizes the righteousness of this upright group in terms of very concrete scriptural practices and ascetic laws. Indeed, the Qur'ān employs the same phrase, that the people of the book "bid what is right and forbid what is wrong" (*wa-ya'murūna bi-l-maʿrūfi wa-yanhawna ʿani'l-munkari*, Q3:113), that just three verses earlier it uses to praise its own community (*ta'murūna bi-l-maʿrūfi wa-tanhawna ʿani l-munkari*, Q3:110, cf. Q9:67!). The Qur'ān's claim

[3] Madigan, *The Qur'ān's Self-Image*, 200–9.

that it merely confirms previous tradition invites us to scrutinize its depiction of an "upright nation" with special rigor.

Perhaps we should read the Qurʾān's evocation of an existing group to its liking as part of its general interest in establishing a trustworthy predecessor. We cannot of course take its depiction of this upright nation at face value. Yet the manifold conceptual and lexical commonalities of the Qurʾānic passage about the "upright nation" with the Didascalia suggest a real affinity between the Qurʾān and an existing community. And these commonalities, as Nicolai Sinai points out to me, concern precisely not the Judaeo-Christian ritual lawcode discussed above, but the Didascalia's much more widespread "Christian" practices. For example, in its description of the paschal fast, the Didascalia (DA XXI, 214.8–13) instructs its audience to:

- fast entirely, and taste nothing (*ṣymyn wmdm l' tṭʿmwn*).
- to assemble together and watch and keep *vigil all night* (*lly'*),
- to engage in *prayers* (*bṣlwt'*) and petitions,
- and to recite God's word, namely by engaging in *reading* (*wbqryn'*) of the prophets (*dnby'*) and the Gospel (*wb'wnglywn*) and the psalms (*wbmzmwr'*), "with fear and trembling and with assiduous supplication."

Further on, as we saw earlier, the Didascalia instructs its audience "to *worship* (*dtsgdwn*) God (*l'lh'*)," to be ministered by the "holy *Scriptures*" (*bktb'*), and to "believe" (*wthymnwn*) in the "resurrection" (*bqymt'*) of the dead (DA XXIV, 232.5–8). The Qurʾān's notion of the "the people of the book" (*ʾahl l-kitāb*), the fact that they "prostrate" (*yasǧudūna*) and their "believing in God (*yuʾminū-*

na bi-llāhi) and the Last Day (*al-yawmi l-ʾāḫiri*)" are reminiscent of these expressions, just as the Didascalia's language of cultic observance in general resembles that of the Qurʾān. Perhaps most importantly, the Didascalia routinely refers to its own community as *ʿm*ʾ, as "the people," as we saw in Chapter Four, a term similar in meaning and pronunciation to the Qurʾān's *ʾumma*.

On their own, the conceptual and lexical commonalities between the two liturgical passages would be merely an illustration of the larger affinities between the Qurʾānic and Christian cultures: the Didascalia's practice of paschal vigils and Bible readings is of course not particular to the Didascalia, but defines the ascetic tradition more generally. Yet the commonalities between the Qurʾān and the Didascalia here adduced are much more intimate than the broader associations between the Qurʾān and the Syriac ascetic tradition at large, which are helpfully pointed out by Madigan (see above). In the context of the results presented in the previous chapters, we can state that once again the Didascalia may be the best witness of the type of worship, and especially the widespread Syriac tradition of the nightly reading (*wbqryn*ʾ), that the Qurʾān (which of course refers to itself as *al-qurʾān*, Q2:185) describes as a practice among the people of the book. The practices and narratives in question and the lexemes used to describe them can be found throughout Late Antique Aramaic discourse, yet nowhere clustered, arranged, and inflected quite the way they are in the two texts under consideration.

To return to our question, the Qurʾānic passage above seems to reflect the existence of a discrete group among the people of the book. In order to identify the subgroup, one should first identify the group: the question of course arises whether the "people of the book" here would self-identify as Christians, as Judaeo-Christians, or as Jews. Just before singling out the *ʾummatun qāʾimatun*, the "upright nation" (Q3:113) among them, the Qurʾān accuses members of the people of the book of "killing the prophets unjustly" (Q3:112), a crime with which the Jews are charged occasionally in rabbinic and often in Syriac Christian literature.[4] The theme of killing the prophets, hence, would typically evoke Jews rather than Christians.

While we should therefore not read the Qurʾānic verse above in light of Christianity alone, any categorical distinction between Jews and Christians would not do justice to the continuity the Qurʾān posits between the people of the Torah and the people of the Gospel, as I argued in Chapter Four. I take the Qurʾān's following accusation against Jews and Christians as central to its ethno-religious categories:

The Jews say,
"The Christians stand on nothing,"
And the Christians say,
"The Jews stand on nothing,"
Though they follow the [one] Book.

---

[4] On the Christian context of this theme, see most recently Gabriel Said Reynolds, "On the Qurʾān and the Theme of Jews as 'Killers of the Prophets'," *Al-Bayān* 10 (2012): 9–32. For rabbinic portrayals of the Jews as killers of the prophets, see for example Sifra *Behuqotai* 6, Ekha Rabbah 2:4 and 4:17, Qohelet Rabbah 3:19 and 12:7, Bavli *Gittin* 57b and Bavli *Sanhedrin* 96b. See also Israel Yuval, *Two Nations in your Womb, Perceptions of Jews and Christians in Late Antiquity and the Middle Ages* (Berkeley: University of California Press, 2006 [2000]), esp. pp. 31–91; and Richard Kalmin, "'Manasseh Sawed Isaiah with a Saw of Wood:' An Ancient Legend in Jewish, Christian, Muslim, and Persian Sources," in Mark Geller and Shaul Shaked (eds.), *Talmudic Archaeology in Babylonia* (Leiden: Brill, forthcoming).

So said those who had no knowledge,
similar to what they say.
God will judge between them
On the Day of the Resurrection
Concerning that about which they used to differ (*fī-mā kānū fīhi yaḫtalifūna*) Q2:113

Does the Qurʾān here conceptualize true Jews and Christians as Israelites, reflecting the previously discussed self-identity of both rabbis and church fathers, and does it see both as the recipients of Jesus' message? Above, we saw that the Qurʾān expects God to judge between Jews and Christians "on the Day of the Resurrection concerning that about which they used to differ (*yaḫtalifūna*)" (Q16:124), namely Shabbat.[5] Now we see that He will also judge between them in general – implying that what divides them is not part of the true religion, even if the identification of the erroneous elements will only occur at the end of days.

In pointing to the sameness of true religion, the Qurʾān continues a tradition of which the Clementine Homilies are equally part: as discussed in the Introduction, the Homilies explicitly state that, "there being one teaching by both [Jesus and Moses], God accepts him who has believed either of these" (Clementine Homilies 8:6). Likewise, its "upright nation" would likely share the Qurʾān's notion that any distinction between true Judaism and true Christianity is false. The Qurʾān speaks elsewhere of a "righteous nation" (*ʾummatun muqtaṣidatun*) among the

[5] On the Christian claim to Israel in general and the Didascalia's in particular, see page 163, on the differences regarding Shabbat, see pages 107–110.

People of the Book who *did* observe "the Torah and the Gospel Q5:66."[6] The way in which the Qur'ān perceives of this "upright nation," hence, stands in the tradition of the Clementine Homilies. Yet the Qur'ān here recasts Jews and Christians as two groups of *one* people; unlike the Clementine Homilies that distinguish between Jews and gentiles and unlike the Didascalia that almost fully collapses them. The Qur'ān, however, upholds such a distinction only until the Day of Judgment, making its difference with its predecessors one of eschatology more than of socio-religious taxonomy.

The Qur'ān's terminology is stable and precise: the "people of the book" is only *one* people, the Israelites, even if there is discord between the Jews and the people of the Gospel. If the "upright" sub-group among the people of the book is called an *'umma*, a "people," or "nation" or otherwise distinct community, this implies that this group does have a distinct "code of law and a custom" (Q5:48). And, in as far as they are termed "upright," we can assume that this sub-group, real or perceived, observes its group's lawcode according to the Qur'ān's liking. In turn, to the degree that we can determine the "code of law" and "cus-

[6] This upright nation seems to have a predecessor in Biblical times. In *Sūrat al-'A'rāf*, we learn that "among the people of Moses (*min qawmi Mūsā*) is a nation (*'ummatun*) who guide by the truth and do justice thereby" (Q7:159). According to Rubin, this group should be identified "with contemporary Jews who have embraced Islam" (see idem, "Children of Israel," in McAuliffe (ed.), *Encyclopaedia of the Qur'ān*, ad loc). This reading does not fully do justice to the context of the passage; the sequel explicitly states that "we split them up into twelve tribal communities" (Q7:160), indicating the primitive Israelite context of the verse – lest perhaps some Jews among the Qur'ān's audience claimed to belong to some of the lost tribes.

tom" of the Qur'ān's upright nation, we can identify the group. We have seen that the Qur'ān conceptualizes of the people of the book *only* in terms of Jews and Christians, as *yahūd* and *naṣārā*. There are no distinct Judaeo-Christians in the Qur'ān's taxonomy; the proximity of the Qur'ān's upright nation with the Didascalia hence suggests that it here depicts the behavior of Christians to its liking (as reiterated in Q5:83, see below).

The Qur'ān considers the Jewish food laws as partially abrogated by Jesus, constructing one set of Israelite food laws that God decreed on the Qur'ān's own community as well as on the entire people of the book, yet it maintains the distinction between Jews and Christians with regard to the Shabbat, and of course in its taxonomy. While the difference between Jews and Christians may be false, God will judge between them at the end of times only. Lessing's famous "Parable of the Ring" is not so far from the Qur'ān's attitude here. In between Jews, Christians, and its own community, Judaeo-Christians are not a distinct category for the Qur'ān. The "upright nation," to reiterate, is described in its scriptural and ascetic practices, not in terms of its ritual lawcode. The upright nation's observance of "the Torah and the Gospel" (in Q5:66) reflects the Didascalia's concomitant endorsement of the primary Law and of Jesus' message. The Qur'ān's idea of an "upright nation" is based on a real group; they are Christians, and the Didascalia may again be a central historical source for reconstructing this group.

Hence, we can equate the Qur'ān's "upright nation" among the people of the book with neither the Didascalia's Judaeo-Christian group nor with a putative community constituted by the Clementine Homilies. The believers in question should not be depicted as a group that is socially distinct or even clearly distinguishable from the broader Christian (or Jewish) communities of their time. The evidence presented in this volume instead suggests Judaeo-Christianity to be a discrete religious *tendency* endorsed to varying degrees by individual members of established Christian or Jewish groups, best described by the Didascalia and the Clementine Homilies. The Judaeo-Christian ritual lawcode is a distinct phenomenon, yet those endorsing it may not have stood apart with regard to their social cohesion and self-identity.

On the strength of the Qur'ān's broad legal affinity with the Didascalia's Christian group and the Didascalia's depiction of Judaeo-Christian practices, I make the following claim: the Qur'ān is familiar both with a Christian and a rabbinic majority and with the Judaeo-Christian tendencies among these majorities, especially the Christian one. The enduring vitality of Judaeo-Christian practices up to the seventh century – and their plausible absorption into the early Muslim community – can in turn be corroborated by the Qur'ān.

It is hence no wonder that the Christians, the *naṣārā* of the Qur'ān, as well as its "people of the Gospel," are difficult to grasp. They are part of the one people of the book; hence, they are Israelites – which corresponds very well to the Didascalia's self-identity as Israelite and as "the people" established in Chapter Four. Yet it seems to me that the group that most closely corresponds to the Qur'ān's *naṣārā* is that of the Didascalia's Christian authors – the group that stands accused within the Qur'ān of having "forgotten" or "neglected" part of its covenant for its rejection of the purity laws the Qur'ān sees as incumbent on the entire People of the Book. This group, while constituting a Jewish-leaning form of Christianity, calls itself "Christian" and I endorse the conventional translation of *naṣārā* as such.

It should be noted that the Didascalia designates the bishops to whom the apostles address the Didascalia (on whom more below) as "helpers of God," akin to the Qurʾān's term for the apostles. The Arabic word for helpers, *ʾanṣār*, in turn, evokes the term *naṣārā*.[7] The Qurʾān accuses the *naṣārā* of associationism and of taking Jesus as Lord (the Didascalia's views on this will be discussed in the epilogue).[8] Indeed, these *naṣārā* did "neglect" part of what

---

[7] Note that while the Qurʾān describes the disciples as "helpers of God" (*ʾanṣāru llāhi*), the Didascalia designates the bishops, to whom the apostles address the Didascalia, to be "helpers of God" (*m'drn' 'm 'lha*, DA XII, 143.15). On the bishops among the Qurʾān's *naṣārā*, see my Epilogue. Pointing in turn to the linguistic proximity of the Qurʾānic terms for "helpers" and "Nazarenes," Sidney Griffith has pointed out that "one might .... assume that the Naṣārā of the Qurʾān are thought to be the spiritual descendants of Jesus' first disciples" (idem, "al-Naṣārā in the Qurʾān: A Hermeneutical Reflection," 302). *Naṣārā* is the standard term that the Qurʾān uses to describe Christians, e.g. in *Sūrat al-Tawbah*, where it laments the fact that these "Christians call the Messiah the Son of God" (*qālati n-naṣāra l-masīḥu bnu llāhi*, Q9:30). The term "helper," of course, is quite common in the Qurʾān and used in many other ways. For example, the emigrants "help" the believers in Q8:72 and 74; in Q59:8; they even "help God" (*yanṣurūna llāha*) and his apostle. Yet the terminology and description for the "helpers" passages, Q61:14 and Q43:65, suggest a specific designation. This in turn makes an association with the "helpers for/towards God" in Q3:52 and Q61:14 very suggestive. Cf. also J. M. F. Van Reeth, "Le Prophète musulman en tant que Nâsir Allâh et ses antécédents: le 'Nazôraios' évangélique et le livre des Jubilés," *Orientalia Lovaniensia Periodica* 23 (1992): 251–274.

[8] The Qurʾānic concept of *shirk* ("associationism"), defined as the association of God with other divine powers, is sadly missing from

the Qurʾān understands as their covenant – in my view, their food laws especially. The *naṣārā* hence are behaving like most Late Antique Christians.

De Blois has taken the Qurʾān's accusation of associationism and its legislation on food laws as indication that the *naṣārā were* Judaeo-Christians, in line with the patristic reports of Judaeo-Christian "Nazarenes," a term indeed akin to the Arabic *naṣārā*.[9] Yet de Blois' valuable study neglects the fact that the Qurʾān, rather than describing them, legislates on the *naṣārā*. Griffith correctly points out that the rhetoric of the Qurʾān's view of Jesus "is seen to be polemically corrective," rather than descriptive of actual Christian views of Jesus.[10] The same holds true for the Qurʾān's view of purity. The Qurʾān's Christians did *not* observe "the Jewish laws of purity," as de Blois suggests they may have; instead, the Qurʾān enjoins Christians to observe the purity laws instituted by itself – as well as,

European languages (outside of the "associationism" in abstract algebra). On "associationism" and "associators" see Gerald Hawting, *The Idea of Idolatry and the Emergence of Islam: From Polemic to History* (Cambridge: Cambridge University Press, 1999); see also idem, "Idolatry and Idolaters," in McAuliffe (ed.), *Encyclopaedia of the Qurʾān*, ad loc. Missing here is Patricia Crone, "The Quranic *Mushrikūn* and the Resurrection (Part II)," *Bulletin of the School of Oriental and African Studies* 76 (2013), 1–20; eadem, "The Quranic *Mushrikūn* and the Resurrection (Part I)," *Bulletin of the School of Oriental and African Studies* 75 (2012): 445–472; and eadem, "The Religion of the Qurʾānic Pagans: God and the Lesser Deities," *Arabica* 57 (2010), 151–200; see note 153.

[9] De Blois, "Naṣrānī (Ναζωραῖος) and ḥanīf (ἐθνικός)," esp. 11–6 and 25–7; see also Petri Luomanen, "Ebionites and Nazarenes," in Matt Jackson-McCabe (ed.), *Jewish Christianity Reconsidered* (Minneapolis, MN: Fortress Press, 2007), 81–118.

[10] Griffith, *The Bible in Arabic*, 33, reiterated more forcefully on 37.

incidentally, by the Didascalia's Judaeo-Christian group and by the Clementine Homilies.[11]

De Blois and Griffith adduce good evidence that the term *naṣārā* simply meant "Christian" in the usage of the "pagan" non-Christians in Persia and Syria (de Blois dismisses this evidence when it comes to the Qur'ān's *naṣārā*).[12] Both scholars also mention in passing the Talmudic use of the Hebrew term *nṣrym*, but neither considers the evidence for the most widespread use of any cognate to the Arabic term *naṣārā* in the time of the Qur'ān: the rabbinic so-called "blessing of the heretics," or *Birkat haMinim*.[13] The twelfth of the nineteen "blessings" in the rabbinic *Amidah* prayer is actually more of a curse. It asks for the uprooting of the *mlkwt zdwn*, the "empire of in-

---

[11] De Blois, "Naṣrānī (Ναζωραῖος) and ḥanīf (ἐθνικός)," 16. De Blois here suggests that "the picture that emerges is thus that at one stage, early in the history of Islam, Muslims, Jews and Nazoraeans all shared the same dietary restrictions" (ibid.), yet he takes this as the early stage before Muhammad's own abrogation of food laws. Rather, according to my reading of the Qur'ān, it holds that all three groups already *should* share the same dietary restriction since the coming of Jesus, as confirmed by Muhammad, only that the Jews and the Christians fall short of realizing it. See also page 160, note 5.

[12] See Griffith, "*Al-Naṣārā* in the Qur'ān," 302–6; De Blois, "Naṣrānī (Ναζωραῖος) and ḥanīf (ἐθνικός)," 1–15; see also Sebastian P. Brock, "From Antagonism to Assimilation: Syriac Attitudes to Greek Learning," in Nina Garsoïan *et al.* (eds.), *East of Byzantium: Syria and Armenia in the Formative Period* (Washington, DC: Dumbarton Oaks Center for Byzantine Studies, 1982), 17–34; and *idem*, "Christians in the Sasanid Empire: A Case of Divided Loyalties," in Stuart Mews (ed.), *Religion and national identity: papers read at the nineteenth summer meeting and the twentieth winter meeting of the Ecclesiastical History Society* (Oxford: Basil Blackwell, 1982), 1–19.

[13] De Blois correctly points out that the Talmudic evidence (mainly Babylonian Talmud *Ta'anit* 27b) is of limited relevance; see also Griffith, "*Al-Naṣārā* in the Qur'ān," 303.

solence," likely to be understood as the Byzantine Empire, thereby pointing to the "Christian" context of the curse. It also asks for the destruction of the *mynym* and the *nṣrym*, distinguishing between heretical Jews and gentile Christians.[14] The liturgical prominence of the prayer, recited daily in private and in Synagogues on Shabbat, points to the *Jewish* background of the Arabic term *naṣārā*, in addition to its Syriac Christian and pagan usage.

Jews, Christians, and pagans all use a cognate of *naṣārā* to mean Christian, not Judaeo-Christian. Griffith rightly sees the Qurʾān's *naṣārā* as mainstream Christians and correctly emphasizes the Qurʾān's portrayal of them as "polemically corrective." De Blois, however, is right in pointing out that the Qurʾān's *naṣārā* are *associated* with Judaeo-Christian food laws. Put simply, I submit for con-

[14] While the manuscript evidence for the actual wording of the "Birkat haMinim" dates to the post-Qurʾānic period, the consensus is that the wording, "may the *nṣrym* and the *mynym* immediately perish," had long been established; it is also part of almost all prayer books both from Palestine and from Babylonia. Ruth Langer convincingly argues that *nṣrym* means "Christians" (see eadem, *Cursing the Christians: A History of the Birkat HaMinim* (Oxford: Oxford University Press, 2012), 57–63; see also Yaakov Teppler, *Birkat haMinim: Jews and Christians in Conflict in the Ancient World* (TSAJ 120; Tübingen: Mohr Siebeck, 2007), esp. 48–61; cf. Reuven Kimelman, "'Birkat ha-minim' and the Lack of Evidence for an anti-Christian Jewish Prayer in Late Antiquity," in E.P. Sanders et al., *Jewish and Christian Self-Definition* (Philadelphia: University of Pennsylvania Press, 1981), 226–244. Note that *hnwṣry* is the rabbis' standard designation of Jesus from early on. On the term *mynym*, see Zellentin, *Rabbinic Parodies*, 172. Before the coming of Islam, the term *myn* shifted from denoting any non-rabbinic Jewish heresy to Jesus-belief and then even to gentile Christianity (then paralleling *nṣry*) without ever leaving behind any of the previous meanings. In the Islamic period, the term *myn* developed further to denote Karaites; see Langer, *Cursing the Christians*, 60.

sideration that the Qurʾān's main rebuke against the *naṣārā* is that they *are* Christians and thereby neglect the Judaeo-Christian ritual lawcode. God, it states, "loves those who keep pure" (Q2:222).

The textual triangle of the Qurʾān, the Didascalia, and the Clementine Homilies suggests that the Judaeo-Christian ritual lawcode would be commensurate with that of the Qurʾān and that some people within the established Jewish and Christian communities, but by no means the communities as a whole, observed these laws. This scenario does not prove, of course, the traditional Muslim narrative that Islam is the original form of worship endorsed by the historical Jesus. Yet it does suggest that anyone propounding such a view of Christianity in the seventh century of the Common Era would have something to offer in support of it; further, the broad overlap between the Qurʾānic and Judaeo-Christian lawcodes indicates that at least some of the historical claims of the Qurʾān are well worth considering from the point of view of critical historiography.

If the "upright nation" that the Qurʾān favors (whose practices it mostly confirms and then again alters in few but fundamental ways) believed in Jesus, and if some of its members stand in continuity with the Judaeo-Christian legal culture of the Didascalia and the gentile believers of the Clementine Homilies, then future studies may have to link the discussions about "Judaeo-Christianity" with those of "Islamic Origins" – first of all by presenting these terms and the methodologies associated with them as fundamentally flawed.[15] "Judaeo-Christian" is a term

[15] On the general importance of Judaeo-Christianity for the Qurʾān, see Gnilka, *Die Nazarener und der Koran*; Edouard-Marie

scholars developed based on ancient Christian heresiology. As a result, scholars tend to comb Late Antiquity in search of an elusive phenomenon that never quite seems to fit the categories they apply.[16] Indeed, the construct of "Judaeo-Christianity" either follows ancient heresiological paradigms or orients itself along the lines of Jewish and Christian ethnic, ritual, and theological categories. These categories were in turn developed by rabbis and church fathers precisely during their sustained attempt to separate their communities from each other and to ostracize anyone transgressing the newly established borders of orthodoxy.[17]

Gallez, *Le Messie et son prophète: aux origines de l'islam* (Versailles: Éditions de Paris, 2005); de Blois, "Elchasai – Manes – Muḥammad," 31–48; Pines, "Notes on Islam and on Arabic Christianity and Judaeo-Christianity," 135–52; and Youssef Durrah al-Haddad, *The Qur'an is a (Nazarite) Mission* (Jounieh: Librairie pauliste, 1969 [Arabic]; see also idem, *Al-ʾInjīl fī-l-Qurʾān* (Jounieh: Librairie pauliste, 1982 [Arabic]). Cf. also the Joseph Azzi, *Le prêtre et le prophète: Aux sources du Coran* (Trans. Maurice S. Garnier) (Paris: Maisonneuve et Larose, 2001), which is a translation of Abu Musa al-Hariri, *Priest and Prophet: Research on the Rise of Islam* (n.p., 1979) [Arabic, both published under pseudonyms]; and Schoeps, *Theologie und Geschichte des Judenchristentums*, 342; see also page 25, note 33 and page 79, note 4.

[16] Recent works on the topic include Edwin K. Broadhead, *Jewish Ways of Following Jesus: Redrawing the Religious Map of Antiquity* (WUNT 266; Tübingen: Mohr Siebeck, 2010); Oskar Skarsaune and Reidar Hvalvik (eds.), *Jewish Believers in Jesus: The Early Centuries* (Peabody, MA: Hendrickson Publishers, 2007); Peter J. Tomson and Doris Lambers-Petry (eds.), *The Image of the Judaeo-Christians in Ancient Jewish and Christian Literature* (Tübingen: Mohr Siebeck, 2003); and Simon Mimouni (ed.), *Le Judéo-christianisme dans tous ses états* (Paris: Éditions du Cerf, 2001). A more modest and in my view more fruitful approach is found in the volume edited by Matt Jackson-McCabe, *Jewish Christianity Reconsidered* (Minneapolis: Fortress Press, 2007).

[17] E.g. Iricinschi and Zellentin (eds.), *Heresy and Identity in*

These categories are particularly ill-suited to doing justice to the tradition of the communities that endorsed both Jesus' elevated status *and* the ritual lawcode I termed Judaeo-Christian – such as those who may have adhered to principles like those of the Didascalia's alleged converts from "the people," its Judaeo-Christian group, and the authors of the Clementine Homilies.[18] When seek-

Late Antiquity; Daniel Boyarin, *Border Lines: The Partition of Judaeo-Christianity* (Philadelphia: University of Pennsylvania Press, 2004); cf. idem, "Rethinking Jewish Christianity: An Argument for Dismantling a Dubious Category (to which is Appended a Correction of my Border Lines)," *Jewish Quarterly Review* 99 (2009): 7–36.

[18] The methodological problems associated with the construction of Judaeo-Christianity both as a concept and as a distinct group are exacerbated when transferring the discussion to the issue of Islamic origins. Griffith's trenchant criticism is worth quoting in full: "Heretofore researchers have identified a number of different Christian communities as the likely [Qurʾānic] Christians whose views they have found reflected in the Qurʾān. For the most part, their methodology has been first to articulate what they take to be the Qurʾān's own Christology, and consequent theology, and then to match it with the creedal formulae and reports of the beliefs of some historically attested earlier Christian community, usually much earlier than the seventh century and usually not otherwise known to have been in the Arabic-speaking milieu of the Qurʾān's own day. The problem for these scholars has then been to advance a rationale for how the chosen community could have been present to the nascent Islamic community, whose scripture then, on the usual hypothesis, adopted the chosen Christian community's Christological and theological position" (idem, "al-Naṣārā in the Qurʾān: A Hermeneutical Reflection," 312). Griffith rightly points to the lack of independent communities, but ignores the persistence of evidence of "Judaeo-Christianity" within established Jewish and Christian groups, and especially the continuity of Judaeo-Christian law and ritual. In my view, the legal culture we see directly and indirectly attested in the Didascalia and in the Clementine Homilies serves as one of the legal outsets of the Qurʾān; the explicit and implicit testimony of the Qurʾān in turn corroborates the ongoing presence of this culture in the Arabic-speaking milieu of its

ing to understand "Judaeo-Christianity," we should rely on testimony closer to the Judaeo-Christian insider's and close Christian and early Muslim outsider's perspectives offered to varying degrees in the Clementine Homilies, the Didascalia, and the Qur'ān. Given the broad continuity between the practices described in these texts, it may make as much sense to call the Judaeo-Christian observances "proto-Muslim" as it does to state that the Qur'ān presupposes familiarity with "Judaeo-Christian" practice. Both statements are defensible, yet both bear the danger of side-tracking the primary discussion – about what people practiced and believed where and when – by a premature focus on name-calling, which should be postponed until the evidence is sifted more thoroughly. Regardless of the terminology we use, it seems that Muhammad kept alive part of the Jesus movement that Christianity did not.

The term "Judaeo-Christianity," of course, will not go away simply because it is a fuzzy remnant of ancient religious polemics.[19] For the time being, I therefore embraced

time. The ongoing development of Judaeo-Christian literature past the fourth century, as discussed by Reed and others (see above page 97, note 32), as well as the spread of the Didascalia and the Clementine Homilies in all languages and cultures surrounding the Arabian Peninsula, are in my view sufficient proof of the near-certainty that the texts were part of the oral discourse in seventh-century Arabia. This does not prove a distinct community, but points to a Judaeo-Christian legal culture within groups of Jews and Christians under the rule of rabbis and bishops to whom I will return in the epilogue.

[19] The history of scholarship regarding the term "Gnosticism" may demonstrate the limits that apply to our liberty to do away with a term like "Judaeo-Christianity." In 1996, Michael Williams rightfully sought to eliminate the category, showing how ill-suited it is to describing the texts of the Nag Hammadi library; see idem, *Rethinking "Gnosticism": An Argument for Dismantling a Dubious Category*

it and tried to specify what it means for the sake of a more efficient argument: the endorsement by gentile believers in Jesus of ritual purity beyond the strictures of the Decree of the Apostles. In this broad sense, then, the Qurʾān emancipates itself from a Judaeo-Christian *nomos* that can be reconstructed with the help of the Didascalia's alleged "Judaeo-Christian" group and the Clementine Homilies.

It is this Judaeo-Christian legal culture that the Qurʾān takes as one of its points of departure – yet the Qurʾān at the same time abrogates such Judaeo-Christian legal culture by modifying views on key issues such as the direction of prayer and the celebration of festivals, issues which carve out the Qurʾān's independent self-identity. This identity, needless to say, simultaneously sets the Qurʾānic community apart from rabbinic Jews and from the practices of those Christians who likewise rejected Jewish festivals, but who celebrated their belief in Jesus' divinity with Passover and the Eucharist. I would like to stress one more time that the necessary emphasis on continuity of law and narrative in the present study should not be perceived as undermining the fundamental independence of Qurʾānic

---

(Princeton: Princeton University Press, 1996). No consensus, however, has materialized following his efforts; instead, in 2003, Karen King reinvigorated the category of Gnosticism and reconstructed it based on insiders' testimony, carefully distinguishing between "Sethian" and "Valentinian" strands of Gnosticism; see eadem, *What Is Gnosticism?* (Cambridge, MA: Belknap Press of Harvard University Press, 2003). A similar attempt, i.e. a reconstruction of "Jewish" vs. "gentile" strands of Judaeo-Christianity, perhaps better termed "Christian Judaism" and "Jewish Christianity," would now seem possible based on texts such as the Clementine Homilies, the Didascalia and the Qurʾān. What remains clear is that the nominalist perspective is extremely limited; the Judaeo-Christian ritual lawcode seems a more stable basis for our inquiry.

thought. To the contrary, the more one reads the Qur'ān in light of the Didascalia and the Didascalia in light of the Qur'ān, the more familiar both sound; the more familiar they sound, the more we can appreciate, against the background of a shared legal culture, how distinct and distinctive each text really is.

The Qur'ān in Light of Late Antiquity – and Late Antiquity in Light of the Qur'ān

The close legal commonalities between the Qur'ān and the Didascalia here presented have, to the best of my knowledge, been noted only very partially in previous scholarship. The core of the evidence is a simple comparison of the selection of biblical laws and narratives endorsed by both texts. Detractors from my arguments may well bring evidence that the Didascalia, far from being a unique document, simply constitutes evidence of "orthodox" Late Antique Syriac Christianity, and that finding Christian aspects in the Qur'ān is hardly noteworthy. Such people would not be entirely misguided in my view, for the Didascalia certainly constitutes evidence of some type of Christianity, even if we have a hard time locating it more precisely before the seventh century. The precise role of the Didascalia in Syriac patristic discourse over the early centuries is a question that will hopefully be revisited. Yet the only argument that would fully dislodge the Didascalia (be it in Syriac or in a lost Arabic or Ethiopic translation) from a central place in future historical discussions of the Qur'ān's legal culture would be to point to another document that would cluster, arrange, and inflect laws and narratives in a way as closely related as those of the Qur'ān and the Didascalia are to each other. Since I consider the Didascalia as the best, but by no means as a full witness to the legal culture of the Qurʾān, I am inclined to believe that many such documents may well once have existed, though I am not sure traces of any of them would have been preserved.

The evidence of the Judaeo-Christian lawcode – the further development of the Decree of the Apostles – is more complex. Attributed to the formerly Jewish believers in the Didascalia, and corroborated as gentile practices by the Clementine Homilies and by the Qurʾān, these laws show a stable set of legal observances (in addition to the Decree of the Apostles) from the fourth century at the latest to the seventh: ritual washing after intercourse and before prayer, the prohibition of intercourse during the menses, the strict and expanded prohibition of carrion, and the avoidance of pork. Momentous on their own, the specific continuities of Judaeo-Christian ritual law are provided with a robust context by the broader continuity of law and narrative between the Didascalia and the Qurʾān.

This continuity should lead scholars of Late Antique religions to reassess the evidence for "Judaeo-Christianity" especially past the fourth century. My argument for the persistence of Judaeo-Christian legal culture as a discourse disembedded from specific independent churches or synagogues surely is messy. The alternative minimalist and maximalist readings of the evidence – either the complete disappearance of Judaeo-Christianity or the existence of hidden Judaeo-Christian communities in the sands of Arabia – have the advantage of apparent clarity. Yet the price of dismissing as irrelevant the ample evidence of a persisting Judaeo-Christian legal culture, or in turn of the

Christian, rabbinic, and Qur'ānic silence on any distinct group, seems too high. The Judaeo-Christian lawcode is complex enough to allow us to posit legal continuity, but it is also simple and unobtrusive enough to be maintained by any number of people in a given Christian community without attracting negative responses by higher authorities – who, after all, could well be following similar practices. The emphatic endorsement of ritual purity *per se* by Athanasius of Bālād, discussed in the Introduction, is not a long way off from its importance in the Clementine Homilies or in the Qur'ān.

In terms of law, the present study may therefore make as much of a difference for the study of Late Antiquity as for the study of the Qur'ān. The Qur'ān often explicates its continuity with the preceding tradition; we can now simply affirm this claim to a certain degree. The suggestion here that the Qur'ān's legal material seems to stand in dialogue with a concrete contemporaneous legal corpus, however, may well contribute to the discussion of the internal dating of the Qur'ān's surahs. For the fact that much of its legal materials are preserved in its longer surahs, traditionally seen as later and as "Medinan" surahs, dovetails nicely with the plausible scenario of the emerging Muslim community's interaction with concrete bodies of Christian, Judeao-Christian, and rabbinic law. The Qur'ān's internal abrogations as well as its abrogation of previous law (as briefly discussed regarding the cases of alms, prayer, and festivals) may be more open to a more concrete historical contextualization.

In terms of understanding legal narrative, it is clearly our reading of the Qur'ān that may benefit from the present study, as it is benefitting from the evidence of Jacob of Serugh and other Syriac authors. In the case of the original giving of the law, the punishment of the Israelites with further laws after their sins, and of Jesus' (and in turn Muhammad's) abrogation of these further laws, we have seen that the Didascalia bears much explanatory potential for the Qurʾān.

This explanatory potential is the result of the Qurʾān's allusive nature – it implies that its audience is familiar with a broad spectrum of Jewish and Christian traditions, to which it often responds forcefully. The Didascalia presents an important source for such narratives and legal traditions, yet its importance should not be considered as exclusive. I maintain, and have repeatedly evoked the plausible relevance of many of the traditional explanations of Qurʾānic law. In the epilogue, I will sketch another brief example of the simultaneous importance of the rabbinic tradition.

The present study, hence, does not offer any simple answers on such questions as the origins of Islam or the persistence of Judaeo-Christian groups. The Qurʾān clearly stands in intimate dialogue with mainstream rabbis and Christians, as the historical evidence would suggest in any case. With the help of the Didascalia and the Clementine Homilies, we can reconstruct with more specificity a Judaeo-Christian legal culture that the Qurʾān endorses. Yet it is clear at the same time that these two texts are not themselves literary sources for the Qurʾān in any form. It is the triangle of all three texts that allows us to understand an otherwise lost Judaeo-Christian legal culture – a culture whose very existence is in my view the most important result of this study.

Epilogue

The Qurʾān between Christianity and Rabbinic Judaism

The triangular relationship in the above title posits that the Qurʾān, much like the Judaeo-Christian tradition, should best be conceived of as situating itself in between Christianity and rabbinic Judaism. The Qurʾān engaged in a multi-vocal dialogue with a varied selection of its contemporaries, be they Jewish, Christian, Zoroastrian, Mandean, Samaritan, or Manichean. My emphasis on the pertinence of the Didascalia for the construction of the Qurʾān's interlocutors, to the degree here suggested, may well be read as presuming a sterile exchange between two parties, or worse, between two texts. Understanding my readings this way would surely miss my point (as the many references to other Christian and especially rabbinic voices throughout this book will hopefully have shown). One could indeed bring countless examples of the importance of rabbinic, other Christian, and other biblical and post-biblical literature to the understanding of the Qurʾān. Yet I do, in fact, argue that Judaeo-Christian legal culture, as reconstructible with the help of the Didascalia, the Clementine Homilies, and the Qurʾān itself, holds a central place among the direct interlocutors of the longer surahs of the Qurʾān, often attributed to its "Medinan" period of composition.

My claim does not discount the equally privileged pertinence of the broader Aramaic tradition for the understanding of the Qurʾān's narratives and theology. On the contrary, the importance of this tradition becomes ever more apparent in present scholarship – writings such as those of Philoxenus of Mabbug and of Jacob of Serugh have not yet been fully explored in their own contexts, let alone in their Qurʾānic reception history. The Qurʾān, likewise, cannot be historically understood in ignorance of the rabbinic tradition. This epilogue – in its focus on more technical philology than is found in the rest of this volume – is set out to extend the discussion to include the rabbis more fully as interlocutors with the Qurʾān, both balancing and enhancing the role I attribute to the Didascalia's Christians.

One last set of examples illustrates the perhaps crucial, though by no means exclusive, position of the Didascalia for our reconstruction of the Qurʾān's legal culture. The following discussion shows how the Qurʾān positions itself vis-à-vis the Didascalia's Christian hierarchy next to that of its second central interlocutor: the *yahūd* (e.g. Q5:18) or *allaḏīna hādū* (Q6:146, see also Q2:62 and Q6:26), the rabbinic Jews.[1] The Qurʾān's longer surahs engage the rab-

[1] Note that elsewhere the Didascalia understands the word "Jews" in an active sense to be a "confessor" (*mwdynwtʾ*), even though they do not "confess" (*mwdynʾ*, DA XIII, 150.15–6) the killing of Christ – a word play that must have originated in a Semitic language and is accordingly missing from the Latin. There is some grammatical resemblance of the Didascalia's folk etymology and the Qurʾānic verbal forms denoting "to be Jewish" such as *allaḏīna hādū*. According to Horovitz, these terms denote an active self-identification with Judaism ("sich zum Judentum bekennen;" see idem, *Koranische Untersuchungen*, 153); one may equally consider the Hebrew and Syriac verb *yhd*, denoting conversion to Judaism (see Sokoloff, *Syriac Dictionary*, 567). The context in the Qurʾān, however, does not allow a distinction

binic Jews in intimate dialogue as the other group, together with the Christians, the *naṣārā*, that comprises the "people of the book." Furthermore, as we have seen already, the Qurʾān employs a number of rabbinic teachings.[2]

In the following example, I will suggest a reading strategy for the Qurʾān that may be applicable to many of the instances in which the text *simultaneously* relates to its contemporaneous Jewish and Christian traditions. As I have sketched above e.g. in the case of the patriarchs' observance of the Torah *avant la lettre*, most Qurʾānic references to the traditions of "the people of the book" are twofold, combining a critique of the rabbis with a critique of Christianity.[3] Initially, the Qurʾān's apparent divergenc-

---

between Jews and converts. See Uri Rubin, "Jews and Judaism," in McAuliffe (ed.), *Encyclopaedia of the Qurʾān*, ad loc.

[2] See already page 152, note 31; see also Mishna *Sanhedrin* 4:5 and Q5:32. A full discussion of the often polemical Qurʾānic use of rabbinic teachings remains a desideratum to which I hope to respond in due course. For a good summary, see Reuven Firestone, "Jewish Culture in the Formative Period of Islam," in David Biale (ed.) *Cultures of the Jews: A New History* (New York: Schocken Books, 2002), 267–302, and the classical piece by Shlomo Dov Goitein, "Who were the notable teachers of Muhammad? (Offering a new solution for an old problem)," *Tarbiz* 23 (1951/52): 146–59 [Hebrew]. The most prolific scholar on the Jews of Arabia is undoubtedly the student of Meir Jacob Kister, Michael Lecker; see for example his collection of articles *Jews and Arabs in Pre- and Early Islamic Arabia* (Aldershot: Ashgate, 1998). In my view, the early Muslim historiography cannot be dismissed, but must be read with more caution than Lecker tends to do, as is perhaps most apparent in idem, *The 'Constitution of Medina': Muḥammad's First Legal Document* (Princeton, NJ: Darwin Press, 2004).

[3] See pages 162–3. Further examples illustrating the simultaneous pertinence of rabbinic and Judaeo-Christian traditions will appear in the framework of my contributions to the *Notre Dame Qurʾān Seminar*; for publication details see page XXII, note 3.

es from rabbinic and Christian teachings may be perceived as vague polemics or as indicative of a lack of precise familiarity with these traditions. Closer consideration, however, allows us to see that the Qurʾān's simultaneous dialogue with rabbinic literature displays the same precision we saw when the Qurʾān addresses the oral tradition encapsulated by the Didascalia.

I will seek to illustrate how the Qurʾān's intentional distortion of rabbinic tradition generates a polemical message for those who can tell the difference. Most importantly, considering that the Qurʾān deals with its two most central interlocutors in the same way allows us to transfer insights between the ways in which it engages both, as in the following verse:

> The Jews and the Christians (*an-naṣārā*) say:
> "We are God's sons (*ʾabnāʾu-llāhi*), and his beloved ones (*ʾaḥibbāʾuhū*)."
> Say: "Then why does He punish you for your sins?
> Rather you are humans from among His creatures." (Q5:18)

The Qurʾān here laments that the Jews and the Christians call themselves "sons of God;" elsewhere, it charges that the Christians call Jesus this.[4] In my view, the Qurʾān here addresses both the rabbinic and the Christian oral traditions with great precision and patent familiarity: the rabbis indeed explicitly state that "Israelites are beloved (*ḥbybyn*) as they are called 'the sons (*bnym*) of God'" (Mishna *Avot* 3:14).[5] The pertinent Christian tradition can

[4] For the Quran's polemics against portraying God as a father, see also Q2:116–117; Q10:68–69; Q17:111; Q19:88–95; Q23:91; Q43:81–83; and Q72:3.

[5] Mishna *Avot* 3:14 is quoting Deuteronomy 14:1 as proof. For divine sonship, see also Exodus 4:22, Shemot Rabbah 33:17, Bemid-

again best be reconstructed with the help of the Didascalia, which addresses its members explicitly as "sons of God" (e.g. *bnwhy d'lh'* in DA II, 14.15 or *bny' … d'lh'* in DA XI, 129.15) and its audience as "beloved sons" (*bnyn ḥbyb'*, DA VI, 70.5).[6] The Qur'ān seems aware of this broad overlap of traditions and, when it accuses the Jews and Christians of claiming divine "sonship" for themselves, it reflects these teachings accurately enough to generate a precise message of polemical difference. What is the sonship worth, the Qur'ān asks, if it does not protect from punishment?

Elsewhere, the Qur'ān again accuses the Jews and Christians by polemicizing against the role of two official titles whose precise nature has yet to be determined:

They have taken their *'aḥbārahum* and their *ruhbānahum* as lords (*'arbāban*) besides God,

---

bar Rabbah 9:14, but see Bereshit Rabbah 26:5 for rabbinic polemics against *individual* claims to being a son of God. See also Zellentin, *Rabbinic Parodies*, 201–2 and 213–36 and Peter Schäfer, *The Jewish Jesus: How Judaism and Christianity Shaped Each Other* (Princeton: Princeton University Press, 2012), 150–9 and idem, *Jesus in the Talmud*, 49. For Israel as beloved, see also Shemot Rabbah 27:9, Midrash Zuta Shir haShirim 3:4, and Pesikta Rabbati 20:3.

[6] Note that the full phrase in DA II, 14.15 is "servants and sons of God" (*'bdwh bnwhy d'lh'*). While the Qur'ān rejects the language of divine sonship, it calls the faithful "servants of God" (*'ibāda-llāhi*, Q37:40; see also Q37:74, 128, 160, 169, and Q44:18). Communal claims to divine sonship are of course not exclusive to the Didascalia, but reflect a Matthean tradition; see Matthew 5:9 and Marcus, "The *Testaments of the Twelve Patriarchs* and the *Didascalia Apostolorum*," 611–12. Most notably, just as God the Father has become a central element of the Jewish and Christian liturgy, the Didascalia equally depicts God and the bishop as fathers and Jesus, as well as any male member of its community, as a "Son of God" (*br' l'lh'*, DA IX, 109.16); see also the similar wording in chapters DA X, DA XVIII, and DA XXI.

and also the Messiah, Mary's son,
though they were commanded to worship only one God
There is no god except Him;
He is far too immaculate
To have any partners that they associate (*yušrikūna*) with Him (Q9:31).

On the surface, the Qurʾān here seems merely to polemicize against attributing lofty status to religious leaders, the *ʾaḥbār* and *ruhbān*. The Qurʾān likely turns the table on Christians by echoing the tradition of Matthew, who depicts Jesus as denouncing those who like to be called "lord," "*rby*" (Peshitta on Matthew 23:7–8). This tradition is also recorded in the Clementine Homilies' statement that there is no salvation in "believing in teachers (διδασκάλοις) and calling them lords (κυρίους)" (Clementine Homilies 8:5). In addition, however, the Qurʾān engages both sides of the porous linguistic border between Aramaic and Arabic by simultaneously addressing its own audience and its adversaries in their own respective idioms. A close reading first of the rabbinic literature and then of the Didascalia will illustrate the Qurʾān's strategy in addressing its interlocutors and help us determine the identity of the *ʾaḥbār* and *ruhbān*, as well as allowing us historically to contextualize the charges leveled against these figures. This literary and philological inquiry will allow us once more to situate the Qurʾān more precisely vis-à-vis the Didascalia and the rabbinic literature.

Taking the ʾaḥbār *as lords beside God*

As has long been observed, the term the Qurʾān uses above to designate the Jewish dignitaries, *ʾaḥbār* (often translated as "scribes"), is a term known from the rabbinic tradition. There, the Aramaic *ḥbry* or the Hebrew *ḥbrym* are members of the rabbinic movement, suggesting that the Qurʾān uses an insiders' term.[7] Moreover, while "rabbis" are not named explicitly in the passage cited, the Qurʾān elsewhere associates the *ʾaḥbār* with the rabbis (see Q5:44 and 64), indicating that the audience should consider both titles here as well: that is, the accusation of taking the *ʾaḥbār* as "lords," *ʾarbāban*, evokes the very title "rabbi."

The fact that the Aramaic and Arabic root for "lord," *rb*, denotes both God and the rabbis then leads to the Qurʾān's first message: the title rabbi is already hubristic.[8]

---

[7] In Aramaic, the term *ḥbr* often denotes a *rabbinic* "colleague;" see Sokoloff, *A Dictionary of Jewish Babylonian Aramaic*, 428–9 and idem, *A Dictionary of Jewish Palestinian Aramaic*, 184. In Hebrew, the term can also denote a member of a pious group within the rabbinic movement; in Syriac, it only denotes a friend or "another" more generally (see idem, *A Syriac Lexicon*, 410). How far the Hebrew is pertinent here depends on the weight one wants to attribute to the Qurʾānic evidence for the rabbinic usage of this term in seventh-century Arabia – a topic that can hardly be addressed here (but see pages 213–4). Note that the Qurʾān's term for "rabbis," *rabbāniyyūna*, is a plural whose formation is also cognate to one of the Aramaic plural forms for "rabbi," *rbnn*. See Abraham Geiger, *Was hat Mohammed aus dem Judenthume aufgenommen?* (Bonn: Baaden, 1833), 49–50; Horovitz, *Koranische Untersuchungen*, 63.

[8] Note that *rb* in Aramaic and Syriac can also denote the deity or divine epithets; e.g. *'lh' rb'* ("great God," Bavli *Sanhedrin* 96a; see Sokoloff, *A Dictionary of Jewish Babylonian Aramaic*, 1052), *rbwn kl 'lmy'* ("Lord of the universe," i.e. God, M. L. Klein, *Genizah Manuscripts of the Palestinian Targum to the Pentateuch* (Cincinnati: Hebrew Union College Press, 1986) on Genesis 38:24, cited by Sokoloff, *A Dictionary of Jewish Palestinian Aramaic*, 513). On the meanings of *rb* in Syriac, see below. As Joseph Witztum reminds me, *rb* can of course also denote a secular lord in Qurʾānic Arabic, especially in Q12.

The Qur'ān hence accuses the rabbis of perhaps the most outrageous variant of *shirk*, of associating another deity with God: it accuses them of playing gods themselves.[9] This charge of course seems flatly to contradict the monotheism of the rabbinic corpus.[10] Would the Qur'ān have

[9] On the Qur'ānic concept of *shirk* ("associationism") and of the "associators" see above, page 190–1, note 8.

[10] Similarly, the Qur'ān's charge that the Jews call *ʿUzayr* the son of God (Q9:30) or that the Christians deify Mary along with Jesus (Q5:116) as part of the Trinity may not be based on either Qur'ānic misapprehension or on peculiarities of Arab Judaism and Christianity (which certainly existed; see Epiphanius' often noted description of Arabian Collyridianism in *Panarion* 79), but may rather be based on subtle polemics. The infancy gospels, for example, exalt Mary in a way that is only minimally shy of her deification; similarly, it does not take a giant leap to recast Mary's Byzantine status of *theotokos* as anthropolatry; see Averil Cameron, "The Cult of the Virgin in Late Antiquity: Religious Development and Myth-Making," in Robert N. Swanson (ed.), *The Church and Mary* (Woodbridge: Boydell Press, 2004), 1–21, and Jaroslav Pelikan, *Mary Through the Centuries: Her Place in the History of Culture* (New Haven: Yale University Press, 1996), 55. As Griffith concisely puts it, "the underlying problem here, in my view, is to have mistaken the Qur'an's religious critique of Christian beliefs and practices, and the polemical rhetoric in which it is expressed, for historical reports or accounts of these same beliefs and practices" (idem, "al-Naṣārā in the Qur'ān: A Hermeneutical Reflection;" see also Griffith's useful comments on the Qur'ān's view of the trinity in ibid., "Syriacisms in the 'Arabic Qur'ān'" and in ibid., *The Bible in Arabic*, 29–36). See also Neuwirth, *Der Koran als Text der Spätantike*, 723–768. Likewise, one could see in the alleged rabbinic praise for *ʿUzayr* an exaltation akin to that of Mary (see G. D. Newby, *A History Of The Jews Of Arabia*, 59). If this person denotes the traditional Ezra (rather than an angelic figure), one could consider that in Fourth Ezra (14:9), God states that Ezra would "live with my Son and with those who are like you, until the times are ended" (see also Fourth Ezra 14:14, and Horovitz, *Koranische Untersuchungen*, 127f; Fourth Ezra was widely circulating in various

expected its audience really to believe that the rabbis saw themselves as "lords beside God"?

A close reading of the above cited surah in dialogue with the rabbinic tradition suggests that at least part of the Qurʾān's audience would have grasped a reference to very specific rabbinic tradition; the reference would then generate the Qurʾān's message as precise polemical hyperbole. To reiterate, in the preserved literature, explicit self-deification is not known as a hallmark of rabbinic Judaism. To the contrary, God ostentatiously flogs an angel just because a rabbi mistook it as a deity. The rabbi may well be a stand-in for mystically or Christian-inclined Jews, yet the flogging drives home the point of the unity of God regardless.[11]

While it may seem at first sight that the Qurʾān does not grasp the theology of its adversaries, consideration of the rabbinic tradition allows for a deeper understanding: indeed, the deification of *ʾaḥbār* and of rabbis reflects the Qurʾān's polemical engagement with rabbinic claims to authority. The following example from a rabbinic saying is widely attested in Palestine as well as in Babylonia and can therefore be safely assumed to be part of the rabbinic oral tradition:

---

languages in Qurʾānic times). For a recent discussion, see also Viviane Comerro, "Esdras est-il le fils de Dieu?," *Arabica* 52 (2005): 165–181.

[11] Bavli *Hagiga* 15a and Schäfer, *The Jewish Jesus*, 103–49. On Metatron in general, see Saul Lieberman, "Metatron: the Meaning of His Name and His Functions," in Ithamar Gruenwald (ed.), *Apocalyptic and Merkavah Mysticism* (Leiden: Brill, 1980), 235–241; for rabbinic polemics against individuals claiming divine sonship, see also page 206, note 5.

Rabbi El'azar ben Shammu'a says: "Let the honor of your disciple be as dear to you as your own, and the honor of your colleague (*ḥbr*) as the fear of your *rb*, and the fear of your *rb* as the fear of Heaven." (Mishna *Avot* 4.12)[12]

Rabbi El'azar defines the honor due to a teacher in typically climactic fashion, suggesting that each status of rabbinic society should be elevated by one step: disciples should be honored as equals, equals as teachers, and teachers as God. Within rabbinic discourse, there would be no danger here of confusing the subject of divine honor, one's teacher (*rb*), with God himself – the teacher is honored only since he embodies the rabbinic tradition that as a whole is endorsed by God. Yet the tradition, with which the Qur'ān seems familiar, is wide open for polemical recasting from a critical outside perspective. For the teachings of Q9:31 and of the rabbis overlap doubly, both associating both the roots *ḥbr* and *rb* with God ("heaven" in rabbinic parlance).[13]

The rabbinic tradition thereby allows us to correct our course towards assuming that the Qur'ān engages a specific Jewish saying known to its audience, which it criticizes without spelling it out. The Qur'ān very likely implies that its audience knows a tradition akin to the one preserved, which it criticizes through hyperbole. If so, the audience will understand the charge not as claiming that the Jews actually take the rabbinic "colleagues" to be "lords besides God." Instead, the charge is very precise: if one needs to

---

[12] See Mekhilta *Amaleq* 1, Yerushalmi *Nedarim* 9.1 (41b), 35–6, Bavli *Pesahim* 108a, Avoth de Rabbi Nathan 27, Tanhuma *Beshalah* (Warsaw) 26, Shemot Rabbah 3:17, cf. also Bavli *Nedarim* 41b and *Pesachim* 22b.

[13] See Sokoloff, *A Dictionary of Jewish Babylonian Aramaic*, 1157, and idem, *A Dictionary of Jewish Palestinian Aramaic*, 557.

fear the colleagues *as if* they were God, well, they may as well be thought of *as* God, leading to the said charge of *shirk*. Read against the rabbinic literature, the Qurʾān's charge becomes reasonable – which of course does not adjudicate the ultimately theological question whether the charge would have been justified or not.

In this case and others, the Qurʾān's divergence from rabbinic tradition seems not to be motivated by ignorance, but by issuing a "polemically corrective" statement, to use Griffith's felicitous term. In emphasizing that they should not be taken as "lords beside God," the Qurʾān by no means dismisses the authority of the rabbis and the *ʾaḥbār* as such. Elsewhere the Qurʾān explicitly states that they judged by the book and were charged to preserve it (Q5:44), even if it later complains that the rabbis and the *ʾaḥbār* do not exercise their authority properly (Q5:53).

The Qurʾān also charges that the rabbinic "colleagues," the *ʾaḥbār* (as well as the *ruhbān*, whose role is to be determined) "wrongfully eat up the people's wealth"

"O you who have faith!
Indeed many of the colleagues (*al-ʾaḥbāri*) and the *ruhbāni*
Wrongfully eat up the people's wealth,
And bar [them] from the way of God
Those who store up gold and silver
And do not spend it in the way of God
Inform them of a painful punishment." (Q9:34)

When it comes to the rabbinic *ḥbrym*, the accusations against the *ʾaḥbār* are plausible in light of rabbinic practice. Charges of abuse of the priestly tithe are as old as the practice itself, as the prophetic laments of the Hebrew Bible amply illustrate. Yet, after the destruction of the Temple, the tithes, originally reserved for priests and Levites, went increasingly to scholars, and the *ḥbrym* were especially scrupulous with respect to tithing.[14] While we do not know about Jewish practices in Arabia in the seventh century, these communal payments to the scholars (or at least the discourse about them) may well be the historical background against which we should read the accusation that the rabbinic officials misuse these funds. (The Qurʾān does not explicate its opposing idea of how these funds should be spent; likely it has charity in mind – as discussed in Chapter One – and simply opposes any accumulation of funds.) Likewise, much of the Qurʾān's engagement with rabbinic Judaism and Christianity is geared towards purging contemporaneous tradition from perceived transgression of a stringent stance on the first biblical commandment of avoiding *shirk*.

The example of deified rabbis is also helpful in adjusting our focus: just as in the case of the Didascalia, in no way should we assume that the Qurʾān makes direct use of rabbinic writing. The rabbinic saying cited above had become part of the broader Jewish tradition in the time of the Qurʾān; there is, however, no trace of direct contact between the Qurʾān and rabbinic literature. Rather, we should see both the Qurʾān and the rabbinic saying as reflecting an oral Jewish culture that stretched from Palestine to Sasanian Babylonia, as well as to the large area south of both lands, Arabia.[15] The cumulative evidence of allusions

---

[14] See e.g. Mishna *Demai* 4:1–6, Bavli *Gittin* 30b and A'hron Oppenheimer, "Terumot and Maʿaserot," in Michael Berenbaum and Fred Skolnik (eds.), *Encyclopaedia Judaica* (Detroit: Macmillan Reference, 2007) 19:652–654; see also above, page 209, note 7.

[15] See Newby, *The Jews of Arabia*, 33–77 and above, page 205, note 2.

to this and other rabbinic sayings suggests that the Qurʾān presumes its audience's familiarity with aspects of rabbinic traditions when the text challenges them. This also holds true for the Qurʾān's expectations towards its audience's knowledge of the Christian tradition. And in this, as in many other cases, the Qurʾān's critical references reflect a twofold engagement with both parties of "the people of the book," the rabbinic Jews and the Christians in the mold of the Didascalia. Few among the people of the book, as I discussed in the conclusion, are exempted from this criticism.

Taking the ruhbān *as lords beside God*

The Qurʾān's precise response to the rabbinic tradition in the previous examples invites an examination of whether the critical address to the Christians regarding their veneration of religious leaders reflects aspects of the Didascalia's tradition in similar terms. As we saw in Q9:31, in addition to accusing the Jews of taking their *ʾaḥbār* as lords besides God, the Qurʾān accuses Christians of taking their *ruhbān* as such. Further, after accusing the *ʾaḥbār*, the rabbinic officials, of wrongfully eating up the people's wealth, the Qurʾān in turn accuses the *ruhbān* of doing so. It seems, then, that the *ruhbān* held a position of esteem and fiscal authority in the Christian community akin to that of the *ʾaḥbār* in the rabbinic community. Just as was the case in the Qurʾān's use of rabbinic titles and teachings, we may be able to identify its use of Christian titles and teachings with the help of the Didascalia, which will again allow for a more precise reading of the Qurʾān's polemical engagement of contemporaneous Christians.

The term *ruhbān* can indeed be contextualized in relation to the Didascalia when considering the following Qur'ānic passage:

Surely you will find the most hostile people towards the faithful
to be the Jews (*al-yahūd*) and the associators (*allaḏīna 'ašrakū*)
and surely you will find the nearest of them in affection to the faithful
those who say "we are Christians (*naṣārā*)"
That is because there are *qissīsīna* and *ruhbānan* among them
And they are not arrogant.
When they hear what has been revealed to the Apostle,
You see their eyes fill with tears
Because of the truth they recognize. (Q5:82–3)

This verse makes it clear that, just as we encountered two titles of rabbinic officials, the Christians also seem to employ two titles: that of the *ruhbān* and that of the *qissīsīn*. As was the case with the rabbinic titles, the Qur'ān's positive evaluation here endorses the two offices designated by the two titles in principle at the same time as pointing to the undue veneration of their holders, as well as to the embezzlement of public funds.

The Qur'ān's term *qissīs*, often translated as "priest," has already been broadened to denote "elder;" this term is well-attested in Arabic inscriptions and ancient poetry and is akin to the Syriac *qšyš*.[16] In the Didascalia – as throughout much of the Christian tradition – "elders" are depicted as the church leadership, under the bishop:

[16] See Geiger, *Was hat Mohammed*, 50–1 and especially Horovitz, *Koranische Untersuchungen*, 64. For the Syriac term, see Sokoloff, *A Syriac Dictionary*, 1419–20.

And for the elders (*lqšyšʾ*) let there be separated a place on the eastern side of the house, and let the chair of the bishop (*dʾpysqwpʾ*) be among them and let the elders (*qšyšʾ*) sit with him.
(DA XII, 143.23–5)

Indeed, the Didascalia portrays the bishop as the head of the council of elders; the two offices are codependent throughout the text:

But concerning the bishops, hear likewise. The shepherd (*rʿyʾ*) is who is appointed bishop (*ʾpysqwpʾ*) and head among the council of elders (*bqšyšwtʾ*) in the church and in every congregation.
(DA IV, 52.6–7)

The church leadership hence is made up of a group of elders who are headed by a bishop, a common Christian structure at least since the time of Ignatius of Antioch, similarly endorsed by the Clementine Homilies.[17] Each time that the Didascalia mentions the elders, it actually does so in conjunction with the bishop to whom they are ranked second. In chapters IX, XI, and XII, the Didascalia specifies the roles and privileges of these two offices, together with those of the various lesser roles in the church, such as deacon, subdeacon and lector. It is important to note that the Didascalia presupposes a very local ecclesiastical struc-

[17] The ecclesiastical hierarchy of the Clementine Homilies, like that of the Didascalia, consists of the bishop, elders, deacons, and widows; see Clementine Homilies 3:64–7 and 11:36; see also 7:5 and 20:23. The Homilies' endorsement of such a hierarchy invites us in turn to speculate whether Judaeo-Christian tendencies would have been found among all strata of Christian society, or whether the Qurʾān's positive image of elders would in turn shed light on this question. There is, however, not enough evidence to sustain such an inquiry.

ture: every congregation has a bishop, who is a married man, but no higher office is mentioned.[18]

Given this description of the church leadership as a bishop surrounded by a council of elders, the intriguing possibility arises that we can use the Didascalia in order to understand the Qurʾān's two titles for Christian officials. We have seen that despite its close affinity with much of the Didascalia, the Qurʾān seems to make no reference to the bishopric – indeed, ecclesiastical hierarchy is the one element of the Didascalia's teaching that so far seemed conspicuously absent from the Qurʾān's engagement with this tradition. Given the attestation of Arabian bishops for centuries before the Qurʾān, the silence is noteworthy.[19] Does the Qurʾān, when speaking about the elders (*qissīsīna*) and *ruhbān*, assume its audience's knowledge of the Didascalia's hierarchy that places the bishop as the first among the elders (*qšyšʾ*)? The answer depends on the meaning of the term *ruhbān*, or *rāhib* in the (post-Qurʾānic) singular. If we are to answer the question in the positive, then we can relate the Qurʾān's legal culture in one further aspect to the legal culture of the Didascalia.

---

[18] On church hierarchy in the Didascalia, see also Wayne Meeks, "Social and Ecclesial Life of the Early Christians," in Margaret M. Mitchel and Frances M. Young (eds.), *The Cambridge History of Christianity: Origins to Constantine* (Cambridge: Cambridge University Press, 2006), 145–73; Georg Schöllgen, *Die Anfänge der Professionalisierung des Klerus und das kirchliche Amt in der syrischen Didaskalie* (Münster: Aschendorff, 1998); and Allen Brent, "The Relations between Ignatius and the Didascalia," *The Second Century* 8 (1991), 1–29.

[19] See Theresia Hainthaler, *Christliche Araber vor dem Islam* (Leuven: Peeters, 2007); see also page 190, note 7.

The term *rāhib* is well-attested in Arabic inscriptions and poetry where it is usually understood to denote "monk" or "anchorite." This reading makes good sense as a possible meaning in Late Antique Arabic; given the spread of monasticism, monks were as prominent in Arabia as bishops, and the Qurʾān elsewhere speaks of monks' cells (*ṣawāmiʿ*, Q22:40).[20] Likewise, the two charges of the Qurʾān – that the *ruhbān* were venerated as if they were God and that they misused funds – can easily be related to the broader evidence: monks were often accused of embezzlement; and there is no shortage of evidence for the Christian veneration of holy men, which can easily appear excessive to outsiders.[21] There is hence no doubt – and no way to disprove – that the term *ruhbān* can denote monks. Yet a closer reading of the respective Qurʾānic passages in dialogue with the Didascalia and with the rabbinic tradition suggests that one should at least broaden the term's meaning to include church officials such as the Didascalia's bishops, as has been proposed by Abraham Geiger and confirmed by de Blois.

---

[20] See Griffith, *The Bible in Arabic*, 12; idem, "Monasticism and Monks," in McAuliffe (ed.) *Encyclopaedia of the Qurʾān*, ad loc.; Horovitz, *Koranische Untersuchungen*, 64; and the extensive discussion in Jane Dammen McAuliffe, *Qurʾānic Christians: An Analysis of Classical and Modern Exegesis* (Cambridge: Cambridge University Press, 1991), 221–37.

[21] See e.g. Peter Brown's substantial article, "Holy Men," in Averil Cameron et al(eds.), *The Cambridge Ancient History. Volume 14: Late antiquity: Empire and successors, A.D. 425–600* (Cambridge: Cambridge University Press, 2000), 781–810; for a central text depicting the veneration of a holy man, see Robert Doran (ed. and trans.), *The Lives of Simeon Stylites* (Kalamazoo: Cistercian Publications, 1992; see also the Introduction by Susan Ashbrook-Harvey).

To begin with, the bishops and the elders, just like the rabbis, were the recipients of the tithes in their respective communities; and they were seen as comparable to God, as the Didascalia often repeats, e.g. as follows:[22]

Indeed, great power, heavenly, that of the Almighty, is given to [the bishop]. Nevertheless, love the bishop and be afraid of him (*wdḥlyn*) as of a king, and honor him as God (*dl'lh'*). Your fruits and the works of your hands present to him, so that you may be blessed. Your first fruits and your tenths and your vows and your oblations give to him. For it is required that he may be sustained from them, and that he may provide also for those who are in want, to each as it is right for him. (DA IX, 111.22–112.8.)

But today the offerings that are presented through the bishops to the Lord God, for they are your high priests (*rby khnykwn*).... [The bishop] is a servant (*mšmšn'*) of the word and mediator (*wtlyty'*), but to you a teacher, and your father after God ... This is your chief (*ryškwn*) and your leader and he is a mighty king (*wmlk'*) to you. He guides in the place of the Almighty (*'ḥyd kl*). But let him be honored (*myqr*) by you as God, because the bishop sits for you in the place of the Almighty God (*'lh' 'ḥyd kl*) ....
(DA IX, 103.15–25)[23]

---

[22] See also Ignatius' *Letter to the Magnesians* and Didache 4:1, as already noted by Marmorstein, "Judaism and Christianity in the Middle of the Third Century," 232 [10], note 46; Marmorstein also notes the affinity between the Didascalia and the rabbis on bestowing divine honors on their leaders. See also page 88, note 14.

[23] The Qur'ān's accusation of Jewish and Christian anthropolatry becomes even more poignant when considering the Didascalia's attributes for the bishop in the previous quotation, such as "teacher," "king," and "father." The first two terms can both evoke divine attributes in the Qur'ān (even though both are also used in a secular context, as Joseph Witztum reminds me), one of them even homophonously (*malik* e.g. Q59:23, 20:114, for "teacher;" see Q2:31). Associating the terms with a bishop rather than with God seems therefore especially outrageous; the Qur'ān likewise explicitly and repeatedly dismisses God's role as father; see page 207, note 6.

The bishops, like the rabbis, thus receive tithes and their authority is compared to that of God. Given the close parallels with the treatment of the rabbinic literature with respect to Q9:31 – the bishops' portrayal in association with the elders, their God-like veneration and their reception of tithes – it then seems that "bishop" is a much more likely reading of the Qur'ānic *ruhbān* than "monks." This is also suggested by the Didascalia's pairing of bishops and elders in likely parallel to the Qur'ān's pairing of *ruhbān* and elders. The Didascalia even anticipates the Qur'ān's charge of "wrongfully eating the wealth of the people" when warning the bishops as follows:

> As good stewards (*rb' bt'*) of God, therefore, do well in dispensing those things that are given and come into the congregation .... Thus distribute and give to all who are in want. But be you also nourished and live from these things which come into the church. And do not swallow (*tbl'wn*) them by yourself alone, but let those who are in want be sharers with you, and you shall be without offence with God. (DA VIII, 94.13–24)

The warning against embezzlement of the church funds, paired with the imagery of swallowing, and the stern warning that follows in both texts speaks of a discourse shared with the Qur'ān. If there is such a significant overlap between the Didascalia's attitude towards the office of the bishop and the Qur'ān's attitude towards the *ruhbān*, the identity of the offices seems likely. Unlike *qšyš* for "elder," however, the term *rhb* is not associated with the episcopacy anywhere in the Syriac literature. While we have learned that we must not read any Syriac etymology as necessarily determinative of the meaning of any word in Qur'ānic Arabic, the broader deictic field of the term *ruhbān* and the associated Qur'ānic word *ri'āya*, "care" (Q57:27) – a cognate to the Syriac term *r'y'*, "shepherd" – is still worth considering, as we will soon do.[24]

If understood broadly as determining the complexities of the semantic context, however, then Syriac and Aramaic can be helpful to establish the meaning of certain Arabic words; etymology is a technique which the rabbinic as well as the Muslim exegetical traditions themselves discovered a long time ago. The root *rhb*, indeed, is well-attested both in Arabic and in Syriac, as denoting "fear." The term connotes the "fear of God," also a central Qurʾānic concept that is usually expressed with the words *ḫašya* and *ḫawf* (see Q2:74, Q2:150 among others). It should be noted that the "fear of God" (Syriac *dḥlt' 'lh'* and Hebrew *yr't hšm*) constituted one of the most central theological concepts of the Syriac as well as the rabbinic traditions.[25] It is thus not surprising that a term for a Christian official would conote "fear" – indeed, Theodor Nöldeke already suggested that the Qurʾān's term *ruhbān*, as the "God-fearing" ones, parallels the Pahlavi term *tarsāk*, which also originally denoted the "fear of God," but came to stand simply for Christians *tout court* as well.[26]

---

[24] On risks inherent to applying etymology uncritically, see pages 35–6, note 44.

[25] See Adam Becker "Martyrdom, Religious Difference, and 'Fear' as a Category of Piety in the Sasanian Empire: The Case of the *Martyrdom of Gregory* and the *Martyrdom of Yazdpaneh*," *Journal of Late Antiquity* 2 (2009): 300–336 and idem, *Fear of God and the Beginnings of Wisdom: The School of Nisibis and the Development of Scholastic Culture in Late Antique Mesopotamia* (Philadelphia: University of Pennsylvania Press, 2006).

[26] See Theodor Nöldeke's "Review of Friedrich Schulthess, *Homonyme Wurzeln im Syrischen*," in *Zeitschrift der Deutschen Morgenländischen Gesellschaft* 54 (1900): 163; see also Horovitz, *Koranische Untersuchungen*, 64; and Siegmund Fraenkel, *Die Aramäischen*

More specifically, however, the Didascalia connects the concept of the "fear of God," with the fear of the bishop, as we have already seen above. Namely, it calls not only for the "fear of God" (*dḥlt' 'lh'*) repeatedly, but it specifically presents anyone ascending to the episcopacy as having to be "fearful" (*dḥwltn*, DA IV), that is of God. More importantly, the bishop must be an object of fear himself: by his household (DA IV, 54.12) and by his community (DA VII, 74.19). The laymen are indeed judged according to whether "the layman loves the bishop and honors him and fears (*wdḥl*) him as father and lord (*wmr'*) and god after God Almighty" (DA VII, 75.12–14, see also DA IX, 112, 3 and DA XV, 164.5). If the bishop fears and must be feared (as "god after God"!), it would thus not be surprising that its Arabic rendering would not reflect the Greek origin of the Syriac term, *'pysqwp'*, "overseer." Rather, it seems plausible that the Arabic term *ruhbān*, if it designated the

---

Fremdwörter im Arabischen (Leiden: Brill, 1886), 267–8; as well as Shlomo Pines, "The Iranian Name for Christians and the 'God-Fearers,'" *Proceedings of the Israel Academy of Sciences and Humanities* 2 (1968): 143–52. A good example of the uses of the term *tarsāk* can be found in the *Shāyast lā-shāyast*, where it can denote either "reverence" (XII.30) or a "Christian" (VI.7). See Edward W. West (ed. and trans.), *Pahlavi Texts. Volume 1: The Bundahis, Bahman Yast, and Shāyast lā-shāyast* (Cambridge: Cambridge University Press, 2012 [1880]. De Blois criticizes the lexical association as "semantically tenuous; whereas the Persian term encompasses the Christians as a whole, the Arabic word [*rāhib*] has a much narrower meaning" (see idem, "Naṣrānī (Ναζωραῖος) and ḥanīf (ἐθνικός)," 9). While the objection undoubtedly weakens Nöldeke's case, it seems to me that etymology should not be constructed as tracing words to single origins – the Persian term may well have influenced the Arabic usage; moreover, a bishop would easily be seen to represent Christianity as a whole.

"bishop" in the Qur'ān, would reflect one of its inevitable Syriac associations, "fear," as expressed in Arabic.[27]

Geiger suggested that one should "derive" the Arabic term *not* from "fear," but from the Syriac root *rb*, which denotes "rabbis," "lords," "leaders" or "high officials" – despite the medial *hā'* of *rhb*. For Geiger, *ruhbān* simply denotes "clerics."[28] This procedure could of course be perceived as a cavalier dismissal of the integrity of the Arabic word. Still, the centrality of the "fear of God" in Syriac Christianity and the Pahlavi term for Christian based on "fear" (which was first proposed long after Geiger) strongly suggests that the audience of the Qur'ān would likewise have associated the title of a bishop, as well as the term *ruhbān* with "fear" first and foremost.

Geiger's suggestion, recently reiterated more carefully by de Blois, to hear an echo of *rwrbn'*, the plural form (with a doubling of the initial *resh*) of the Syriac *rb*, "leader," in the Arabic *ruhbān*, may guide us to a better appreciation not of the etymology of the term, but of the Qur'ān's subtle use of homophony.[29] For what de Blois reconstructs,

---

[27] There are indeed many Syriac loanwords in Qur'ānic Arabic, yet far fewer, if any, Greek loanwords; see the helpful summary by Rippin, "Foreign Vocabulary," *Encyclopaedia of the Qur'ān*, ad loc.

[28] Geiger, *Was hat Mohammad*, 51.

[29] De Blois suggests that "the Arabic plural *ruhbān* comes from the (reduplicated) Syriac plural *rawrßānē* (also *rabbānē*), either with dissimilation of *r-r-* to *r-h-*, or by popular etymological attachment to the (Arabic, not Aramaic) root *r-h-b*, with back-formation of the singular *rāhib*." See idem, "Naṣrānī (Ναζωραῖος) and ḥanīf (ἐθνικός)," 9. The intriguing study of Emran Al-Badawi, "From 'Clergy' to 'Celibacy:' The Development of *rahbaniyyah* between the Qur'an, Hadith and Church Canon," forthcoming in *Al-Bayān* reached me too late to comment upon it.

the Qurʾān makes explicit. It charges the Christians to have taken their *ruhbān* as *ʾarbāban*, as lords beside God, doubly evoking the multi-lingual term *rb* at the center of the polemic against rabbinic and Christian leaders in Q9:31. Indeed, one of the Didascalia's terms for Jesus is *rbʾ* (DA XIX, 190.11), just as the Qurʾān claims when accusing the Christians of taking Jesus as Lord (Q9:31). An audience familiar with the designation of the bishops as *rbʾ btʾ* (as "stewards," or "lords of the house") or as *rby khnykwn* ("high priests," which we saw above), would likely have understood the Qurʾān's accusation against the veneration of the *ruhbān*, and their alleged embezzlement of funds, as at least conceivably applicable to the bishops. Geiger was certainly right in observing that *ruhbān* sounds a lot like *rb* and that the Qurʾān uses this homophony in order to convey its message against bishops and rabbis. There is no need, however, to invent yet another etymology – similarity of sound already conveys the message.

If the *ruhbān* are bishops, then the Qurʾānic passage proscribing *rahbāniyya* – likely a term describing the institution of being one of the *ruhbān* – should then also be read more broadly. God here is reported as stating (in the first person *pluralis majestatis*):

Then we followed [Noah and Abraham] with Our apostles
And We followed [them] with Jesus son of Mary,
And We gave him the Gospel,
And We put in the hearts of those who followed him
kindness (*raʾfatan*) and mercy (*raḥmatan*) and *rahbāniyya*,
They innovated it,
– We had not prescribed it (*katabnāhā*) for them –
Only seeking God's pleasure.
Yet they did not observe it (*mā raʿawhā*) with due observance (*ḥaqqa riʿāyatihā*)

So we gave the faithful among them their reward,
But many of them are transgressors. (Q57:27)

The institution of *rahbāniyya* is again associated with the followers of Jesus, the Christian community. The Qur'ān describes this institution either as a divine ordinance that was then corrupted, or as a human innovation in order to please God, which may have had its merits, but was not duly observed – both readings seem plausible.[30] The offences associated with the institution are likely the ones explicated in Q9:31: the undue veneration of those exercising it and the misuse of the funds of the congregation. There is, *prima facie*, not much we can learn from this passage about the precise meaning of the term – in the traditional view, the innovation is "monasticism;" in my broader reading, it would include any official church office.

If we read the term *rahbāniyya* to denote the ecclesiastical hierarchy as such, however, the passage takes on a very clear message, especially about the office of bishop, which can again be appreciated in light of the lexical and conceptual overlaps between this passage and the Didascalia. The Didascalia calls the bishop *r'y'*, "shepherd" (DA IV, 52.6,

[30] The more commonly accepted reading of the verse, "And We put in the hearts of those who followed him kindness and mercy – and *rahbāniyya*, they innovated it, we had not prescribed it for them," implies that the institution of *rahbāniyya* was not originally a divine one that subsequently became corrupted. This reading may grammatically be slightly sounder than its alternative cited above and attractive in principle. While the reading remains to be solved, I would assume that the episcopacy is conceivable as being "put in the hearts" of Jesus' followers as much as the rabbis were given authority over the Jews. See McAuliffe, *Qur'ānic Christians*, 260–84; and Griffith, "Monasticism and Monks," in McAuliffe (ed.), *Encyclopaedia of the Qur'ān*, ad loc.

a common Syriac term for bishops)[31], a central metaphor that is drawn out in many verses (DA VII, 78.5–80.18; see also DA IV, IX, and X), and instructs the bishops to judge "as it was prescribed" (*ktb'*): "with kindness (*bnyḥ'*) and mercy (*wbrḥm'*)" (DA VI, 71.17–8). The Qur'ān, in turn, complains that even though God put "kindness (*ra'fah*) and mercy (*raḥmah*)" into the hearts of Jesus' followers, many of the *ruhbān* are transgressors and innovated something that God has not prescribed (*katabnāhā*) for them (Q57:27), negatively reflecting the language of the Didascalia.

The Qur'ān's choice of language points to a shared conceptuality: it charges that the holders of the office of *rahbāniyya* did not "care (*mā ra'awhā*) with due care (*ḥaqqa ri'āyatihā*)." The Arabic verb for "care," *r'y*, occurs elsewhere in the legal context of keeping a covenant (see Q23:8); it derives from the Arabic root for shepherd, *rā'in* (see Q28:23). The cognate Syriac root *r'y* likewise denotes the "shepherd" and the bishop. The Qur'ān's lexical association of the *ruhbān* with "shepherds" to whom "kindness" and "mercy" are "prescribed" contributes yet another hint for the suggested reading of *ruhbān* as "bishops" and *rahbāniyya* as "episcopate."

Moreover, as mentioned before, the Qur'ān's charges against the bishops have a long tradition in the Didascalia itself: the entire eighth chapter of the Didascalia warns the bishops not to devour the wealth of the people and informs them that they will be held accountable by God on Judgment Day, should they transgress: "you are they

---

[31] See Sokoloff, *A Syriac Dictionary*, 1480; *r'ywt'* denotes the episcopate.

who have heard how the word is furious, hard against you if you despise and do not preach God's will, you are those who are in grave danger of destruction if you despise your people" (DA VIII, 96:13–17). The Qurʾān concurs, informing "of a painful punishment" for those of the *ruhbān* who "wrongfully eat up the people's wealth," "storing up gold and silver and not spending it in the way of God" (Q9:34).

As we have seen throughout this book, the affinities between the Didascalia and the Qurʾān do not point to literary contact, but they make eminent sense of both texts when taking the Didascalia as one of the points of departure for the Qurʾān's legal culture. The Didascalia calls the bishops "helpers of God" (*m'drn' 'm 'lha*, DA XII, 143.15) and entrusts them with the teaching of Jesus' disciples, the Apostles. The Qurʾān, in turn, calls Jesus' disciples *ʾanṣāru llāhi*, "helpers to God" (Q61:14), yet it takes issue with the actions of some of the bishops, the leaders of the *naṣārā*, the Christians.

This brief epilogic discussion illustrates well that reading the Qurʾān in dialogue with more than one of its many interlocutors among the panoply of Late Antique religions is vastly more rewarding, as well as more accurate, than the reductionism inherent in the focus on one outside source alone. My exclusive focus on the Didascalia (along with the Clementine Homilies) in the main body of this study seems necessary to begin constructing the legal culture in which we have to situate and appreciate the Qurʾān. Yet the present study aspires to being no more than another point of departure for the ongoing inquiry into the Late Antique context of the Qurʾān's legal culture.

Bibliography

Ahrens, Karl. "Christliches im Qoran: Eine Nachlese." *Zeitschrift der Deutschen Morgenländischen Gesellschaft* 84 (1930): 15–68 and 148–90.

al-Badawi, Emran. "From 'Clergy' to 'Celibacy:' The Development of *rahbaniyyah* between the Qur'an, Hadith and Church Canon." *Al-Bayān* (forthcoming).

al-Badawi, Emran. *Sectarian Scripture: The Qur'an's Dogmatic Re-Articulation of the Aramaic Gospel Traditions in the Late Antique Near East*. PhD Dissertation. Chicago, IL: University of Chicago, 2011.

al-Haddad, Durrah. *Al-Injīl fi-l-Qur'ān*. Jounieh: Librairie pauliste, 1982.

Andrae, Tor. *Der Ursprung des Islams und das Christentum.* Uppsala: Almqvist & Wiksells, 1926.

Azzi, Joseph. *Le prêtre et le prophète: Aux sources du Coran*. Translation of Abu Musa al-Hariri's *Priest and Prophet: Research on the Rise of Islam* (n.p., 1979) [Arabic] by Maurice S. Garnier. Paris: Maisonneuve et Larose, 2001.

Baumstark, Anton. "Aegyptischer oder antiochenischer Liturgietypus in AK I–VII?" *Oriens Christianus* 7 (1907): 388–407.

Beck, Edmund, ed., *Des heiligen Ephraem des Syrers: Hymnen de Virginitate. Corpus Scriptorum Christianorum Orientalium.* Volume 224. Louvain: Secrétariat du CorpuSCO, 1962.

Becker, Adam. "Martyrdom, Religious Difference, and 'Fear' as a Category of Piety in the Sasanian Empire: The Case of the *Martyrdom of Gregory* and the *Martyrdom of Yazdpaneh.*" *Journal of Late Antiquity* 2 (2009): 300–336.

Becker, Adam. *Fear of God and the Beginnings of Wisdom: The School of Nisibis and the Development of Scholastic Culture in Late Antique Mesopotamia*. Philadelphia, PA: University of Pennsylvania Press, 2006.

Berenbaum, Michael and Fred Skolnik, eds. *Encyclopaedia Judaica* Detroit: Macmillan Reference, 2007.

Berger, Peter L. *The Sacred Canopy: Elements of a Sociology of Religion*. New York, NY: Doubleday, 1967.

Bishai, Wilson B. "Sabbath Observance from Coptic Sources." *Andrews University Seminary Studies* 1 (1963): 25–31.

Bladel, Kevin van. "The Legend of Alexander the Great in the Qur'ān 18:83–102." In *New Perspectives on the Qur'ān: The Qur'ān in Its Historical Context 2*, edited by Gabriel Said Reynolds, 175–203. Abingdon: Routledge, 2011.

Blois, François de. "Elchasai – Manes – Muḥammad: Manichäismus und Islam in religionshistorischem Vergleich." *Der Islam* 81 (2004): 31–48.

Blois, François de. "Naṣrānī (Ναζωραῖος) and ḥanīf (ἐθνικός): Studies on the Religious Vocabulary of Christianity and of Islam." *Bulletin of the School of Oriental and African Studies* 65 (2002): 1–30.

Bobzin, Hartmut. "The 'Seal of the Prophets': Towards and Understanding of Muhammad's Prophethood." In *The Qur'ān in Context: Historical and Literary Investigations into the Qur'ānic Milieu*, edited by Nicolai Sinai, Angelika Neuwirth, and Michael Marx, 565–584. Leiden: Brill, 2009.

Bockmuehl, Markus. "The Noachide Commandments and New Testament Ethics, with Special Reference to Acts 15 and Pauline Halakhah." *Revue Biblique* 102 (1995): 72–101.

Boddens Hosang, F. Jacob Eliza. *Establishing Boundaries: Christian-Jewish Relations in Early Council Texts and the Writings of Church Fathers.* Leiden: Brill, 2010.

Borret Marcel, ed. and trans. *Origène. Contre Celse.* Sources chrétiennes 132, 136, 147, 150. Paris: Éditions du Cerf, 1967–1969.

Bourdieu, Pierre. *Outline of a Theory of Practice.* Cambridge: Cambridge University Press, 1979.

Bowman, John. "The Debt of Islam to monophysite Syrian Christianity." *Nederlands Theologisch Tijdschrift* 19 (1964/5): 177–201.

Boyarin, Daniel. "Rethinking Jewish Christianity: An Argument for Dismantling a Dubious Category (to which is Appended a Correction of my Border Lines)." *Jewish Quarterly Review* 99 (2009): 7–36.

Boyarin, Daniel. *Border Lines: The Partition of Judaeo-Christianity*. Philadelphia: University of Pennsylvania Press, 2004.

Boyce, Mary, ed. and transl. *The Letter of Tansar.* Rome: Istituto Italiano per il Medio ed Estremo Oriente, 1968.

Brent, Allen. "The Relations between Ignatius and the Didascalia." *The Second Century* 8 (1991): 1–29.

Brinner, William M. "An Islamic Decalogue." In *Studies in Islamic and Judaic Traditions. Volume 1*, edited by William M. Brinner and Stephen D. Ricks, 67–84. Atlanta: Scholars Press, 1986.

Broadhead, Edwin K. *Jewish Ways of Following Jesus: Redrawing the Religious Map of Antiquity.* WUNT 266; Tübingen: Mohr Siebeck, 2010.

Brock, Sebastian P. "Christians in the Sasanid Empire: A Case of Divided Loyalties." In *Religion and national identity: papers read at the nineteenth summer meeting and the twentieth winter meeting of the Ecclesiastical History Society*, edited by Stuart Mews, 1–19. Oxford: Basil Blackwell, 1982.

Brock, Sebastian P. "From Antagonism to Assimilation: Syriac Attitudes to Greek Learning." In *East of Byzantium: Syria and Armenia in the Formative Period*, edited by Nina G. Garsoïan, Thomas F. Matthews and Robert W. Thomson, 17–34. Washington, DC: Dumbarton Oaks Center for Byzantine Studies, 1982.

Brock, Sebastian, Aaron Butts, George Kiraz and Lucas Van Rompay, eds. *Gorgias Encyclopedic Dictionary of the Syriac Heritage.* Piscataway, NJ: Gorgias Press, 2011.

Broshi, Magen. "Was There Agriculture at Qumran?" In *The Site of the Dead Sea Scrolls: Archaeological Interpretations and Debates, Proceedings of the Conference Held at Brown University, November 17–19, 2002*, edited by K. Galor, J.-B. Humbert, and J. Zangenberg, 249–81. Leiden: Brill, 2006.

Brown, Peter. "Holy Men." In *The Cambridge Ancient History. Volume 14: Late Antiquity: Empire and Successors, A.D. 425–600*, edited by Averil Cameron, Bryan Ward-Perkins and Michael Whitby, 781–810. Cambridge: Cambridge University Press, 2000.

Buell, Denise Kimber. *Why This New Race? Ethnic Reasoning in Early Christianity.* New York, NY: Columbia University Press, 2005.

Burkert, Walter. *Greek Religion.* Translated by John Raffan. Cambridge, MA: Harvard University Press, 1985 [1977].

Burton, John. *The Sources of Islamic Law: Islamic Theories of Abrogation*. Edinburgh: Edinburgh University Press, 1990.

Byrskog, Samuel. *Story as History – History as Story: The Gospel Tradition in the Context of Ancient Oral History.* WUNT 123; Tübingen: Mohr Siebeck, 2000.

Cameron, Averil. "The Cult of the Virgin in Late Antiquity: Religious Development and Myth-Making." In *The Church and Mary,* edited by Robert N. Swanson, 1–21. Woodbridge: Boydell Press, 2004.

Camplani, Alberto. "A Coptic Fragment from the Didascalia Apostolorum (M579 F.1)." *Augustinianum* 36 (1996): 47–51.

Cohen, Shaye J.D. "Antipodal Texts: B. Eruvin 21b–22a and Mark 7:1–23 on the Tradition of the Elders and the Commandment of God." In *Envisioning Judaism: Studies in Honor of Peter Schäfer on the Occasion of his Seventieth Birthday,* Volume 1, edited by Annette Y. Reed, Ra'anan S. Boustan, Klaus Hermann, Reimund Leicht, Guiseppe Veltri and Alex Ramos, 965–83. Tübingen: Mohr Siebeck, 2013.

Cohen, Shaye J.D. "Menstruants and the Sacred in Judaism and Christianity." In *Women's History and Ancient History*, edited by Sarah. B. Pomery, 273–299. Chapel Hill, NC: University of North Carolina Press, 1991.

Cohen, Shaye J.D. *From the Maccabees to the Mishnah*. Louisville, KY: Westminster John Knox Press, 2006 [1987].

Cohen, Shaye J.D. *The Beginnings of Jewishness. Boundaries, Varieties, Uncertainties.* Berkeley, CA: University of California Press, 1999.

Cohn-Sherbok, Dan. "Modern Hebrew Christians and Messianic Judaism." In *The Image of the Judaeo-Christians in Ancient Jewish and Christian Literature*, edited by Peter J. Tomson and Doris Lambers-Petry, 287–298. Tübingen: Mohr Siebeck, 2003.

Comerro, Viviane. "Esdras est-il le fils de Dieu?" *Arabica* 52 (2005): 165–181.

Connolly, R.H. "The Use of the *Didache* in the *Didascalia*." *Journal of Theological Studies* OS 24 (1923): 147–157.

Connolly, R.H., ed. and trans. *Didascalia Apostolorum: The Syriac Version Translated and Accompanied by the Verona Latin Fragments*. Oxford: Clarendon Press, 1929.

Cover, Robert. "The Supreme Court, 1982 Term – Foreword: Nomos and Narrative." *Harvard Law Review* 97 (1983): 4–68.

Cox, James John Charles. "Prolegomena to a Study of the Dominical Logoi as Cited in the Didascalia Apostolorum. II: Methodological Questions." *Andrews University Seminary Studies* 15 (1977): 1–15 and 17 (1979): 137–167.

Crone, Patricia. "The Religion of the Qur'ānic Pagans: God and the Lesser Deities." *Arabica* 57 (2010): 151–200.

Crone, Patricia. "Islam, Judeo-Christianity and Byzantine Iconoclasm." In *From Kavād to al-Ghazālī: Religion, Law, and Political Thought in the Near East, c. 600–c. 1100*, by Patricia Crone, 59–96. Aldershot: Ashgate, 2005.

Crone, Patricia. "The Quranic *Mushrikūn* and the Resurrection (Part I)." *Bulletin of the School of Oriental and African Studies* 75 (2012): 445–472.

Crone, Patricia. "The Quranic *Mushrikūn* and the Resurrection (Part II)." *Bulletin of the School of Oriental and African Studies* 76 (2013): 1–20.

Crone, Patricia. "What do we actually know about Mohammed?" Accessed on October 30, 2012 at http://www.opendemocracy.net/faith-europe_islam/mohammed_3866.jsp.

Crone, Patricia and Silverstein, Adam. "The Ancient Near East and Islam: The Case of Lot-Casting." *Journal of Semitic Studies* 55 (2010): 423–50.

Dawson, Timothy. "Propriety, Practicality, and Pleasure: the Parameters of Women's Dress in Byzantium, A.D. 1000–1200." In *Byzantine Women: Varieties of Experience 800–1200*, edited by Lynda Garland, 41–75. Aldershot: Ashgate, 2006.

Déroche, François. *Qur'ans of the Umayyads: A Preliminary Overview.* Leiden: Brill, 2014 (forthcoming).

Deines, Roland. "Das Aposteldekret – Halacha für Heidenchristen oder Christliche Rücksichtnahme auf jüdische Tabus?" In *Jewish Identity in the Greco-Roman World*, edited by Jörg Frey, Daniel R. Schwartz and Stephanie Gripentorg, 323–395. Leiden: Brill, 2007.

Deines, Roland. *Die Gerechtigkeit der Tora im Reich des Messias: Mt 5,13–20 als Schlüsseltext der matthäischen Theologie.* WUNT 177; Tübingen: Mohr Siebeck, 2005.

Doran, Robert, ed. and trans. *The Lives of Simeon Stylites*. Foreword by Susan Ashbrook-Harvey. Kalamazoo: Cistercian Publications, 1992.

Doumato, Eleanor A. "Hearing Other Voices: Christian Women and the Coming of Islam." *International Journal of Middle East Studies* 23 (1991): 177–199.

Dunn, Geoffrey. *Tertullian*. London: Routledge, 2004.

Ekenberg, Anders. "Evidence for Jewish Believers in 'Church Orders' and Liturgical Texts." In *Jewish Believers in Jesus: The Early Centuries*, edited by Oskar Skarsaune and Reidar Hvalvik, 649–652. Peabody, MA: Hendrickson, 2007.

Feltoe, Charles Lett, ed. *The Letters and Other Remains of Dionysius of Alexandria*. Cambridge: University Press, 1904.

Fiensy, David A. "Redaction History and the Apostolic Constitutions." *Jewish Quarterly Review* 72 (1982): 293–302.

Firestone, Reuven. "Jewish Culture in the Formative Period of Islam." In *Cultures of the Jews: A New History*, edited by David Biale, 267–302. New York, NY: Schocken Books, 2002.

Fonrobert, Charlotte Elisheva. "Jewish Christians, Judaizers, and Christian anti-Judaism." In *Late Ancient Christianity*, edited by Virginia Burrus, 234–254. Minneapolis, MN: Fortress Press, 2005.

Fonrobert, Charlotte Elisheva. "The Didascalia Apostolorum: A Mishnah for the Disciples of Jesus." *Journal of Early Christian Studies* 9 (2001), 483–509.

Fonrobert, Charlotte Elisheva. *Menstrual Purity: Rabbinic and Christian Reconstructions of Biblical Gender.* Stanford, CA: Stanford University Press, 2000.

Fraenkel, Siegmund. *Die Aramäischen Fremdwörter im Arabischen.* Leiden: Brill, 1886.

Fraipont, J. and D. De Bruyne, eds. *Augustinus, Quaestionum in Heptateuchum libri VII. Locutionum in Heptateuchum libri VII. De octo quaestionibus ex veteri testament.* Leuven: Brepols, 1958.

Françon, J. "The Didascalie éthiopienne traduit en français." *Revue de l'Orient Chrétien* 16 (1911): 161–166 and 266–70; 17 (1912): 199–203 and 286–293; and 19 (1914): 183–87.

Frankfurter, David. "Jews or Not? Reconstructing the 'Other' in Rev. 2:9 and 3:9." *Harvard Theological Review* 94 (2001), 403–427.

Freidenreich, David M. *Foreigners and Their Food: Constructing Otherness in Jewish, Christian, and Islamic Law*. Berkeley, CA: University of California Press, 2011.

Funk, Franz Xaver von, ed. *Didascalia et Constitutiones Apostolorum. 2 Vols.* Paderborn: Ferdinand Schoeningh, 1905.

Gallez, Edouard-Marie. *Le Messie et son prophète: aux origines de l'islam*. Versailles: Éditions de Paris, 2005.

Galtier, Paul. "La date de la Didascalie des Apôtres." *Revue d'histoire ecclésiastique* 42 (1947): 315–351.

Geiger, Abraham. *Was hat Mohammed aus dem Judenthume aufgenommen?* Bonn: Baaden, 1833.

Gero, Stephen. "The So-Called Ointment Prayer in the Coptic Version of the Didache: A Re-Evaluation." *The Harvard Theological Review* 70 (1977): 67–84.

Gibb, Hamilton A.R., ed. *The Encyclopaedia of Islam*. Leiden: Brill, 1960–2009.

Gibson, Margaret Dunlop, ed. *The Didascalia Apostolorum in Syriac, Edited from a Mesopotamian Manuscript with Various Readings and Collations of Other MSS.* Cambridge: Cambridge University Press, 2011 [1903].

Gilliot, Claude. "Reconsidering the Authorship of the Qur'ān: is the Qur'ān Partly the Fruit of a Progressive and Collective Work?" In *The Qur'ān in its Historical Context*, edited by Gabriel Said Reynolds, 88–108. London: Routledge, 2008.

Glover, T.R., ed. and trans. *Tertullian: Apology; De spectaculis. Loeb Classical Library 250*. London: Heinemann, 1931.

Gnilka, Joachim. *Die Nazarener und der Koran: Eine Spurensuche*. Freiburg: Herder, 2007.

Gobillot, Geneviève. "Der Begriff Buch im Koran im Licht der pseudoklementinischen Schriften." In *Vom Koran zum Islam*, edited by M. Gross and K.-H. Ohlig, 339–445. Berlin: Hans Schiler, 2009.

Gobillot, Geneviève. *La conception originelle, ses interprétations et fonctions chez les penseurs musulmans: la fiṭra.* Cairo: Institut Français d'Archéologie Orientale, 2000.

Goitein, Shlomo Dov. "Prayer in Islam." In *Studies in Islamic History and Institutions* by Shlomo Dov Goitein, 73–89. Leiden: Brill, 1966.

Goitein, Shlomo Dov. "The Birth-Hour of Muslim Law." *The Muslim World* 50 (1960): 23–29.

Goitein, Shlomo Dov. "Who were the outstanding teachers of Muhammad? (Offering a new solution for an old problem)." *Tarbiz* 23 (1951/52): 146–59. [Hebrew]

Goldziher, Ignaz. *Vorlesungen über den Islam*. Heidelberg: Carl Winter's Universitätsbuchandlung, 1925.

Goodman, Martin D. "Jews and Judaism in the Second Temple Period." In *The Oxford Handbook of Jewish Studies*, edited by Martin D. Goodman, 53–78. Oxford: Oxford University Press, 2002.

Graf, Georg. *Geschichte der christlichen arabischen Literatur.* Rome: Biblioteca Apostolica Vaticana, 1944.

Grégoire, Henri. "Mahomet et le monophysitisme." In *Mélanges Charles Diehl: Études sur l'histoire et sur l'art de Byzance*, 107–119. Paris: Ernest Leroux, 1930.

Griffith, Sidney H. "*Al-Naṣārā* in the Qurʾān: a Hermeneutical Reflection." In *New Perspectives on the Qurʾān: The Qurʾān in Its Historical Context 2*, edited by Gabriel Said Reynolds, 301–322. Abingdon: Routledge, 2011.

Griffith, Sidney H. "Christian Lore and the Arabic Qurʾān: The 'Companions of the Cave' in Surat al-Kahf and in Syriac Christian Tradition." In *New Perspectives on the Qurʾān: The Qurʾān in Its Historical Context* 2, edited by Gabriel Said Reynolds, 109–137. Abingdon: Routledge, 2011.

Griffith, Sidney H. "The Prophet Muḥammad, his Scripture and his Message according to the Christian Apologies in Arabic and Syriac from the First Abbasid Century." In *La Vie du prophète Mahomet. Colloque de Strasbourg (octobre 1980)*, edited by Toufic Fahd, 99–146. Paris: Presses universitaires de France, 1983.

Griffith, Sidney H. *The Bible in Arabic: the Scriptures of the People of the Book*. Princeton, NJ: Princeton University Press, 2013.

Griffith, Sidney H. "Syriacisms in the 'Arabic Qurʾān': Who were those who said 'Allāh is third of three' according to al-Mā'ida

73?" In *A Word Fitly Spoken: Studies in Mediaeval Exegesis of the Hebrew Bible and the Qur'ān, Presented to Haggai Ben-Shammai*, edited by Meir M. Bar-Asher, 83*–110*. Jerusalem: The Ben Zvi Institute, 2007.

Günther, Sebastian. "Muḥammad, the Illiterate Prophet: An Islamic Creed in the Qur'ān and Qur'ānic Exegesis." *Journal of Qur'anic Studies* 4 (2002): 1–26.

Günther, Sebastian. "O People of the Scripture! Come to a Word Common to You and Us (Q. 3:64): The Ten Commandments and the Qur'an." *Journal of Qur'anic Studies* 9 (2007): 28–58.

Gwynn, John, ed. and trans. *Selections Translated into English from the Hymns and Homilies of Ephraim the Syrian, and from the Demonstrations of Aphrahat the Persian Sage. Nicene and post-Nicene Fathers of the Christian Church.* Series 2 Volume 13. Grand Rapids, MI: Eerdmans, 1956.

Haldon, John F. *Byzantium in the Seventh Century: The Transformation of a Culture.* Cambridge: Cambridge University Press, 1990.

Hallaq, Wael B. *The Origins and Evolution of Islamic Law*. Cambridge: Cambridge University Press, 2005.

Hamburger, Jeffrey F. and Susan Marti, *Crown and Veil: Female Monasticism from the Fifth to the Fifteenth Centuries.* New York, NY: Columbia University Press, 2008.

Harden, J.M., ed. *The Ethiopic Didascalia*. London: Society for Promoting Christian Knowledge, 1920.

Hauler, Edmund, ed. *Didascaliae Apostolorum fragmenta Veronensia latina*. Leipzig: Teubner, 1900.

Hawting, Gerald R. "The Origins of the Muslim Sanctuary at Mecca." In *Studies on the First Century of Islamic Society*, edited by G.H.A. Juynboll, 23–47. Carbondale, IN: Southern Illinois University Press, 1982.

Hawting, Gerald R. *The Development of Islamic Ritual*. Aldershot: Ashgate, 2006.

Hawting, Gerald R. *The Idea of Idolatry and the Emergence of Islam: From Polemic to History.* Cambridge: Cambridge University Press, 1999.

Hayman, A.P. "The Image of the Jew in Syriac Anti-Jewish Polemical Literature." In "*To See Ourselves as Others See Us:*" *Christians, Jews, and "Others" in Late Antiquity*, edited by

Jacob Neusner and E.S. Frerichs, 423–441. Chico, CA: Scholars Press, 1985.

Heinz, Ohme. "Sources of the Greek Canon Law to the Quinisext Council (691/2)." In *The History of Byzantine and Eastern Canon Law to 1500*, edited by Wilfried Hartmann and Kenneth Pennington, 24–114. Washington, DC: The Catholic University of America Press, 2012.

Hendel, Ron. "Away from Ritual: The Prophetic Critique." In *Social Theory and The Study Of Israelite Religion: Essays in Retrospect and Prospect*, edited by Saul M. Olyan, 59–80. Atlanta, GA: Society of Biblical Literature, 2012.

Hengel, Martin and Roland Deines. "E P Sanders' 'Common Judaism', Jesus, and the Pharisees." Translated by D.P. Bailey. *Journal of Theological Studies* 46 (1995): 1–70.

Himmelfarb, Martha. *A Kingdom of Priests: Ancestry and Merit in Ancient Judaism.* Philadelphia, PA: University of Pennsylvania Press, 2006.

Horovitz, Josef. *Koranische Untersuchungen*. Berlin: de Gruyter, 1926.

Hoyland, Robert G. *Seeing Islam as Others Saw It: A Survey and Evaluation of Christian, Jewish and Zoroastrian Writings on Early Islam.* Princeton, NJ: Darwin, 1997.

Hoyland, Robert. "The Jews of the Hijaz in the Qurʾān and in their Inscriptions." In *New Perspectives on the Qurʾān: The Qurʾān in Its Historical Context 2*, edited by Gabriel Said Reynolds, 91–116. Abingdon: Routledge, 2011.

Iricinschi, Eduard and Holger Zellentin, eds. *Heresy and Identity in Late Antiquity.* Tübingen: Mohr Siebeck, 2008.

Jackson-McCabe, Matt, ed. *Jewish Christianity Reconsidered*. Minneapolis, MN: Fortress Press, 2007.

Jaffee, Martin. "What Difference Does the 'Orality' of Rabbinic Writing Make for the Interpretation of Rabbinic Writings?" In *How Should Rabbinic Literature Be Read in the Modern World?*, edited by Matthew Kraus, 11–33. Piscataway, NJ: Gorgias Press, 2006.

Jean-Paul Migne (ed.), *Dionysii Exigui justi, facundi opera omnia. Patrologia Latina* 67. Paris: Migne, 1848.

Jeffery, Arthur. *The Foreign Vocabulary of the Qurʾān*. Leiden: Brill, 2007 [1938].

Joannou, Périclès-Pierre *Discipline générale antique (IVe–IXes.)* 2 volumes. Grottaferratta-Rome: S. Nilo, 1962–1964.

Jones, Stanley F. "Evaluating the Latin and Syriac Translations of the Pseudo-Clementine Recognitions." *Apocrypha* 3 (1992): 237–257.

Jones, Stanley F. "The Pseudo-*Clementines*: a History of Research, Part I." *The Second Century* 2 (1982): 14–33.

Jones, Stanley F. *Pseudoclementina Elchasaiticaque inter judaeo-christiana: Collected Studies*. Leeuven: Peeters, 2012.

Kalmin, Richard. "'Manasseh Sawed Isaiah with a Saw of Wood': An Ancient Legend in Jewish, Christian, Muslim, and Persian Sources." In *Talmudic Archaeology in Babylonia*, edited by Mark Geller and Shaul Shaked. Leiden: Brill, forthcoming.

Kaufhold, Hubert. "La littérature pseudo-canonique syriaque" In *Les apocryphes syriaques*, edited by M. Debié, A. Desreumaux, C. Jullien and F. Jullien, 147–167. Paris: Geuthner, 2005.

Kaufhold, Hubert. "Sources of Canon Law in the Eastern Churches." In *The History of Byzantine and Eastern Canon Law to 1500*, edited by Wilfried Hartmann and Kenneth Pennington, 215–342. Washington, DC: The Catholic University of America Press, 2012.

Kimelman, Reuven. "'Birkat ha-minim' and the Lack of Evidence for an anti-Christian Jewish Prayer in Late Antiquity." In *Jewish and Christian Self-Definition*, edited by E.P. Sanders, 226–244. Philadelphia, PA: University of Pennsylvania Press, 1981.

King, Karen *What Is Gnosticism?* Cambridge, MA: Belknap Press of Harvard University Press, 2003.

Kister, Menahem. "Law, Morality, and Rhetoric in Some Sayings of Jesus." In *Studies in Ancient Midrash*, edited by James L. Kugel, 150–154. Cambridge, MA: Harvard University Press, 2001.

Klein, M.L. *Genizah Manuscripts of the Palestinian Targum to the Pentateuch.* Cincinnati, OH: Hebrew Union College Press, 1986.

Klijn, A.F.J. and G.J. Reinink, *Patristic Evidence for Jewish-Christian Sects*. Leiden: Brill, 1973.

Lagarde, Anton de, ed. *The Pseudo-Clementine Recognitions and Homilies (10–14) in Syriac*. Piscataway, NJ: Gorgias Press, 2012 [1861].

Lagarde, Paul de, ed. *Didascalia apostolorum syriace*. Leipzig: Teubner, 1854.

Lange, Nicholas R. M. de. "A Fragment of Byzantine Anti-Christian Polemic." *Journal of Jewish Studies* 41 (1990): 92–100.

Langer, Ruth. *Cursing the Christians: A History of the Birkat HaMinim*. Oxford: Oxford University Press, 2012.

Larin, Sr. Vassa. "Ritual Impurity." *St Vladimir's Theological Quarterly* 52 (2008): 275–292.

Lasker, Daniel J. "The Jewish Critique of Christianity under Islam in the Middle Ages." *Proceedings of the American Academy for Jewish Research* 57 (1990–1991): 121–153.

Lawson, Todd. *The Crucifixion and the Qur'an: A Study in the History of Muslim Thought*. Oxford: Oneworld, 2009.

Lazarus-Yafeh, Hava. "The Religious Dialectics of the Ḥadjdj." In *Some Religious Aspects of Islam* by Hava Lazarus-Yafeh, 17–37. Leiden: Brill 1981.

Lecker, Michael. *Jews and Arabs in Pre- and Early Islamic Arabia*. Aldershot: Ahsgate, 1998.

Lecker, Michael. *The 'Constitution of Medina': Muḥammad's First Legal Document*. Princeton, NJ: Darwin Press, 2004.

Leicht, Reimund. "Das Schriftlichkeitsgebot bei Darlehensverträgen im Koran." In *"Im vollen Licht der Geschichte": Die Wissenschaft des Judentums und die Anfänge der kritischen Koranforschung*, edited by Dirk Hartwig, Walter Homolka, Michael J. Marx, Angelika Neuwirth, 203–222. Würzburg: Ergon, 2008.

Leicht, Reimund. "The Qur'anic Commandment of Writing Down Loan Agreements (Q2:282) – Perspectives of a Comparison with Rabbinical Law." In *The Qurʾān in Context: Historical and Literary Investigations into the Qurʾānic Milieu*, edited by Nicolai Sinai, Angelika Neuwirth, and Michael Marx, 593–614. Leiden: Brill, 2009.

Lieberman, Saul. "Metatron: the Meaning of his Name and his Functions." In *Apocalyptic and Merkavah Mysticism*, edited by Ithamar Gruenwald, 235–241. Leiden: Brill, 1980.

Limor, Ora and Guy Stroumsa. *Contra Iudaeos: Ancient and Medieval Polemics between Christians and Jews.* Tübingen: Mohr Siebeck, 1996.

Lowry, Joseph E. "When Less is More: Law and Commandment in *Sūrat al-Anʿām.*" *Journal of Qurʾānic Studies* 9 (2007): 22 42.

Luomanen, Petri. "Ebionites and Nazarenes." In (ed.), *Jewish Christianity Reconsidered. Rethinking Ancient Groups and Texts*, edited by Matt Jackson-McCabe, 81–118. Minneapolis, MN: Fortress Press, 2007.

Madigan, Daniel A. *The Qurʾān's Self-image. Writing and Authority in Islam's Scripture.* Princeton, NJ: Princeton University Press, 2001.

Maghen, Ze'ev. *After Hardship Cometh Ease: The Jews as Backdrop for Muslim Moderation*. Berlin: de Gruyter, 2006.

Marcus, Joel. "The *Testaments of the Twelve Patriarchs* and the *Didascalia Apostolorum*: A Common Jewish Christian Milieu?" *Journal of Theological Studies* 61 (2010), 596–626.

Marmorstein, Arthur. "Judaism and Christianity in the Middle of the Third Century." *Hebrew Union College Annual* 10 (1935): 223–265.

Marmorstein, Arthur. *Religionsgeschichtliche Studien. 1 Die Bezeichnungen für Christen und Gnostiker im Talmud und Midras.* Skotschau: Marmorstein, 1910.

Marsham, Andrew. "Public Execution in the Umayyad Period: Early Islamic Punitive Practice and its Late Antique Context." *Journal of Arabic and Islamic Studies* 11 (2011): 101-136.

Marx, Michael. "Glimpses of a Mariology in the Qur'an: From Hagiography to Theology via Religious-Political Debate." In *The Qurʾān in Context: Historical and Literary Investigations into the Qurʾānic Milieu,* edited by Nicolai Sinai, Angelika Neuwirth, and Michael Marx, 533–563. Leiden: Brill, 2009.

Mayer, Ann Elizabeth. "Islam Inside and Out". Review *The Anthropology of Justice: Law as Culture in Islamic Society* by Lawrence Rosen. *The Journal of Interdisciplinary History* 22 (1991): 89–100.

McAuliffe, Jane Dammen, ed. *Encyclopaedia of the Qurʾān.* Washington DC: Brill, 2011.

McAuliffe, Jane Dammen. *Qur'ānic Christians: An Analysis of Classical and Modern Exegesis*. Cambridge: Cambridge University Press, 1991.

Meeks, Wayne. "Social and Ecclesial Life of the Early Christians." In *The Cambridge History of Christianity: Origins to Constantine*, edited by Margaret M. Mitchel and Frances M. Young, 145–173. Cambridge: Cambridge University Press, 2006.

Meßner, Reinhold. "Die 'Lehre der Apostel' – eine syrische Kirchenordnung." In *Recht – Bürge der Freiheit. Festschrift für Johannes Mühlsteiger SJ zum 80. Geburtstag*, edited by Konrad Breitsching and Wilhelm Rees, 305–335. Berlin: Duncker & Humblot, 2006.

Methuen, Charlotte. "Widows, Bishops, and the Struggle for Authority in the *Didascalia Apostolorum*." *The Journal of Ecclesiastical History* 46 (1995): 197–213.

Metzger, Marcel, ed. *Les constitutions apostolique. Sources Chrétiennes* 320, 329, and 336. Paris: Le Cerf, 1985–1987.

Mezey, Naomi. "Law as Culture." *The Yale Journal of Law & the Humanities* 13 (2001): 35–67.

Migne, Jean-Paul ed. *Joannis Chrysostomi Opera Omnia. Patrologiae Graeca* 47–64. Paris: Migne, 1862.

Mimouni, Simon, ed. *Le Judéo-christianisme dans tous ses états*. Paris: Éditions du Cerf, 2001.

Morony, Michael G. *Iraq after the Muslim Conquest.* Piscataway, NJ: Gorgias Press, 2005 [1984].

Mourad, Suleiman A. "Mary in the Qur'an: A Reexamination of her Presentation." In *The Qur'ān in its Historical Context*, edited by Gabriel Said Reynolds, 163–174. London: Routledge, 2008.

Mueller, Joseph G. "The Ancient Church Order Literature: Genre or Tradition?" *Journal of Early Christian Studies* 15 (2007): 337–380.

Murray, Michele. "Christian Identity in the Apostolic Constitutions: Some Observations." In *Identity and Interaction in the Ancient Mediterranean: Jews, Christians and Others: Essays in Honour of Stephen G. Wilson*, edited by Zeba A. Crook and Philip A. Harland, 179–194. Sheffield: Sheffield Phoenix Press, 2007.

Nau, François. "Littérature canonique syriaque inédite." *Revue de l'Orient Chrétien* 14 (1909): 1–49 and 113–141.

Nau, François. "'Note sur le prologue de la Didascalie arabe et sur quelques apocryphes arabes pseudo-clémentins" *Journal asiatique* X, 17 (1911): 319–323.

Neuwirth, Angelika. "Meccan Texts-Medinan Additions? Politics and the Re-Reading of Liturgical Communications." In *Words, Texts, and Concepts Cruising the Mediterranean Sea: Studies on the Sources, Contents, and Influences of Islamic Civilization and Arabic Philosophy. Dedicated to Gerhard Endress on his sixty-fifth birthday*, edited by Rüdiger Arnzen and Jörn Thielman, 71–93. Leuven: Peeters, 2004.

Neuwirth, Angelika. "Qur'an and History – A Disputed Relationship. Some Reflections on Qur'anic History and History in the Qur'an." *Journal of Qur'anic Studies* 5 (2003): 1–18.

Neuwirth, Angelika. "The Discovery of Evil in the Qur'an: Contemplating Qur'anic Versions of the Decalogue in the context of Pagan-Arab Late Antiquity." (forthcoming)

Neuwirth, Angelika. "The House of Abraham and the House of Amram" In *The Qur'ān in Context: Historical and Literary Investigations into the Qur'ānic Milieu,* edited by Nicolai Sinai, Angelika Neuwirth, and Michael Marx, 499–532. Leiden: Brill, 2009.

Neuwirth, Angelika. "Three Religious Feasts Between Narratives of Violence and Liturgies of Reconciliation." In *Religion Between Violence and Reconciliation*, edited by Thomas Scheffler, 49–82. Würzburg: Ergon, 2002.

Neuwirth, Angelika. "Two Faces of the Qur'ān: Qur'ān and Muṣḥaf." *Oral Tradition* 25 (2010): 141–156.

Neuwirth, Angelika. *Der Koran als Text der Spätantike. Ein europäischer Zugang.* Berlin: Insel Verlag, 2010.

Neuwirth, Angelika. *Der Koran: Handkommentar mit Übersetzung. Band 1: Poetische Prophetie. Frühmekkanische Suren.* Berlin: Verlag der Weltreligionen, 2011.

Newby, Gordon. *A History of the Jews of Arabia: From Ancient Times to Their Eclipse Under Islam.* Columbia, SC: University of South Carolina Press, 2009 [1988].

Nöldeke, Theodor. Review of *Homonyme Wurzeln im Syrischen* by Friedrich Schulthess. *Zeitschrift der Deutschen Morgenländischen Gesellschaft* 54 (1900): 152–164.

Ong, Walter J. *Orality and Literacy: The Technologizing the Word*. New York, NY: Methuen, 1982.

Paret, Rudi, trans. *Der Koran.* Stuttgart: Kohlhammer, 2004 [1962].

Parisot, Jean. "Aphraatis Sapientis Persae Demonstrationes." In *Patrologia Syriaca*, edited by René Graffin. Paris: Firmin-Didot, 1894.

Pelikan, Jaroslav. *Mary Through the Centuries: Her Place in the History of Culture.* New Haven, CT: Yale University Press, 1996.

Périchon, Pierre, G. C. Hansen and Pierre Maraval, eds. and trans. *Socrate de Constantinople, Histoire ecclésiastique. Livres I–VII.* Sources chrétiennes 477, 493, 505, 506. Paris: Éditions du Cerf, 2004–2007

Pines, Shlomo and Shaul Shaked, "Fragment of a Jewish-Christian Composition from the Cairo Geniza." In *Studies in Islamic History and Civilization in Honour of Professor David Ayalon*, edited by M. Sharon, 307–318. Leiden: Brill, 1986.

Pines, Shlomo. "Gospel Quotations and Cognate Topics in Abd al-Jabbar's *Tathbit* in Relation to Early Christian and Judaeo-Christian Readings and Traditions." *Jerusalem Studies in Arabic and Islam* 9 (1987): 195–278.

Pines, Shlomo. "Judaeo-Christian Materials in an Arabic Jewish Treatise." *Proceedings of the American Academy for Jewish Research* 35 (1967): 187–217.

Pines, Shlomo. "Notes on Islam and on Arabic Christianity and Judaeo-Christianity." *Jerusalem Studies in Arabic and Islam* 4 (1984): 135–52.

Pines, Shlomo. "The Iranian Name for Christians and the 'God-Fearers.'" *Proceedings of the Israel Academy of Sciences and Humanities* 2 (1968): 143–152.

Pines, Shlomo. *The Jewish Christians of the Early Centuries of Christianity According to a New Source*. Jerusalem: Israel Academy of Sciences and Humanities, 1966.

Piovanelli, Pierliuigi. "Exploring the Ethiopic Book of the Cock, an Apocryphal Passion Gospel from Late Antiquity." *Harvard Theological Review* 96 (2003): 427–454.

Piovanelli, Pierliuigi. "The Book of the Cock and the Rediscovery of Ancient Jewish-Christian traditions in Fifth-Century Palestine." In *The Changing Face of Judaism, Christianity and Other Greco-Roman Religions in Antiquity*, edited by Ian H. Henderson and Gerbern S. Oegema, 308–322. Gütersloh: Gütersloher Verlagshaus, 2005.

Platt, Thomas Pell, ed. and trans. *The Ethiopic Didascalia: or, the Ethiopic Version of the Apostolical Constitutions, Received in the Church of Abyssinia*. London: Richard Bentley, 1834.

Poirier, Paul-Hubert and Yves Tissot, eds. *Écrits apocryphes chrétiens I*. Paris: Gallimard, 1997.

Post, Robert C. "Law and Cultural Conflict." *Chicago-Kent Law Review* 78 (2003): 485–508.

Post, Robert C. *Law and the Order of Culture*. Berkeley, CA: University of California Press, 1991.

Pregill, Michael. *The Living Calf of Sinai: Orientalism, "Influence," and the Foundation of the Islamic Exegetical Tradition.* PhD Dissertation. New York, NY: Columbia University, 2007.

Puin, Elisabeth. "Ein früher Koranpalimpsest aus Ṣanʿāʾ (DAM 01–27.1)." In *Schlaglichter: Schriften zur frühen Islamgeschichte und zum Koran, Band 3: Die beiden ersten islamischen Jahrhunderte*, edited by Markus Groß and Karl-Heinz Ohlig, 461–493. Berlin: Hans Schiler, 2008.

Puin, Elisabeth. "Ein früher Koranpalimpsest aus Ṣanʿāʾ (DAM 01–27.1) – Teil II." In *Vom Koran zum Islam: Schriften zur frühen Islamgeschichte und zum Koran, Band 4*, edited by Markus Groß and Karl-Heinz Ohlig, 523–581. Berlin: Hans Schiler, 2009.

Puin, Elisabeth. "Ein früher Koranpalimpsest aus Ṣanʿāʾ (DAM 01–27.1) – Teil III: Ein nicht-ʿuṯmānischer Koran." In *Die Entstehung einer Weltreligion I: Schriften zur frühen Islamgeschichte und zum Koran, Band 5: Von der koranischen Bewegung zum Frühislam*, edited by Markus Groß and Karl-Heinz Ohlig, 233–305. Berlin: Hans Schiler, 2010.

Qara'i, Sayyid 'Ali Quli, ed. and trans. *The Qur'an with an English Paraphrase*. Qom: Centre for Translation of the Holy

Qur'an, 2003. Reprinted as *The Qur'an with a Phrase-by-Phrase English Translation.* Elmhurst, NY: Tahrike Tarsile Qur'an, 2006.

Reed, Annette Y. "Rabbis, Jewish Christians and Other Late Antique Jews: Reflections on the Fate of Judaism(s) after 70 CE." In *The Changing Face of Judaism, Christianity and Other Greco-Roman Religions in Antiquity*, edited by Ian H. Henderson and Gerbern S. Oegema, 323–346. Gütersloh: Gütersloher Verlagshaus, 2005.

Reed, Annette Y. "'Jewish-Christian' Apocrypha and the History of Jewish/Christian Relations" In *Christian Apocryphal Texts for the New Millennium: Achievements, Prospects, and Challenges*, edited by Pierluigi Piovanelli, forthcoming.

Reed, Annette Y. "Heresiology and the (Jewish-)Christian Novel: Narrativized Polemics in the Pseudo-Clementines." In *Heresy and Identity in Late Antiquity,* edited by Eduard Iricinschi and Holger Zellentin, 273–298. Tübingen: Mohr Siebeck, 2008.

Rehm, Bernhard, ed. *Die Pseudoklementinen I: Homilien.* Berlin: Akademie Verlag, 1969.

Reinink, Gerrit J. "Die Muslime in einer Sammlung von Dämonengeschichten des Klosters von Qennešrīn." In *VI Symposium Syriacum 1992*, edited by René Lavenant, 335–346. Rome: Pontificio Istituto Orientale 1994.

Reischl Wilhelm K. and Joseph Rupp, eds. *S. Patris nostri Cyrilli, hierosolymorum archiepiscopi. Opera, quæ supersunt, omnia.* Hildesheim: Georg Olms, 1967 [1848–1860].

Reynolds Gabriel Said and Mehdi Azaiez, eds. *Collaborative Commentary on the Qur'ān. The 2012–2013 Qur'ān Seminar at Notre Dame.* IQSA Publishing, forthcoming.

Reynolds, Gabriel Said, ed. *New Perspectives on the Qur'ān: The Qur'ān in Its Historical Context 2.* London: Routledge, 2011.

Reynolds, Gabriel Said, ed. *The Qur'ān in its Historical Context.* London: Routledge, 2008.

Reynolds, Gabriel Said. "Le problème de la chronologie du Coran." *Arabica* 58 (2011): 477–502.

Reynolds, Gabriel Said. "On the Qur'ān and the Theme of Jews as 'Killers of the Prophets.'" *Al-Bayān* 10 (2012): 9–32.

Reynolds, Gabriel Said. "On the Qur'ānic Accusation of Scriptural Falsification (taḥrīf) and Christian anti-Jewish Polemic." *Journal of the American Oriental Society* 130 (2010): 189–202.

Reynolds, Gabriel Said. "The Quran and the Apostles of Jesus." *Bulletin of the School of Oriental and African Studies* 76 (2013): 209 227.

Reynolds, Gabriel Said. *A Muslim Theologian in a Sectarian Milieu: 'Abd al-Jabbār and the Critique of Christian Origins.* Leiden: Brill, 2004.

Reynolds, Gabriel Said. *The Qur'ān and Its Biblical Subtext.* London: Routledge, 2010.

Richlin, Amy. "Pliny's Brassiere." In *Sexuality and Gender in the Classical World: Readings and Sources*, edited by Laura K. McClure, 225–252. Oxford: Blackwell, 2002.

Riedel, Wilhelm, ed. and trans., *Die Kirchenrechtsquellen des Patriarchats Alexandrien.* Leipzig: Deichert, 1900.

Roberts, Alexander and James Donaldson, eds. *Ante-Nicene Christian Library, Volume XVII: The Clementine Homilies. The Apostolic Constitutions.* Edinburgh, T & T Clark, 1870.

Rosen, Lawrence. *The Anthropology of Justice: Law as Culture in Islamic Society.* Cambridge: Cambridge University Press, 1989.

Rosenblum, Jordan D. "'Why Do You Refuse to Eat Pork?' Jews, Food, and Identity in Roman Palestine." *Jewish Quarterly Review* 100 (2010): 95–110.

Rosenblum, Jordan D. *Food and Identity in Early Rabbinic Judaism.* Cambridge: Cambridge University Press, 2010.

Rosen-Zvi, Ishay. *Demonic Desires: "Yetzer Hara" and the Problem of Evil in Late Antiquity.* Philadelphia, PA: University of Pennsylvania Press, 2011.

Rubin, Uri. *Between Bible and Qur'an: The Children of Israel and the Islamic Self-Image.* Princeton, NJ: The Darwin Press, 1999.

Sadeghi, Behnam and Mohsen Goudarzi. "Ṣan'ā' 1 and the Origins of the Qur'ān." *Der Islam* 87 (2012): 1–129.

Sadeghi, Behnam, "The Chronology of the Qur'ān: A Stylometric Research Program." *Arabica* 58 (2011): 210–299.

Saldarini, Anthony J. *Matthew's Christian-Jewish Community.* Chicago, IL: The University of Chicago Press, 1994.

Saleh, Walid. "The Etymological Fallacy and Qur'anic Studies: Muhammad, Paradise, and Late Antiquity." In *The Qurʾān in Context: Historical and Literary Investigations into the Qurʾānic Milieu,* edited by Nicolai Sinai, Angelika Neuwirth, and Michael Marx, 649–698. Leiden: Brill, 2009.

Samir, Samir Khalil. "The Theological Christian Influence on the Qur'an: A Reflection." In *The Qurʾān in its Historical Context*, edited by Gabriel Said Reynolds, 141–162. London: Routledge, 2008.

Sanders, E. P. *Judaism: Practice and Belief 63 BCE–66 CE*. London: SCM Press, 1992.

Sandnes, Karl Olav. "The Teaching of the Apostles (Didaskalia apostolorum) and the Syriac Tradition: 'Avoid All the Books of the Gentiles'." In *The Challenge of Homer: School, Pagan Poets and Early Christianity*, edited by Karl Olav Sandnes, 102–110. London/New York, NY: T&T Clark, 2009.

Sarat, Austin. "Redirecting Legal Scholarship in Law Schools." Review of *The Cultural Study of Law*, ed. Paul W. Kahn. *The Yale Journal of Law & the Humanities* 12 (2000): 129–150.

Sasson, Jacob M. "Circumcision in the Ancient Near East." *Journal of Biblical Literature* 85 (1966): 473–476.

Schäfer, Peter. "Research into *Rabbinic* Literature: *An Attempt to Define* the Status Quaestionis." *Journal of Jewish Studies* 37 (1986): 139–152.

Schäfer, Peter. *Jesus in the Talmud*. Princeton, NJ: Princeton University Press, 2007.

Schäfer, Peter. *The Jewish Jesus: How Judaism and Christianity Shaped Each Other.* Princeton, NJ: Princeton University Press, 2012.

Schmid, Wolf. *Narratology: An Introduction*. Berlin: De Gruyter, 2010.

Schoeps, Hans Joachim. *Theologie und Geschichte des Judenchristentums*. Tübingen: Mohr Siebeck, 1949.

Schöllgen, Georg. "Die literarische Gattung der syrischen Didaskalie." In *IV Symposium Syriacum, 1984: Literary Genres in Syriac Literature (Groningen – Oosterhesselen 10–12 September)*, edited by Han J. W. Drijvers, 149–59. Rome: Pontificium Institutum Studiorum Orientalium, 1987.

Schöllgen, Georg. *Die Anfänge der Professionalisierung des Klerus und das kirchliche Amt in der syrischen Didaskalie*. Münster: Aschendorff, 1998.

Schöllgen, Georg. "Pseudapostolizität und Schriftgebrauch in den ersten Kirchenordnungen. Anmerkungen zur Begründung des frühen Kirchenrechts." In: *Stimuli: Exegese und ihre Hermeneutik in Antike und Christentum. Festschrift für Ernst Dassmann*, edited by Georg Schöllgen and Clemens Scholten, 96–121. Münster: Aschendorff, 1996.

Schrier, Omert J. "Chronological problems concerning the Lives of Severus bar Mašqā, Athanasius of Balad, Julianus Romāyā, Yoḥannān Sābā, George of the Arabs and Jacob of Edessa." *Oriens Christianus* 75 (1991): 62–91.

Schwartz, Joshua. "Jews at the Dice Table: Gambling in Ancient Jewish Society Revisited." In *Envisioning Judaism: Studies in Honor of Peter Schäfer on the Occasion of his Seventieth Birthday*, Volume 1. Edited by Annette Y. Reed, Ra'anan S. Boustan, Klaus Hermann, Reimund Leicht, Guiseppe Veltri and Alex Ramos, 129–146. Tübingen: Mohr Siebeck, 2013.

Schwartz, Joshua. "Gambling in Ancient Jewish Society and in the Greco-Roman World." In *Jews in the Graeco-Roman World,* edited by Martin Goodman, 145–165. Oxford: Oxford University Press, 1998.

Schwartz, Seth. "Was there a 'Common Judaism' after the Destruction?" In *Envisioning Judaism: Studies in Honor of Peter Schäfer on the Occasion of his Seventieth Birthday*, Volume 1. Edited by Annette Y. Reed, Ra'anan S. Boustan, Klaus Hermann, Reimund Leicht, Guiseppe Veltri and Alex Ramos, 3–22. Tübingen: Mohr Siebeck, 2013.

Schwartz, Seth. *Were the Jews a Mediterranean Society? Reciprocity and Solidarity in Ancient Judaism.* Princeton, NJ: Princeton University Press, 2010.

Shoemaker, Stephen. *The Death of a Prophet: The End of Muhammad's Life and the Beginnings of Islam*. Philadelphia, PA: University of Pennsylvania Press, 2012.

Shah, Prakash. *Legal Pluralism in Conflict: Coping with Cultural Diversity in Law.* London: Glass House Press, 2007.

Simon, Marcel. *Verus Israel: A Study of the Relations Between Christians and Jews in the Roman Empire, AD 135–425*. Translated by H. McKeating. Oxford: Oxford University Press, 1986.

Sinai, Nicolai. "The Qur'ān as Process." In *The Qur'ān in Context: Historical and Literary Investigations into the Qur'ānic Milieu,* edited by Nicolai Sinai, Angelika Neuwirth, and Michael Marx, 407–440. Leiden: Brill, 2009.

Smith, Dennis. *From Symposium to Eucharist: The Banquet in the Early Christian World.* Minneapolis, MN: Fortress, 2003.

Sokoloff, Michael. *A Dictionary of Jewish Babylonian Aramaic of the Talmudic and Geonic periods.* Baltimore: Johns Hopkins University Press, 2002.

Sokoloff, Michael. *A Dictionary of Jewish Palestinian Aramaic of the Byzantine Period.* Baltimore: Johns Hopkins University Press, 1992.

Sokoloff, Michael. *A Syriac Dictionary: A Translation from the Latin, Correction, Expansion, and Update of C. Brockelmann's* Lexicon Syriacum. Winona Lake, IN: Eisenbrauns, 2009.

Stern, S.M. "'Abd al-Jabbār's Account of How Christ's Religion was Falsified by the Adoption of Roman Customs." *The Journal of Theological Studies* 19 (1968): 128–185.

Stern, Sacha. *Calendar and Community: a History of the Jewish Calendar, 2nd cent. BCE – 10th cent. CE.* Oxford: Oxford University Press, 2001.

Stewart-Sykes, Alistair, ed. and trans. *The Didascalia Apostolorum: an English Version with Introduction and Annotation.* Turnhout: Brepols, 2009.

Strecker, Georg, ed. *Die Pseudoklementinen II: Rekognitionen in Rufins Übersetzung.* Berlin: Akademie Verlag, 1994.

Stroumsa, Guy. *The End of Sacrifice: Religious Transformations in Late Antiquity.* Chicago, IL: Chicago University Press, 2009.

Synak, Eva Maria. "Die Apostolischen Konstitutionen – ein 'christlicher Talmud' aus dem 4. Jh." *Biblica* 79 (1998): 27–56.

Tannous, Jack. *Syria between Byzantium and Islam: Making Incommensurables Speak.* Ph.D. Dissertation. Princeton, NJ: Princeton University, 2010.

Taylor, Miriam S. *Anti-Judaism and Early Christian Identity: A Critique of the Scholarly Consensus.* Leiden: Brill, 1995.

Teppler, Yaakov. *Birkat haMinim: Jews and Christians in Conflict in the Ancient World.* TSAJ 119; Tübingen: Mohr Siebeck, 2007.

Tertullien, *Le Voile des vierges (De uirginibus uelandis). Sources Chrétiennes* 424. Introduced by Eva Schulz-Flügel, and translated by Paul Mattei. Paris: Éditions du Cerf, 1997.

Teske, Roland J., ed. and trans. *The Works of Saint Augustine. Answer to the Pelagians*. Hyde Park, NY: New City Press, 1997.

Teske, Roland J., trans. and Boniface Ramsey, ed., *The Works of St Augustine. Answer to Faustus, a Manichean.* Hyde Park, NY: New City Press, 2007.

Thomas, David, Barbara Roggema, Juan Pedro Monferrer Sala, Johannes Pahlitzsch, Mark Swanson, Herman Teule and John Tolan, eds. *Christian-Muslim Relations: A Bibliographical History*. 5 vols. Leiden: Brill, 2009–2013.

Tomson, Peter J. "Jewish Purity Laws as Viewed by the Church Fathers and by the Early Followers of Jesus," *Purity and Holiness: The Heritage of Leviticus*, edited by Marcel J.H.M. Poorthuis and Joshua Schwartz, 73–91. Leiden: Brill, 2000.

Toorn, Karel van der. "The Significance of the Veil in the Ancient Near East." In *Pomegranates and Golden Bells: Studies in Biblical, Jewish, and Near Eastern Ritual, Law, and Literature in Honor of Jacob Milgrom*, edited by David P. Wright, 329–30. Winona Lake, IN: Eisenbrauns, 1995.

Turner, C.H. "Notes on the Apostolic Constitutions" *Journal of Theological Studies* OS 16 (1915), 523–538.

Uhlig, Siegbert, ed. *Encyclopaedia Aethiopica*. Wiesbaden: Harassovitz, 2005.

Unnik, Willem Cornelis van. "The Significance of Moses' Law for the Churches of Christ according to the Syriac Didascalia." *Sparsa Collecta. Part 3: Patristica–Gnostica–Liturgica* by Willem Cornelis van Unnik, 7–39. Leiden: Brill, 1983.

Vacarella, Kevin M. *Shaping Christian Identity: The False Scripture Argument in Early Christian Literature*. PhD Dissertation. Tallahassee, FL: Florida State University, 2007.

Valavanolickal, Kuriakose, trans. and ed. *Aphrahat Demonstrations I*. Changanassery: HIRS Publications, 1999.

Varga, Csaba. *Comparative Legal Cultures*. New York, NY: NYU Press, 1992.

Vaux, Roland de. "Sur le voile des femmes dans l'orient ancien" *Revue Biblique* 44 (1935): 397–412.

Verheyden, Joseph. "'The Demonization of the Opponent' in Early Christian Literature: The Case of the Pseudo-Clementines." In *Religious Polemics in Context: Papers Presented to the Second International Conference of the Leiden Institute for the Study of Religions (LISOR) held at Leiden, 27–28 April 2000*, edited by Theo L. Hettema and Arie van der Kooij, 330–359. Assen: Van Gorcum, 2004.

Vööbus, Arthur, ed. *Syrische Kanonessammlungen. Ein Beitrag zur Quellenkunde. Corpus Scriptorum Christianorum Orientalium.* Volumes 307 and 317. Louvain: Secrétariat du CorpuSCO, 1970.

Vööbus, Arthur, ed. *The Didascalia Apostolorum in Syriac* I–IV, *Corpus Scriptorum Christianorum Orientalium.* Volumes 401–2 and 407–8. Louvain: Secrétariat du CorpuSCO, 1979.

Vööbus, Arthur. "Die Entdeckung der ältesten Urkunde für die syrische Übersetzung der apostolischen Kirchenordnung. Neue Quellen für die syrische Version." *Oriens Christianus* 63 (1979): 37–40

Vossel, Vincent van. "Le moine syriaque et son diable." In *Le monachisme syriaque aux premiers siècles de l'Eglise, IIe – debut VIIe siècle. I: Textes français*, 191–215. Antélias, Lebanon: Éditions du CERP, 1998.

Vyhmeister, Werner. "The Sabbath in Asia." In *Sabbath in Scripture and History*, edited by Kenneth A. Strand and Daniel A. Augsburger, 151–168. Washington, DC: Review and Herald Publishing Association, 1982.

Vyhmeister, Werner. "The Sabbath in Egypt and Ethiopia." In *Sabbath in Scripture and History*, edited by Kenneth A. Strand and Daniel A. Augsburger, 169–189. Washington, DC: Review and Herald Publishing Association, 1982.

Wagner, Georg. "Zur Herkunft der Apostolischen Konstitutionen." In *Mélanges liturgiques offerts au R. P. dom Bernard Botte, O. S. B., de l'Abbaye du Mont César, a l'occasion du cinquantieme anniversaire de son ordination sacerdotale (4 juin*

1972), edited by Bernard Botte, 525–537. Louvain: Abbaye du Mont César, 1972.

Wagtendonk, Kees. *Fasting in the Quran.* Leiden: Brill, 1968.

Wendebourg, Dorothea. "Die alttestamentlichen Reinheitsgesetze in der frühen Kirche." *Zeitschrift für Kirchengeschichte* 95 (1984): 149–170.

West, Edward W., ed. and trans. *Pahlavi Texts. Volume 1: The Bundahis, Bahman Yast, and Shāyast lā-shāyast.* Cambridge: Cambridge University Press, 2012 [1880].

Westbrook, Raymond (ed.). *A History of Ancient Near Eastern Law.* Leiden: Brill, 2003.

Wheeler, Brannon M. "Israel and the Torah of Muḥammad." In *Bible and Qur'ān: Essays in Scriptural Intertextuality*, edited by John C. Reeves, 61–85. Atlanta, GA: Society of Biblical Literature, 2003.

Wilken, Robert L. *John Chrysostom and the Jews: Rhetoric and Reality in the Late 4th Century.* Berkeley, CA: University of California Press, 1983.

Williams, A. Lukyn, ed. and trans. *Justin Martyr: The Dialogue with Trypho.* New York: Macmillan, 1930.

Williams, Frank, ed. *The Panarion of Epiphanius of Salamis. 2 vols.* Leiden: Brill 1987–1994.

Williams, Michael. *Rethinking "Gnosticism": An Argument for Dismantling a Dubious Category.* Princeton, NJ: Princeton University Press, 1996.

Wimpfheimer, Barry. *Narrating the Law: A Poetics of Legal Stories.* Philadelphia, PA: University of Pennsylvania Press, 2011.

Witakowski, Witold. "The Origin of the 'Teaching of the Apostles'." In *IV Symposium Syriacum, 1984: Literary Genres in Syriac Literature (Groningen – Oosterhesselen 10–12 September)*, edited by H.J.W. Drijvers, 161–171. Rome: Pontificium Institutum Studiorum Orientalium, 1987.

Witztum, Joseph. "Joseph Among the Ishmaelites: Q12 in Light of Syriac Sources." In *New Perspectives on the Qur'ān: The Qur'ān in Its Historical Context 2*, edited by Gabriel Said Reynolds, 425–448. Abingdon: Routledge, 2011.

Witztum, Joseph. "The Foundations of the House (Q2: 127)." *Bulletin of the School of Oriental and African Studies* (2009): 25–40.

Witztum, Joseph. *The Syriac Milieu of the Quran: The Recasting of Biblical Narratives.* PhD Dissertation. Princeton, NJ: Princeton University, 2010.

Yadin, Azzan. *Scripture as Logos: Rabbi Ishmael and the Origins of Midrash.* Philadelphia, PA: University of Pennsylvania Press, 2004.

Young, Frances Margaret. "The Apostolic Constitutions: a Methodological Case-Study." In *Studia Patristica, Vol. XXXVI: Papers Presented at the Thirteenth International Conference on Patristic Studies Held in Oxford 1999. Critica et Philologica, Nachleben, First Two Centuries, Tertullian to Arnobius, Egypt before Nicaea, Athanasius and His Opponents*, edited by Maurice F. Wiles and E.J. Yarnold, 105–115. Leuven: Peeters, 2001.

Yuval, Israel. *Two Nations in your Womb. Perceptions of Jews and Christians in Late Antiquity and the Middle Ages.* Berkeley, CA: University of California Press, 2006 [2000].

Zellentin, Holger. "Jerusalem Fell After Betar: The Christian Josephus and Rabbinic Memory." In *Envisioning Judaism: Studies in Honor of Peter Schäfer on the Occasion of his Seventieth Birthday* Volume 1, 319–67, edited by Annette Y. Reed, Ra'anan S. Boustan, Klaus Hermann, Reimund Leicht, Guiseppe Veltri and Alex Ramos, Tübingen: Mohr Siebeck, 2013.

Zellentin, Holger. "Jesus and the Tradition of the Elders: Originalism and Traditionalism in Early Judean Legal Theory." In *Beyond the Gnostic Gospels: Studies Building on the Work of Elaine H. Pagels,* edited by Eduard Iricinschi, Lance Jennot, Nicola Denzey Lewis and Philippa Townsend, 379–403. *Studies and Texts in Antiquity and Christianity*, Tübingen: Mohr Siebeck, 2013.

Zellentin, Holger. "The End of Jewish Egypt- Artapanus's Second Exodus" In *Antiquity in Antiquity, Jewish and Christian Pasts in the Greco-Roman World*, edited by Gregg Gardner and Kevin Osterloh, 29–73. TSAJ 123; Tübingen: Mohr Siebeck, 2009.

Zellentin, Holger and Eduard Irichinsci, "Making Selves and Marking Others: Identity and Late Antique Heresiologies" in *Heresy and Identity in Late Antiquity*, edited by eidem, 1–27. TSAJ 120; Tübingen, Mohr Siebeck, 2008.

Zellentin, Holger. *Rabbinic Parodies of Jewish and Christian Literature*. TSAJ 120; Tübingen: Mohr Siebeck 2010.

Zellentin, Holger. Review of *Food and Identity in Early Rabbinic Judaism* by Jordan D. Rosenblum. *Journal for the Study of Judaism* 44 (2013): 123–5.

Zellentin, Holger. Review of *Narrating the Law* by Barry Wimpfheimer. *The Journal of Religion* 93 (2013): 117–119.

Zmygrider-Konopka, Zdzislaw. "Les Romains et la circoncision de juifs." *Eos* 33 (1931): 334–350.

Citation Index

Hebrew Bible

Apocrypha and Pseudepigrapha

New Testament

New Testament Apocrypha

Apostolic Fathers

Anonymous and Pseudepigraphic Patristic Literature

Patristic Literature

Rabbinic Literature

Pahlavi Literature

Qur'ān

Author Index

Subject Index